*The Anglo-Dutch
Naval Wars*
1652–1674

Detail of the Prince *from Royal Visit to the Fleet on the Thames by Willian Van de Velde the Younger (National Maritime Museum, Greenwich, London)*

Who ever commands the ocean commands the trade of the world, commands the riches of the world, and whoever is master of that commands the world itself . . . they are not, therefore, small matters, you see, which men so much contend about, when they strive to improve commerce . . . and set their empire in the Deep.

John Evelyn. From his prologue to an unfinished history of the Dutch Wars but printed separately as *Navigation and Commerce, their Original and Progress*, 1674.

The Anglo-Dutch Naval Wars 1652–1674

ROGER HAINSWORTH AND
CHRISTINE CHURCHES

SUTTON PUBLISHING

First published in 1998 by
Sutton Publishing Limited · Phoenix Mill
Thrupp · Stroud · Gloucestershire · GL5 2BU

Copyright © Roger Hainsworth and Christine Churches, 1998

All rights reserved. No part of this publication may be reproduced, stored in a retrieval system, or transmitted, in any form, or by any means, electronic, mechanical, photocopying, recording or otherwise, without the prior permission of the publisher and copyright holders.

The authors have asserted the moral right to be identified as the authors of this work.

British Library Cataloguing in Publication Data
A catalogue record for this book is available from the British Library

ISBN 0-7509-1787-3

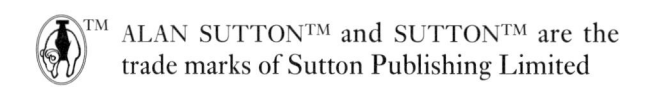

™ ALAN SUTTON™ and SUTTON™ are the trade marks of Sutton Publishing Limited

Typeset in 11/12pt Ehrhardt.
Typesetting and origination by
Sutton Publishing Limited.
Printed in Great Britain by
Butler & Tanner, Frome, Somerset.

Contents

List of Illustrations   vii

List of Maps   ix

Preface   xi

Book One: The First Dutch War

1	First Blood	3
2	The Rival Republics	7
3	First Campaigns: From the Shetlands to the Casquets	23
4	From Triumph to Defeat	35
5	Portland	57
6	The Last Battles	71
7	The Peacemakers	89

Book Two: The Later Wars

8	The Uneasy Peace	97
9	A New War: Lowestoft	103
10	The Four-Day Fight	129
11	From Success to Humiliation	149
12	A Conspiracy of Princes	169

Epilogue   191

Notes   195

Bibliography   203

Index   207

List of Illustrations

The *Prince* in 1672	*Frontispiece*
The *Brederode*	5
A parliamentary fourth-rate	20
The *Speaker*	21
Sir George Ayscue	27
A Dutch East Indiaman and two men-of-war	32
Sir William Penn	38
Witte de With	40
Michiel Adrianszoon de Ruyter	42
The *Sovereign*	45
The battle of Leghorn	49
Maarten Tromp and the battle of Dungeness	54
The *Portland*	60
Robert Blake	67
The battle off the Gabbard	78
George Monck	84
Oliver Cromwell	91
King Charles II	100
Sir Robert Holmes	105
Plan of Manhattan, Long Island	107
Samuel Pepys	109
Jan Evertsen	112
James Duke of York	114
The *Eendracht* and other Dutch ships	118
Jacob van Wassenaer, Lord of Obdam	119
The battle of Lowestoft	122
Cornelis Tromp	126
Sir Edward Montagu	130
Sir Thomas Teddiman	132
Prince Rupert	136
The *Zeven Provincien*	138
The Four-Day Fight	140
The surrender of the *Royal Prince*	145
The damaged *Swiftsure*	147
The emblem of the King's ship	151

The St James's Day Fight	153
The Dutch raid on the Medway	158
The *Royal Charles* carried off by the Dutch	164
Cornelis de Witt	166
The *Superbe*	170
Model of the *St Michael*	173
The burning of the *Royal James*	175
The first battle of Schooneveld	182
Sir Edward Spragge	184
The battle of the Texel	188

List of Maps

The United Provinces in the seventeenth century	9
The battles of the First Dutch War	24
The Kentish Knock, 28 September 1652	44
The battle of Portland, 18 February 1653	63
The battles of the Second and Third Dutch Wars	102
Events around the North Atlantic, 1664–5	106
The battle of Lowestoft, 3 June 1665	121
The Four Days Fight, 1–4 June 1666. Day One	143
The assault on the Medway, 1667	162
The battle of Sole Bay, 28 May 1672	176
The battle of the Texel, 11 August 1673	187

Preface

The great naval battles of the Anglo-Dutch Wars of the seventeenth century have chiefly impinged on the modern consciousness not through historical writing but through contemporary painting. Outstanding here has been the legacy of the van de Veldes, father and son, who painted their magnificent battlescapes for both the Dutch and the English, uninhibited by the claims of patriotism when they clashed with the imperatives of patronage. Some of these paintings and drawings are reproduced in this book. The neglect of historians in more recent times is perhaps due to a sense that these wars were unnecessary, indeed unnatural, should have been avoided and achieved nothing but loss of blood and treasure on both sides. Recently, however, as the bibliography reveals, historians have begun to examine these wars in more detail, sometimes in the course of writing biographies of individual statesmen or admirals, sometimes as part of larger studies of naval warfare across a much longer period. Dr J.R. Jones has recently published a searching analysis of the diplomatic and political background to all three wars, and there have been separate and important studies of the navies of the Commonwealth and Protectorate and of Charles II, and of the causes of the First Dutch War and of Anglo-Dutch commercial rivalry. There has been less detailed attention to the naval battles themselves, to the policies and actions of the commanders, both English and Dutch, and to the difficulties they sought to surmount. These difficulties were considerable because the naval battles of the Dutch Wars were unlike any that had been fought before in terms of the number of ships engaged in the rival fleets and the extraordinary and unprecedented firepower they carried into battle. The sonorous sounds of those distant encounters were heard fearfully by awed and wondering folk on the coasts of England, the Netherlands and France, drifting in like a distant thunder. It is the aim of this book to recall these naval campaigns and to try to show not merely how they were won or lost but also how they were experienced by those who courageously endured them.

The authors are grateful to the History Department of the University of Adelaide and to their colleagues in it for much encouragement, to the staff of the Barr-Smith Library of the university for much helpful support, particularly in locating sources, and to their editor, Anne Bennett of Sutton's for all her efforts on their behalf.

Book One
The First Dutch War

CHAPTER 1
First Blood

The bloody beginning of an unhappy breach.

Anon.[1]

On 12 May 1652, a fine spring day, Captain Anthony Young was sailing down-Channel towards Plymouth to join the Western Guard, a flotilla whose prime duty was to protect the Western Approaches. He commanded a flotilla of two English warships, the *President*, 40 guns, the *Nightingale*, 26, and an armed merchantman, the *Recovery*. Off Start Point a cloud of grey canvas thrusting above the western horizon betrayed the presence of approaching ships. Young at first thought the oncomers must be Sir George Ayscue's squadron which was daily expected from the Barbados but it soon stood revealed as a convoy of seven Dutch merchantmen from the Mediterranean escorted by three Dutch men-of-war. The Dutch commander was Commodore Huyrluyt, the second escort was commanded by Captain Joris van der Zaanen. These two flotillas would unwittingly fire the opening shots of the First Dutch War although war would not be officially declared for several weeks. Young had been commanded to assert England's claim to 'sovereignty of the seas' which foreign ships must recognise by lowering their flags in salute. This Dutch commanders were forbidden to do. However, when Young sent a boat to Huyrluyt making this demand he obligingly agreed, possibly more concerned for his valuable convoy than for the imperatives of national pride, and lowered his flag and fired three guns in salute. Van der Zaanen was made of sterner stuff. Although he also fired a salute, he broke the rules of navigation in the Channel by approaching Young on the windward side (a course with an implied threat). Moreover he refused to strike his flag because, as he told Young's messenger, he would 'lose his head' if he disobeyed his instructions, and defied Young to come and lower it himself if he could. To this Young responded with a broadside which was returned, and others followed during a confused exchange which lasted for an hour and a half. Finally van der Zaanen thought better of it and struck his flag. The third escort lowered its flag without dispute. The firing ceased and Young demanded that van der Zaanen should surrender and bring his ship into port to answer the damage he had done to Young's ship. (The *President* had lost one man killed, four wounded and she had sustained damage to her hull, spars and rigging.) Huyrluyt declared that the Dutch would fight to prevent this and Young's fellow captains counselled that the English should pursue the quarrel no further. Young dispatched an account of the affray to the Council of State from Plymouth. If he was worried about endangering a fragile peace – or that he might be thought not to have gone far enough – he need not have worried. The Council decided on 17 May that it was 'very well satisfied' with what Young had done 'in making the Dutchmen strike'.[2]

The second act of the drama began on 18 May. At that time Admiral Robert Blake with a flotilla of thirteen ships lay off Rye.[3] A second flotilla of nine warships commanded by Nehemiah Bourne, lay at anchor behind the Goodwin Sands to the north of the port of Dover.[4] At about one o'clock lookouts alerted Bourne to the approach of a Dutch fleet of forty-one men-of-war which then cruised slowly outside the Downs heading south towards Dover. In command was Maarten Harpertszoon Tromp, Lieutenant Admiral of the United Provinces from 1636 to 1653 and accounted the greatest seaman of the age. Tromp had been sent to sea with orders not to lower his flag at the demand of English warships and to protect Dutch merchant convoys from being stopped and searched for alleged 'contraband', that is, goods intended for France. He had no warlike designs against the English navy. However, although he was not supposed to provoke hostilities, if he strictly followed his instructions war was likely to follow. A proud man, famed for his victories against the Spanish, while he would not heedlessly cause a war, Tromp would not disobey his orders so as to avoid it. He had been anchored off Nieuport after a cruise along the Dutch coast, but a worsening north-easterly gale, which cost several of his ships' anchors and cables, and the perils of a lee shore persuaded him to cross the Channel and seek shelter behind the South Foreland. Tromp detached two frigates which made their way round the sandbanks to where Bourne's flagship lay and their captains went in person to greet him. They explained their purpose in making for Dover road with much courtesy and Bourne replied to this with cautious affability. However, immediately they departed he dispatched a ketch to alert Blake to the presence of these formidable visitors, and ordered his captains to haul up to their anchors so that they would be ready to weigh at a moment's notice. Meanwhile Tromp's fleet had anchored off Dover. His flagship, the *Brederode*, 56 guns, an 800-ton ship and conspicuous by its size, did not dip its flag in salute and from Dover Castle a cannon boomed its outrage at this neglect. There the Dutch remained quietly all night watched with suspicion by Bourne's flotilla and with some anxiety by the Dover garrison.

Either during the night or at first light Blake weighed and began his painfully slow advance up-Channel towards Dover, tacking laboriously against the strong north-easter. He had already sent the ketch back to Bourne with instructions to come downwind to join him. The Dutch remained at anchor all morning, watched by Dover's inhabitants whose apprehension was increased when Tromp tactlessly had his men engage in noisy musket practice. At noon they sailed once more, standing off for the French coast in sight of Blake's fleet, still laboriously tacking up towards them. Bourne, who had received Blake's order at ten o'clock but had been unable to weigh until almost noon, must have been still negotiating the south end of the Goodwin Sands when Tromp sailed. Tromp was at least halfway to the French coast when he saw a Dutch vessel approaching which had obviously been involved in a sea fight. This was van der Zaanen who had sailed in

The Brederode, *Tromp's flagship in the battles of 1652–3 (National Maritime Museum, Greenwich, London)*

search of Tromp's fleet to report the skirmish off the Start and to seek his aid for the convoy which was sheltering off the English coast at the Fairlight with a number of English men-of-war nearby.[5] Believing from van der Zaanen's report that the convoy, whose cargoes together were said by Tromp to be worth fifty tons of gold, were being searched or seized, Tromp put his fleet about and headed back across the Channel to rescue them. In fact Blake had ignored the Dutch convoy which had simply been sheltering. It may be that van der Zaanen was dramatising events to excuse his being worsted off the Start.

Nevertheless, van der Zaanen had now lit the fuse, for seeing the Dutch bearing down on him Blake cleared for action and put his ships in a better posture for defence by ordering a turn downwind. This meant that his flagship, the *James*, previously in the van was now the rearmost vessel and the one which the Dutch fleet would first encounter. Blake ordered a reduction in sail so that it would be easier for Bourne, who was in sight but more distant than the Dutch, to catch up. Bourne was coming downwind but his ships as he later reported, 'sailed very heavy by reason they are foul', that is, made sluggish by a heavy growth on their hulls. Tromp's *Brederode*, his fleet streaming behind, was within musket shot by 4.30 p.m. Precisely what happened next is uncertain because the two admirals later gave contradictory accounts. Tromp always insisted that he had no warlike intentions and his purpose was simply to pass the English fleet and gather up the precious convoy at the Fairlight. This is probably true because Tromp knew that his masters feared war but hoped to avoid it, unlike the English commanders who expected war and knew that their masters were inclined to embrace it. While Blake later referred to Tromp's 'braving it' on the English coast (that is, throwing down a challenge) in fact he had only sought shelter there. As the *Brederode* closed the *James* fired a shot as a signal for Tromp to strike his flag. This Tromp ignored but replied to a second shot with a signal gun. According to Blake after he fired a third shot the *Brederode* fired a broadside to which the *James* replied and the battle began. Tromp insists that the *James* fired a broadside first through his ship and its spars and rigging. In a much more detailed account written in October 1652 to justify all his actions prior to his resignation, and at a time when he was much beset by his republican enemies, Tromp claimed that Blake's fleet were so scattered that he could not discern whether the convoy was captive among them or not but that he was determined to rescue it if it was.[6] As he approached the *James* he took in his topsails, preparing to send a messenger in the longboat to ask why Blake had opened fire. A third shot then carried off the arm of one of his crew and he responded by firing a signal gun. The *James* had then closed the range and fired a broadside at which the *Brederode* opened fire. While this account, at least in its detail, defies credibility, it seems likely that Blake bears the primary responsibility for what became known as 'the action off Dover'.

Bourne arrived with his flotilla about 4 p.m., and engaged the rear of the Dutch fleet. His ships arrived in an unorganised body and individually drove into the Dutch fleet as the Dutch 'shuffled themselves into clusters' for mutual defence. Firing became general and lasted from 4.30 until dark, those Dutch ships which were at the rear of their fleet finding it 'hot work', as Bourne grimly observed. His ships continued firing until the light faded and the Dutch gradually drew off. As the ships still within range exchanged closing shots, the many spectators on Dungeness and the Downs above the coast would have seen the English fleet anchor to await what the morning should bring. Despite the division of Blake's fleet, prolonged by his turn downwind and the fact that his flotilla had somewhat separated during their long tacks upwind, the English ships had rather the better of the encounter. Bourne's flotilla captured two ships, one being of 30 guns the crew of which were carried off prisoner. The other was stripped of its officers and given a prize crew but the latter abandoned it during the night believing it to be doomed. In fact, although dismasted, it somehow drifted into the path of Tromp's fleet the following morning and was salvaged, a remarkable feat of seamanship. No English ships were lost although the *James* was severely damaged by seventy shot in her hull and more in her rigging, and lost several crewmen and the master and master's mate killed, as ships successively exchanged fire with it as they followed the *Brederode* downwind.[7] In this confused, muddled and unplanned way were fired the opening shots in what the English would later call the First Dutch War.

CHAPTER 2
The Rival Republics

> The English are about to attack a mountain of gold; we are about to attack a mountain of iron.
>
> Adriaen Pauw, Grand Pensionary of Holland

It might seem strange that war should break out between the English Commonwealth and the Netherlands. As Protestant republics they might seem natural allies. Oliver Cromwell considered the war unnatural and continued to detest it. Once he had the power to do so he would find a way to end it. However, the perception of the English radicals that there must be religious and political, indeed ideological, solidarity between the two states ignored much recent history and uncomfortable realities. Some historians have flirted with the same error. The leading authority on the Interregnum navy has observed that the ideological ties linking the republics 'were flimsy compared with the material interests which divided them'.[1] Material interests certainly did divide them as we shall see but the 'ideological ties' were only apparent to the English; to the Dutch they were invisible. The Commonwealth government, like all usurpers, felt environed by enemies. Confronted by Irish Catholics, Scottish Covenanters, royalists everywhere, French hostility and European disdain (at best) it never comprehended how frightening it could appear to the Dutch. Political relations between the two states had disappointed English radicals well before the king's execution in 1649. In 1642 the Long Parliament had sent Walter Strickland to the Hague to seek an alliance. He found the Dutch determined to remain neutral – to the equal disappointment of the royalists since Charles I had married his daughter to William, son of Frederick Henry, Prince of Orange, the year before. During the war the States General only recognised Charles I's ambassador, refusing to acknowledge parliament as a legitimate government or to accord Strickland ambassadorial status. As late as 1648 the Dutch sheltered elements of the English navy which had mutinied and sought refuge at Helvoetsluys from a pursuing squadron commanded by the Earl of Warwick. However, the looseness of the Dutch confederation permitted the legislature of Holland, the largest and wealthiest Dutch state, to accord Strickland ambassadorial status there so that it could negotiate matters relating to trade, prizes of war, etc.

After the Regicide relations grew even colder. Charles II and his exiled court were permitted to shelter in the Netherlands during 1649–50. On 12 May 1649 Isaac Dorislaus, a Dutch-born lawyer and distinguished scholar who had helped to frame the charges against Charles I, whose mission was to mend Anglo-Dutch relations, was murdered by royalists soon after his arrival at the Hague. Despite the protests of anti-Dutch parliamentarians war was narrowly avoided although the easy escape of the murderers made this difficult. Strickland was recalled and the Dutch representative in London sent packing. From the first Holland, always chiefly concerned about its maritime commercial interests and therefore most fearful of war, had urged the recognition of the new republic. The States General would not take that step. It had to balance the competing claims of the rival Orange and republican parties. Not only did the House of Orange support the Stuart cause, the more extreme Orangists dreamed of restoring Charles by force of arms, a threat which the Commonwealth government took seriously. It was one of the reasons why the Commonwealth was engaged in a programme of naval expansion. Meanwhile the stadtholder, William II, was planning to march on Amsterdam to overthrow its republican leaders. Then to the consternation of all royalists, Dutch or English, William II died on 6 November 1650. His heir, William III, was a baby born a week after his father's death.[2] The political situation in the Netherlands was instantly transformed. Holland's republicans seized the opportunity to prevent the appointment of a new stadtholder and five other states followed their example. This period of Orange eclipse became known as the 'True Freedom' and was to last from 1650 to 1672. To the Commonwealth government this reversion to republicanism seemed to open a new, more hopeful era in relations between the two countries. It had dreamed of a union with the Dutch republic ever since 1649, a dream which it clung to long after it should have been obvious that the Dutch would never allow it to be fulfilled. In February 1651 Strickland returned to the Hague accompanied by a weightier negotiator, the Lord Chief Justice, Oliver St John, to offer a union between the two republics to protect their religion and institutions.

The reasons for the Netherlanders' consistent rejection of England's embrace, whether it took the form of some kind of union, or a close alliance or simply a mutual defence pact, do much to explain the political difficulties between the two republics. Firstly the tendency of English radicals to equate the Dutch Reformed clergy with Puritans was illusory. The Dutch Church was profoundly conservative by comparison with the radical sectaries within the English parliament. The clergy were devoted to the House of Orange, detesting the dominant republican culture of Holland. They were more akin to the English and Scottish Presbyterians who had opposed the trial and execution of Charles I and like all royalists saw the Regicide government through a haze of resentment. Their weakness lay in the fact that their Prince of Orange was now an infant from whom nothing could be expected until he reached man's estate. Their congregations were divided between Orangists and republicans, but were united against religious toleration. They saw the English sects, which flourished under the protection of Cromwell's regiments, as dangerous heretics. The clergy lost no time in encouraging their congregations to riot against Strickland and St John. They would have preached rebellion if the States General had consented to a close association with the English Commonwealth. In fact there was no risk of such a policy. The two republics were profoundly different in their organisation

The United Provinces in the seventeenth century

and ethos and the Commonwealth presented a fearsome spectacle to the Dutch of whatever shade of political position. During the two years since the execution of the king the English government had become the government of Britain. Under the generalship of Oliver Cromwell the New Model Army had crushed any threat of a royalist incursion from Ireland, and despite desultory guerilla resistance the Commonwealth and its soldiers governed there. In Scotland the Covenanters had seen their army slaughtered at the battles of Dunbar, Inverkeithing and Worcester and they now resentfully endured the hegemony of Westminster. As the Covenanters had once been allies of parliament this was hardly an encouraging precedent for the Dutch. Throughout the three former kingdoms the Commonwealth's power was virtually complete because garrisons of infantry held in an iron grip most urban centres while squadrons of Ironside cavalry patrolled the countryside. This military strength was not unreasonable in a state with internal enemies and which was little loved by its own people, but although not a military dictatorship it appeared remarkably like it to foreign observers, and especially to the Dutch who lived in a very different polity.

Dutchmen, however divided by religion, politics, provincial resentments and jealousies, had this in common: a detestation of strong central government and its concomitant, weak local government and suppressed local liberties. That recalled the Spanish hegemony which they had heroically thrown off. A union with England, indeed any surrender of Netherlands independence by a treaty with England, would be abhorrent because it would appear to be just another English conquest with their republic reduced to the status of Scotland or Ireland without a shot fired. The government of the United Provinces in 1651 bears a curious resemblance to the government which the former American colonies temporarily adopted under the Articles of Confederation while fighting their war of independence. The Dutch and the Americans after them regarded their states (seven in the Netherlands, originally thirteen in America) as sovereign but in order to achieve victory in a long war and to preserve their independence in peace they formed a union whose constitutional expression was the States General in the Netherlands and the Continental Congress in America. In both these bodies each state was equally represented for the larger states had no more votes than the smaller states. In the States General, unlike the American Congress, decisions usually had to be unanimous to become law. Moreover, the Dutch delegates (significantly not called 'representatives') had no freedom of initiative. If a matter arose on which they lacked instructions from their state governments, they must return home to discover how their state legislature thought they should vote on the issue. In this way the Dutch republic denied itself both the advantages and the perils of strong central government. In 1652 the acting-Grand Pensionary of Holland, Jan de Witt, reproached the Dutch ambassadors in London for allowing parliament to refer to the United Provinces as 'a republic' (*respublica*) singular instead of 'the federated republics' (*Respublicae Foederatae*) plural.[3] His reproach expresses in a nutshell the gulf between the United Provinces and Britain, the most centralised state in Europe.

The United Provinces were more effective in war and peace than might appear possible because, firstly, the stadtholder had provided a unifying focus and military leadership. It should be noted that the stadtholderate was not a hereditary monarchy. It was a salaried office in each state which constitutionally could each have appointed a different stadtholder although in practice they appointed the head of the House of Orange. This system had now ended although two of the states defiantly appointed the head of a cadet branch of the family as their stadtholder. The second unifying force was provided by Holland, wealthiest and most populous of the states, whose leaders, and particularly their chief salaried official, the Grand Pensionary, were capable of organising and to a degree financing war. Significantly Holland was largely responsible for the conduct of foreign policy. This leadership was particularly manifest during the so-called 'True Freedom', the period when the Orange–Nassau stadtholderate was in abeyance between 1650 and 1672. The Grand Pensionary inevitably increased his power and authority when there was no stadtholder to rival him. After the death of Adriaen Pauw in 1653 the office was held by Jan de Witt. No succeeding Grand Pensionary ever equalled his power and prestige and he would prove a most formidable enemy for the English, especially during the 1660s.

So while the English revolutionaries hoped naïvely for a union with the Dutch republic, to the Dutch the Commonwealth appeared like a dangerous, half-mad giant, at once aggressive and fearful, hungry for power and new conquests, possessed of a formidable club, the Ironsides, with which it had destroyed the liberties of its neighbours. Little wonder then that those responsible for the conduct of its foreign policy not only rejected a proposal of union but even the pact of mutual and reciprocal assistance in war which Strickland and St John offered as an alternative. England had few friends and many enemies, the Dutch had no enemies and as a country which had founded its prosperity on carrying merchandise to all countries, needed none. Not only might the giant hug them to death if they accepted its embrace, any association with it would drag the Dutch into wars in which they could lose much and could gain nothing. The trouble was that if England contained eager friends of the Dutch republic it also contained many more inveterate enemies. Radical sectaries, especially the preachers, recognised the 'malignant' royalism of the Reformed Church and denounced its adherents as oppressive 'Presbyterians' while all Puritans expressed horror at the perceived materialism and pursuit of wealth in Amsterdam and other great Dutch cities. Even English Presbyterians had objections – not least to the religious toleration practised particularly in the maritime states. The Dutch resistance to binding treaties tilted the scales toward war because it disillusioned their friends and made the complaints of their enemies more potent.[4] Of these, however, none were more influential than the merchants and shipowners jealous of Dutch trade and perceiving Dutch commerce as a many-armed octopus strangling its English competitors.

English and Dutch commercial rivalry went back at least half a century and had become so intense that it might seem surprising that war did not come earlier than 1652. Dutch prosperity was built on a combination of a huge herring fleet and a large merchant marine capable of moving goods to markets as far apart as the Baltic and Japan. Their herring fleet both fed the Dutch and provided them with a valuable export. The merchant fleet also exported Dutch manufactures, especially cloth woven from Spanish wool, but its most significant function was to bring to the Netherlands the products of Europe, Asia Minor, the East and West Indies and North America and to export them to other markets, chiefly in northern and southern Europe. The Dutch shipowners had a stranglehold on the entrepôt trade and the English shipowners, who could not compete on equal terms, both envied and resented them. In the long war against Spain in Elizabeth's reign the English and Dutch had been allies, with Elizabeth supplying subsidies and an army to the Dutch which she could ill afford. Liberation from old Spanish controls and regulations brought Dutch merchants new opportunities. As early as the 1590s the Dutch had begun to take over a substantial share of England's trade to the Baltic and this alarming competition was soon spreading to other markets. The northern European bulk-carrying trade in timber, tar, grain and salt had long been the foundation of Dutch commerce but in the early seventeenth century the Dutch sought to expand their share of the 'rich trades'. These included the hugely valuable spice trade, especially nutmegs and pepper from the East Indies, sugar from the West Indies, ambergris from the North Atlantic whaling grounds, silks from the Orient and the Levant and gold and slaves from West Africa. It also included Dutch woollen manufactures which expanded in quantity and improved in quality during the seventeenth century. This adversely affected not merely English merchants and clothiers but also those powerful landlords whose tenants relied on weaving for much of their livelihood.

The war with Spain had closed the mouth of the Scheldt which transformed the Low Countries economically and socially. The formerly dominant port of Antwerp was impoverished in wealth and population as thousands of skilled artisans, shipwrights, iron-workers, weavers, goldsmiths, silversmiths, bankers, merchants and shipowners fled north into Holland. As Antwerp declined Amsterdam rose to rank among the wealthiest cities of Europe. This extraordinary concentration of capital, commercial expertise, and maritime and industrial skills, cemented by the ideology of urban independence and the Protestant faith, made the Dutch maritime states, but especially Holland, not only the richest commercial society in Europe, but also the most advanced in specialised ship-building and in such infrastructure as inexpensive credit and insurance. It would also give them that unprecedented combination which so alarmed their competitors: dominance over both the bulk trades and the rich trades. These competitors included the Danes, the cities of the Hanseatic League, the Portuguese and the Venetians but none more than the English. During the early years of the reign of James I Dutch competition was less of a problem to the English than it was to become later. The Spanish war which gave the Dutch their commercial independence, also cut them off from their markets in Spain and Flanders. In England the accession of James I made possible peace with Spain in 1604 and the opening of those markets which were still closed to the Dutch. However, James forgot his merchants' interests in 1609 when he helped to broker a peace between the Dutch republic and Spain. The 'truce' then achieved was to last twelve years and with the Dutch quickly resuming their dominance in the Spanish and Mediterranean trades, relations with England deteriorated to the point that war seemed increasingly likely. Indeed in the East Indies, where Dutch traders believed the English should be exterminated as dangerous interlopers, a brief 'naval war' broke out. This would have continued had not a treaty been negotiated between the rival East India companies giving the English a share in the spice trade. (In fact this treaty, in so far as it conceded anything, was never properly fulfilled by the Dutch on the spot.) In 1622 came the 'massacre' at Amboyna in which ten English traders were tortured to implicate themselves and their chief in a crime in which all were innocent. The London populace howled for a war which James I refused to deliver. There were other disputes: over the whaling at Spitzbergen, over the Muscovy trade, even over the dyeing and finishing of England's exported cloths. However, the danger of war was receding after 1621, despite Amboyna and other quarrels, because in that year war reopened between Spain and the Dutch republic and the commercial situation changed decisively in England's favour. Once more Dutch ships and merchants were denied access to Spanish, Portuguese and Flemish ports, from Spanish-controlled Naples and Sicily, and from Genoa which took its lead from Spain. English merchants swiftly captured their rivals' dominance. The prosperous times which ensued for English merchants, shipowners and manufacturers is often ascribed to England's neutrality during the Thirty Years War. In a sense this is true, but it required not just England at peace but the United Provinces at war. Not only were the Dutch excluded from Spanish markets but their trade with other markets suffered. The depredations of privateers operating from Flemish ports like Dunkirk drove up their costs as insurance rates soared and as ships had to be armed and therefore furnished with larger crews (which meant that munitions and extra supplies took up hold space needed for trade goods). Ships suffered delays if they waited for convoys shepherded by the Dutch navy. They still commanded superior resources to their competitors, including the English, in cheap credit, in their very large merchant fleet and in the network of factors in every European port still open to them. The Dutch still could out-trade the English in pepper and spices in France and northern Europe, for their East Indiamen, huge floating fortresses pierced by many gun-ports, had little to fear from privateers. Nevertheless war cost them their superiority to the English and the war lasted until 1648.

The Thirty Years War caused some dislocation of the northern trade and the competition of the Danes and the Hanseatic League prevented the English from monopolising it, but they could dominate the sale of Baltic tar, timber, salt and grain to the Spanish Netherlands. In the south and the Mediterranean the sun shone indeed. They could trade without serious competition to Spanish and Portuguese ports for wool and wine and Spanish silver not only with English manufactures but also with the 'rich trades' brought home by the East India Company, which also enjoyed a virtual monopoly for spices at Genoa. The Dutch even suffered in their trade with the Levant because they were cut off from the Spanish silver with which they had formerly settled their balances at Aleppo. Thanks to the feckless Duke of Buckingham in Charles I's reign England was briefly at war with Spain and France – something which Cromwell, who, unlike Buckingham, would possess a large army and a powerful fleet, would never have contemplated. Happily this was only a blip in the graph of English prosperity until the English Civil War disrupted commerce after 1642. Even these vicissitudes did not destroy England's commercial advantage but before the war began there was an ominous portent. In 1640 Portugal resumed its independence from Spain and promptly made peace with the Dutch. Within a year their ships entering Lisbon outnumbered the English. Should the Dutch make peace with Spain London merchants knew that their currently bulging order books would rapidly grow slender. In 1648 the blow fell when Spanish and Dutch signed the Peace of Munster. The treaty was unpopular with the Dutch who were sure it could not last but mercantile Holland welcomed it with enthusiasm. With peace all the former Dutch advantages returned: the financial power of Amsterdam with its low interest rates which could not be matched in England; a vastly superior coinage to the clipped, debased English equivalent. (Ironically this last advantage would not be matched until England had a Dutch king.) Then there was the physical plant represented by the Dutch merchant fleet. This fleet was huge and, more importantly, its ships could once more operate more cheaply. The Dutch *fluit* was the container vessel of its day. Large, rounded, simply rigged, it required fewer crewmen and carried more cargo than its English equivalent because, unlike large English merchantmen, *fluits* were not warships in embryo. They carried few or no guns. Their simple but efficient rig needed few mariners. Small crews meant lower costs and holds almost entirely devoted to merchandise. A forest of Dutch masts appeared in ports throughout Spain, Flanders and the Two Sicilies. At Genoa the embargo had ended to Dutch profit and substantial English loss as the Dutch quickly re-established their pre-war dominance in Baltic products. English trade was too well entrenched to be reduced to the levels of 1621 but the impact of Dutch competition was everywhere traumatic and in some markets devastating. While the demand for Northern grain expanded in Western Europe the number of English Baltic voyages fell every year successively from 1647 to 1652. By 1650 the Dutch were reported to be carrying 80 per cent of Spain's exports of fine wool while the long-eclipsed Dutch textile industry now challenged English fine cloth in Iberia, Flanders and the Baltic markets. This also helped to revive the Dutch Levant trade.

A particularly humiliating symptom of the transformation wrought by the Peace of Munster was that Spanish wool and Mediterranean goods now arrived in English harbours in Dutch ships. English merchants found their cheaper freights as attractive as any other customer. Here the English government could intervene on behalf of its shipowners. The Navigation Act of 1651 restricted such produce to the holds of English ships. Historians have long debated the origins and motives of this act. It has been attributed not to commercial but to political motives, the Commonwealth using it as a stick to chastise the Dutch for declining its offer of union or at least a close alliance. Pique may have persuaded some parliamentarians to vote for the measure but it has been convincingly demonstrated that pique did not inspire it.[5] Rather it was an influential if loose association of London merchants, which included parliamentary committee members, whose ambition was to drive back Dutch competition and advance English trade (and their own profits) through the device of a national monopoly. In the past foreign trade in England had been a matter for corporate monopolies such as the Merchant Venturers, the East India Company or the Levant Company. These new men were in favour of the very liberalisation and reform which had earlier fuelled Dutch expansion; an early form of what would later be termed 'imperial preference'. The concept was simple: goods imported into England must be brought directly from the country of origin and in English ships or in ships of the country of origin. Moreover no goods of Africa, Asia or America were to be imported in foreign ships. Similarly the harvest of whaling and fishing must have been extracted by English fishermen, and could only be brought in English ships and fish was only to be exported in English ships. With this last exception the act is directed to the control of imports, and the target is clearly the

Dutch entrepôt trade.[6] The monopoly companies had wanted the Dutch restricted by increases in their own privileges, but the government had listened to the 'free' traders and made the terms of the act general, a significant departure from precedent which heralded the beginning of a gradual decline in the significance of these companies in the nation's commerce.[7]

The act hurt the Dutch and they objected to it, sending an embassy to seek the act's repeal. Of this there was no hope as it would bring so many English advantages. Not only did it encourage the native shipping industry, which would in the end provide more ships and experienced mariners for the navy in time of war, but it was expected to solve the problem of England's adverse balance of trade which sent specie abroad; an evil for which the Dutch were blamed. While the act made war more likely by increasing the tension between the two countries, the act did not cause the war. The Dutch did not make war on the English, whatever the Commonwealth might claim later. They wished to preserve the peace because they knew that war would bring them nothing but loss of ships and treasure. Moreover the English had other causes of economic dissatisfaction, some very close to home. The Newcastle coal fleet frequently passed many hundred sail of herring buses heading northward for the fishing grounds. Inward-bound English vessels often found the Thames estuary thronged with the little craft which had followed the herring shoals south from the Shetlands. Wherever English mariners looked abroad, there the Dutch were usually in much greater numbers. English merchant shipowners had only to peer into their ledgers to perceive the impact of Dutch competition. The Dutch were now embarked on their greatest phase of commercial expansion, making Amsterdam the commercial capital of an empire with trading posts and colonies in North America, the Caribbean, West Africa, around the Indian Ocean and through the East Indies. Of course, others suffered from this Dutch expansion, the Hanseatic towns and the Danes among them, but they were too weak to challenge the Dutch. Indeed the King of Denmark had felt constrained in 1648 to give the Dutch a treaty which provided that in effect they paid no tolls to pass into or out of the Baltic and gave all Dutch ships a cost advantage over all their competitors. However, if these competitors were helpless the Commonwealth was another matter. Possessed of a navy potentially more powerful in size of ships and weight of guns than any afloat it would not long suffer such heavy blows to its trade without being tempted to employ it.

At sea politics and commerce curiously intertwined because of the ancient claim of English kings to command of the seas around the British Isles, a claim which the Commonwealth would extend even further. If other countries accepted this claim, and the Commonwealth insisted repeatedly that the Dutch must do so even when they were most ardently seeking an alliance with them, then logically all merchant or naval ships which passed through the Channel or the North Sea did so only by the Commonwealth government's consent. This is the importance of the apparently insulting claim that all foreign ships should salute English warships by lowering their topsails and flags. The claim to the 'sovereignty of the seas', however unreasonable, was not without practical significance. It empowered English warships and privateers to stop foreign ships and search them for 'contraband', that is, cargoes consigned to any country with which England was at war – even if war had not been officially declared. Since 1649 the Commonwealth had been engaged in an undeclared maritime war with France which chiefly involved English privateers. These were more cruel in their deprivations than the navy. (Some privateersmen had tortured Dutch crews to make them 'confess' that their cargoes were bound for France when they were not.) The Dutch rejected the concept of contraband, insisting that the flag covered ship and cargo. All their cargoes were Dutch until they arrived at their destination. If the ship was neutral so were its contents. The carrying trade would become a nightmare if Dutch *fluits* could be the legitimate prey of anyone at war with the country for which their cargo was destined. The Dutch entrepôt trade was founded on their carrying the goods of all nations. However, the Commonwealth would not concede the Dutch claim because it was so inimical to its interests. Attempts to persuade St John and Strickland to back down on this point were as much a failure as their own proposal of a treaty of union. English privateersmen and occasionally naval vessels continued to seize Dutch ships and cargoes. A Dutch vessel transporting a cargo to Scotland which was carrying 'contraband' to the Commonwealth's Scottish opponents was fired on by a naval flotilla when it refused to permit a search. The gunfire slew the captain and most of his crew and the vessel then burned and sank. The Dutch tried to retaliate but their slender gains could not balance their substantial losses, even when the French permitted Dutch privateers to use the sanctuary of Dunkirk. Large English merchant ships, armed for self-defence, could resist privateers more effectively than the *fluits*. The English seized 140 Dutch ships during 1651 and a further thirty during January 1652.

In the face of such provocation it may seem surprising that the Dutch did not themselves declare war before the close of 1651. After all the Dutch, during military and naval campaigns which extended over a period of eighty-one years (interrupted only by the truce from 1609 to 1621), had successfully achieved their independence from the greatest power in Europe, the Spanish empire. They were the only country to emerge from the Thirty Years War wealthier than when they entered it. They had extended their territories at the expense of the Spanish Netherlands. They had obtained Spain's acknowledgement of their independence and, more remarkably, the right to trade with the Spanish overseas empire. Their admirals were seasoned and experienced both in war and as mariners. By contrast the English navy had not fought a fleet action since the Armada. Charles I's failed expeditions against Cadiz and La Rochelle hardly matched the achievements of admirals like Tromp against the Spanish fleet. Since the execution of Charles I the navy had been 'new-modelled' like the parliamentary army before it. That is it had been reorganised, its leadership changed, its strength increased by new construction. However, although it had mopped up Prince Rupert's privateers, conquered the remaining royalist outposts in the Scilly and Channel Isles, and had even blockaded Lisbon and established a Mediterranean presence, these useful achievements were still hardly comparable to the exploits of the Dutch navy in the Thirty Years War. Contemplating the successful United Provinces, with Amsterdam the financial capital of Europe, with the Dutch perceived as Europe's most industrious, efficient and sophisticated people, defended by an effective army and an undefeated navy, foreign observers believed that the Dutch were the likelier victors in any war with the Commonwealth.

Dutch statesmen were less optimistic, particularly those from Holland, the state which would have to pay the most war taxes and lose the most shipping. When war became certain in 1652 the Grand Pensionary of Holland, Adriaen Pauw, gloomily observed: 'The English are about to attack a mountain of gold; we are about to attack a mountain of iron.' The Dutch merchant marine was much larger and more valuable than its English equivalent, and the English coastline from Lands End to the Wash stooped over its trade routes like a bird of prey. This naval war would be fought in seas which the valuable Dutch convoys were compelled to cross inward and outward. While Dutch naval vessels and privateers would pick up English prizes, they would be few compared to the host of ships which were likely to fall into English hands. The Dutch admirals were experienced. Their opponents were not. Nevertheless even if the Dutch admirals won victories at sea what benefits could this war bring which the Dutch did not possess already, save hopefully a treaty which bound the English to respect the neutrality of the Dutch flag?

This reasoning explains why Dutch negotiators reached London in December 1651 eager to discuss a general settlement of grievances. They were hampered by their States General's demand for the repeal of the Navigation Act although there was no intention of going to war over that issue. The real issue was the English assaults on their ships, and establishing the principle that the flag covered the cargo. Dutch neutrality must protect her maritime commerce, the foundation of her wealth. Naturally the ambassadors sought damages for ships and cargoes already lost and in rejoinder the English brandished claims both real and imaginary for depredations across the oceans and stretching back to the 'massacre' of Amboyna. These protracted negotiations were still in train the following February when the Commonwealth discovered that the States General had voted to fit out a fleet of 150 sail. This was one of the immediate causes of the war. The Dutch had austere notions of profit and loss which persuaded them to keep feeble naval forces in time of peace. To prepare for war was sensible, but to announce so huge a fleet was seen as a threat. Indeed it was intended to persuade the English to moderate their demands. The effect was the reverse and, worst of all, the threat was without substance. The Dutch were incapable of providing so large a fleet in 1652 and that which they could mobilise largely consisted of ships inferior to those they would have to confront.

By May the Commonwealth was still resolutely demanding the recognition of England's sovereignty of the seas, the payment of tribute for fishing in British seas, and the Dutch abandoning their claim that their flag made their cargoes neutral. Admiral Blake was ordered to collect a strong summer guard in the Downs. In retaliation the States General ordered Tromp to sea. However, even after that first, half accidental, engagement between Tromp and Blake off Dover, Grand Pensionary Pauw was sent to England in June as a last-ditch attempt to avoid war. It was in vain. The Commonwealth would not back down while the Dutch government dared not display weakness to its own people, which was clamouring for war, lest it revive the fortunes of the Orange Party. On 6 July the

States General ordered Tromp to lose no opportunity to attack the English fleet and do it 'all imaginable damage'.

What were these fleets which were now to meet in battle? The Dutch fleet was organised and financed by the five admiralties of the United Provinces from customs duties which it was the admiralties' responsibility to collect.[8] These admiralties had been created in 1597 by the Seven Provinces in their States General as a purely temporary measure which was destined to survive until the end of the republic in 1795. Three of these admiralties were within Holland. The most important admiralty was at Amsterdam, Rotterdam had the Admiralty of the Maas (or Meuse) while the Admiralty of the North Quarter was alternately based on Hoorn and Enkhuizen to pacify local jealousies. The other two were in Friesland (at Harlingen) and Zeeland (Middelburg).[9] The navy was a mixture. It included 'states ships' some of which had been built as warships while others had been converted from ocean-going merchant ships. The remainder of the fleet was composed of merchant ships hired from shipowners and converted to naval use by increasing their armament. A fleet so composed might appear unsatisfactory to later generations of naval officers but it had one real advantage in 1651–2: it was simple to re-create. Its re-creation was necessary because after the Peace of Munster the navy had largely been sold off on the principle of beating swords into ploughshares by increasing the merchant fleet and relieving the tax burden. Now those states ships which had survived disarmament could be reactivated. Those which had been sold could be hired back or repurchased as could other merchant ships. In the meantime work could begin on constructing more warships which would come into service if the war lasted longer than was hoped. However, the Dutch learned a lesson from 1651–2. When peace returned they would resolve to maintain a strong peacetime navy.[10]

Dutch warships would prey on English commerce and could capture English naval vessels, especially converted merchantmen, which could be taken into the navy or sold to shipowners for civilian use. Dutch tactics would be based on 'disable and capture' – or burn. Their ships would be packed with armed men. Their aim would be to dismast their opponents with their guns, kill or disable the mariners with musket fire, and then board to suppress all resistance from the survivors. Alternatively, fireships would be employed against vessels which had been dismasted. The Dutch were masters of the use of fireships and expected to use them to great effect against the English. Large crews meant that Dutch warships, especially the smaller ships, and only a minority were larger than 450 tons, could not make long voyages because they could not carry stores for so many hungry mouths. However, they should not need to. Naval battles between Dutch and English would naturally be fought in the southern areas of the North Sea or in the Channel close to their bases. So the Dutch navy as it hastily re-created itself in 1651–2 was strong in numbers of men but weak in numbers and size of guns. Their ships were smaller and of shallower draught than English warships so that they could navigate the shoal-strewn estuaries of the Dutch rivers. Nevertheless, their ships were numerous, fast and manoeuvrable when their bottoms were not foul, and represented a formidable threat to any opponent who possessed a fleet built on the same principles for the same tactics.

The problem was that the English navy was not built on those principles nor, it appears, had it been even in the era of Drake and Hawkins more than half a century earlier. For this we have an unlikely authority, King Phillip II of Spain. Humourless, crippled by gout and excessive piety, conscientious to a fault, the king could be relied on to do his homework. He advised the Duke of Medina-Sidonia, whose unhappy fate it was to command the Armada, that 'the enemy's aim will be to fight from a distance, since he has the advantage of superior artillery . . . while ours must be to attack, and come to grips with the enemy' and he promised the duke should receive a detailed report of the way in which the enemy 'arranges his artillery so as to be able to aim the broadsides low in the hull and so sink his opponent's ships'.[11] Since then little had changed except that English warships had grown larger and their guns, at least in the lower tier, even heavier. The Dutch, therefore, might encounter some of the unhappy experiences of the Spanish in 1588. The English had some very large ships, which were then loosely termed 'great ships' but classified as 'first-rates'. Charles I had created with the 'ship money' tax, which had so alienated his subjects during the 1630s, a small but potentially formidable fleet of large- and medium-sized warships which was first commanded by the Earl of Northumberland, a skilled admiral, and then from 1642 by the parliamentarian Earl of Warwick. Northumberland's second 'ship-money fleet' of 1636 contained 27 ships of which 18 were purpose built, 4 were 'whelps' (smaller support vessels or scouts) and 5 were hired armed merchant-ships. The true warships were of 24 to 42 guns. However, when Warwick took over six years later the fleet had been strengthened. Now it contained two giant ships, the *Sovereign of the Seas*, 110 guns, 1,200 tons, built in 1637, and the *Prince Royal*, 70, 1,187 tons, built in 1641 (renamed *Resolution* under the Commonwealth).[12] There were 12 large warships of 700–900 tons armed with more than 40 guns including the *James*, 48 (but later 66), *Charles*, 44, *Unicorn*, 46, *Henrietta Maria* (later renamed *Paragon*), 42 and 8 smaller ships of between 30 to 40 guns. Warwick commanded until late in 1648 and during his time 7 'frigates' of between 440 and 650 tons and 32 to 46 guns joined the fleet, including the original 'frigate', the privately owned *Constant Warwick* which was built in 1645, hired until 1649 and then purchased. Commonwealth frigates were two-decker warships which took their place in the battle fleet, were classed as third, fourth or fifth-rates according to tonnage and armament, and should not be confused with late eighteenth-century frigates.[13]

This was only the beginning. After serious mutinies inspired by the trial and execution of the king which many officers and crew had never bargained for, the navy was purged of dissidents and 'new-modelled'. New commanders were appointed from the army, styled 'generals-at-sea' when they were of admiral rank, crews were either persuaded into loyalty or replaced. Administration was placed in the hands of commissioners in February 1649. The Navy Commissioners proved indefatigable builders and purchasers. They added forty-one new ships from 1649 to the close of 1651 (including sixteen privateers captured from either the Dutch or the French).[14] Among them were such third-rates (large frigates) as the *Speaker*, 50–56 guns, 778 tons net, the *Fairfax*, 52, 789 tons net, and the *Worcester*, 48, and *Antelope*, 56 and the ship which has the dubious honour of

A parliamentary fourth-rate, similar to the Constant Warwick, *by William van de Velde the Elder (National Maritime Museum, Greenwich, London)*

initiating the first action of the war, the *President* (or *Great President*), 38.[15] With war would come an even heavier expansion as at least 111 ships of all sizes, including prizes, were added between 1652 and 1654. Of these, eleven were third-rates of between 48 and 52 guns, and fifteen fourth-rates of between 38 and 48 guns.

With few Dutch warships armed with more than forty guns this new English fleet was a formidable force, for it was not primarily numbers of ships which made the Commonwealth navy such a dangerous weapon but the guns its ships carried into action. Bruijn states that no less than fourteen ships carried an equal or far greater number of guns than Tromp's *Brederode*, the most formidable Dutch warship (but even that was a converted East Indiaman).[16] Oppenheim lists the 56 guns carried on the large frigates as 4 demi-cannon, 22 culverins, 26 demi-culverins and 8 sakers.[17] (Demi-cannon were 32-pounders, culverins were 24-pounders, demi-culverins were then 18-pounders and sakers 9-pounders.) In fact armament varied from ship to ship, and if the lists are to be believed, the number of guns on a ship might vary over time. Standardisation, even as an objective, had to await the later years of Samuel Pepys's administration. Nevertheless this represents an impressive armament for a third-rate and if Dutch admirals knew these details it should have caused them concern. The 'great ships',

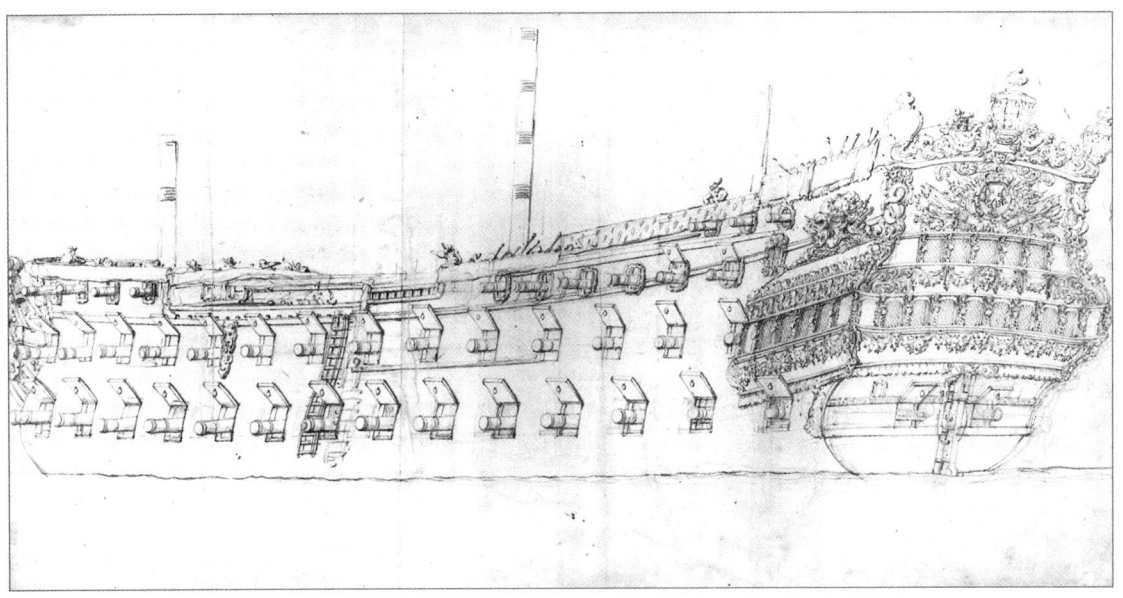

The Speaker, *by William van de Velde the Elder (National Maritime Museum, Greenwich, London)*

the first-rates *Sovereign* and *Resolution* carried cannon (sometimes called 'cannon-drakes') which fired a 42-pound shot, a weapon normally seen on land only at sieges, and the second-rates (among them *Triumph, George, Andrew, Victory* and *Swiftsure*), carried a larger but varying number of the 32-pounder demi-cannon in their bottom tiers. Heavy guns could cause serious, perhaps even fatal, damage to the hulls of ships which were lightly armed not least because lightly constructed. For there was the rub. Ships which were not already armed with heavy guns could not simply be armed with them to meet a new technological situation in time of war. These iron guns, weighing several hundredweight with their carriages, needed heavy beams to reinforce the deck from which they would fire and which would have to withstand the vibrations of their heavy recoil. Ships needed to be built with such forces in mind. Converted merchant ships, which formed the bulk of the Dutch fleet were not built to carry heavy guns but neither were purpose-built Dutch warships. To carry such weight the Dutch would need ships of broader beam than they usually built because more substantial frames and heavier guns on a ship of their normal beam brought more displacement of water and a deeper draught than many of the lesser harbours and broad but shallow estuaries could float. A broader beam spread the weight and lessened the draught but would slow the ship through the water and Dutch officers wanted fast, manoeuvrable ships to effect their captures. As a result sacrifices had to be made and few Dutch ships mounted cannon heavier than 24-pounders and 18-pounders were more usual. Indeed heavy iron guns were not even manufactured in the Netherlands and were difficult to import in time of war.[18]

If the English began the war with a technological advantage, what of their crews? Their merchant marine was considerable but was far smaller than that of the Dutch. They would always be struggling to crew their ships simply because their ships were so large and so heavily armed that they needed large crews if the guns were to be operated on both broadsides. In fact it is clear that some ships with more than 20 guns a side did not have sufficient crewmen to provide gun crews for all the guns at the same time. However, if there was time to reload the guns, run them out and fasten the breechings on both sides, the gunners and other nominated assistants could have fired the guns when the great ship's bell tolled above them. Then it would have taken some time before the gun crews could run the guns in and reload them first on one side, then on the other. Often an attacking ship would come down on an enemy with the wind. Once in range it would put the helm over, fire a broadside, wear round, fire the other broadside and then tack off as the crew busily reloaded before making another attacking run perhaps as long as an hour later. One solution to the lack of men was open to both sides but much more to the English: sending soldiers to sea. The English soldiers were disciplined and battle-hardened. Another advantage possessed by the English navy in 1652 – and we shall see that this is sustained throughout the war – was the high morale of the sailors. Although pay would seem hopelessly irregular to modern eyes, food unpalatable, water and beer often worse, their conditions were vastly superior to those endured by their unpaid, half starved predecessors of Charles I's navy. The Commonwealth had resources of taxation and fines and sales of property unknown to the first Stuart kings and they laboured hard to pay their sailors and to care for the sick or wounded and for the dependants of the slain. The sailors repaid this solicitude by very low rates of desertion compared with the Dutch fleet even though large numbers of the crew were pressed into service against their will. Finally they were well led and they knew it. Robert Blake was a legend among his men long before the Dutch War and his colleagues Deane, Monck, Penn and Lawson (of whom only Penn was a seaman rather than a 'general-at-sea') seem to have been respected by their men and respected by each other, and to have deserved it. During the coming war there would be none of the rivalries and divisions which so frequently characterised the Dutch high command. To the first campaigns of that war we must now turn.

CHAPTER 3

First Campaigns: From the Shetlands to the Casquets

> By a letter from Sir George Ayscue . . . from the Downs the Dutch have appeared there with a fleet consisting of 102 men-of-war, besides 10 fire-ships which are divided into three squadrons, being not far asunder . . .
> Council of State to Admiral Blake, 11 July 1652[1]

The Commonwealth government saw the Dutch merchant marine as the prime target of their navy, not Tromp's battle-fleet. The Netherlands could hardly survive the destruction, or even better the capture, of the bulk of that rich asset and would be compelled to sue for peace while its destruction would give English commerce a huge if only short-term advantage. That is why as early as 10 June the Council of State authorised Blake 'to take and seize upon the Dutch East India Fleet homeward bound and secure the same, or as many as shall be taken' and send them into port as prizes. He should do this in a way which would enable him also to destroy or disrupt the Dutch herring fleet which was fishing off the English and Scottish coasts. He was also to take similar measures against the Dutch 'Eastland' (that is, the Baltic) trade.[2] These orders all demanded the same response: a voyage northward to an area where he could ambush both East India and Baltic convoys before they had entered the North Sea. If all the navy had to do was to wreak havoc among the Dutch merchant marine then this would have been a well-conceived plan, particularly since the government intended to leave a subsidiary fleet in the Downs to ambush Dutch vessels coming home through the Narrow Seas. However, the navy had another role which the orders did not mention: it must face the Dutch navy in battle and hopefully inflict a decisive defeat. Indeed this should come first. Once Tromp and his fellow admirals were crushed there would be nothing to protect the Dutch merchant marine save their own guns which would be no match for Blake's heavily armed men-of-war. If, on the other hand, Blake's fleet should be scattered commerce-raiding, with his ships' companies depleted by the need to furnish prize crews, and Tromp should arrive on the scene with his formidable fleet, united and battle ready, the consequences could be disastrous. Blake himself had never faced an enemy battle-fleet and may have been too inexperienced to perceive the flaws in his masters' strategy. There is no evidence that he questioned his orders and the priorities they reflected.

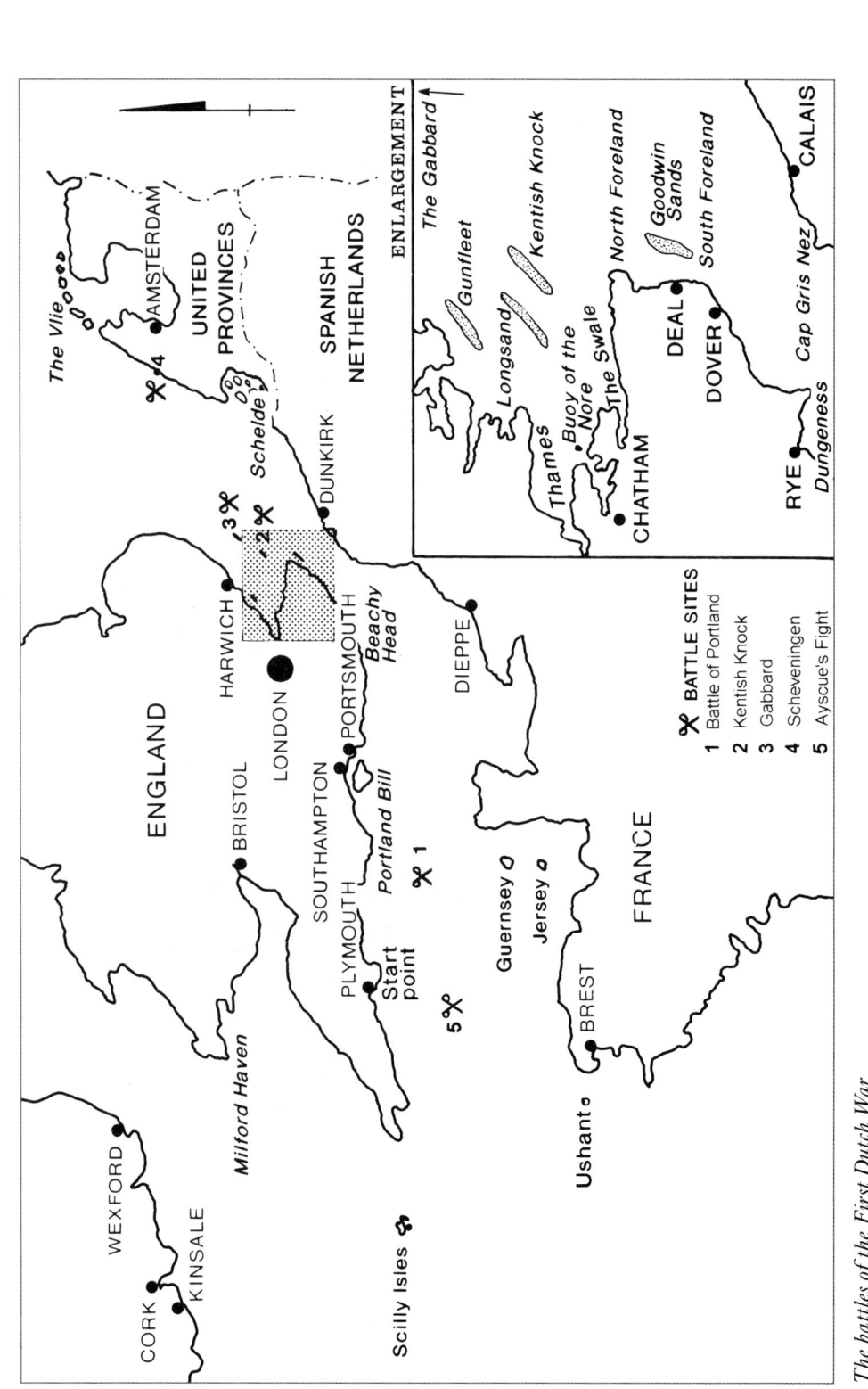

The battles of the First Dutch War

When the war began Blake lay in the Downs with a substantial fleet. The Council of State and even its Navy Committee seems to have been disconcertingly vague as to just how substantial this fleet was, since in the second week of June it sent a Colonel Thompson to 'take an exact account of them' and also to determine how many of them were 'state's ships' (that is, naval vessels) and how many were armed merchantmen.[3] The Council was labouring to organise and equip a fleet of thirty merchantmen in the Thames together with two or three warships, including the *Vanguard* and *Success*, and orders had been issued to mobilise the *Sovereign*, the largest capital ship afloat. Blake was also authorised to take into service four captured Dutch warships. (Three of these may have been armed merchantmen serving as escorts.) On 29 May the Council had informed Blake that a Dutch convoy of sixty sail had passed Weymouth and on 11 June Blake reported that he had captured 'eleven Holland' ships laden with 'salt, etc.' together with 'a cruiser of 22 guns' and sent them into Dover.[4] The Council's correspondence during June contains many references to Dutch prisoners, Dutch prizes and cargoes. All armed vessels, men-of-war, merchantmen and prizes, were to be sent to the Downs as reinforcement as soon as they could be made ready. On 15 June Sir George Ayscue, now returned from the Barbados, was ordered to take his squadron of seven ships to the Downs to join Blake's fleet although (as it later appeared) he would remain there commanding whatever ships Blake left to guard the Narrow Seas when he sailed north. Ten days later the Council, learning that Blake was off the South Foreland and ready for sea, wrote asking him to let them know the names of the ships he would sail with and those he would leave behind under Ayscue. This implies that they had left him to decide how strong a force he would take and how relatively weak a force he would leave watching the Narrow Seas.[5] Unfortunately Blake sailed about the time the letter was written so on 28 June the Council was driven to ask Ayscue what ships he commanded.[6] Ayscue had the seven ships he had taken to the Barbados – the *Rainbow*, 52 (flagship), *Amity*, 36, *Success*, 30, *Increase of London*, 36, *Malaga Merchant*, 30, *Ruth*, 30 and '*Brazil* frigate', 24 – together with the *Paragon*, 42 (the former *Henrietta Maria*), *John and Elizabeth* and the *Mary*, 24, and about eight others whose names are not recorded. The *John and Elizabeth*, *Increase* and *Malaga Merchant* were clearly armed merchantmen. The reinforcements the Council had been preparing throughout June were still in the Thames. By 14 June the Council had learned from its spies abroad that Tromp's fleet 'doth daily increase and is now recruited to considerable numbers' so it seems remarkable that they should allow Blake to divide his fleet with Tromp's fleet just over the horizon.[7] It seems more remarkable still that once Blake had sailed they should then decide that they did not know where he had gone. Nevertheless on 30 June they querulously complained that when Blake had sailed from Dover he had sent no word 'what design' he was upon nor what course he had set, nor could the rest of the fleet inform them either, so that they did not know where to send to him nor how best to direct the ships he had left behind. They also seem to have realised the danger in which Blake might have left Ayscue and even the south-east coast and Thames estuary by his departure, because they anxiously enquired what he had decided to do about Tromp's fleet 'whereunto you are *in the first place* to have respect by your instructions'.[8] Had Blake received this letter his response might well have been that far from giving Tromp's fleet priority, their instructions to him had clearly required a northern voyage against Dutch trade routes and so they should have understood that that was where he was heading. A week later the Council learned where Blake was when he sent Dutch prisoners into Sunderland from ships which he had seized and sent dispatches south over land. It is likely that Blake was prepared to leave Ayscue vulnerable because he reasoned that Tromp must follow him north to defend the vital convoys.

Admiral Ayscue may have made the same calculation for he showed no anxiety about his exposed position. He did beg the Council for a couple of smacks or ketches 'or other small, nimble vessels' for scouting for by 3 July he had learned nothing about Tromp's movements.[9] This ignorance had not inhibited him from a sortie which was certain to bring him to Tromp's attention and might persuade the Dutchman that he had better rid the Narrow Seas of this nuisance before he turned to pursue Blake. When Ayscue learned that a convoy of thirty or forty Dutch merchantmen, homeward bound from Portugal, were approaching with an escort of four warships he had sortied against them with nine ships. His leading vessels came up with the convoy at first light off the French coast. There was little resistance. Ayscue's flotilla captured five, twenty-six ran themselves ashore on Calais sands while a further eight fled north-east. Ayscue's boats' crews fired three despite furious resistance by the French, who were as eager to plunder the stranded ships as were the English to destroy them. The rest Ayscue believed could never be got off, being much battered by cannon fire and of deep draught, while a wind had got up which would 'be as destructive an enemy to them as their French friends'.[10] In fact the French in their eagerness for plunder were observed cutting holes in the helpless vessels' sides and then hauling away the cargoes in carts. The eight who fled were pursued but they only caught one and after a sharp fight in which one of his pursuers, the *John and Elizabeth*, suffered heavy casualties the Dutchman was driven ashore near Gravelines and burned. All the captured ships together with the *John and Elizabeth* were brought into Dover.

The following day the States General reported to Tromp that some English ships still lay in the Downs and since the wind continued northerly, making a pursuit of Blake impossible until it changed, he might as well 'attack, destroy or capture them'. However, he must break off and pursue Blake should the wind turn southerly. The admiral received the same advice from the Dutch plenipotentiary, Pauw, who chanced to fall in with Tromp while returning from his fruitless embassy. Pauw boarded the *Brederode* and gave Tromp accurate intelligence of English naval dispositions. Tromp approached the North Foreland slowly during the 5th and 6th, much hindered by light winds. His plan was to send Witte Cornelis de With, the Vice-Admiral of Holland who had just joined him with a flotilla of eight ships, and Pieter Floriszoon, Vice-Admiral of the North Quarter, with his squadron to stop up the southern entrance to the Downs. Ayscue would then be trapped when Tromp entered the Downs with the main fleet from the north and he could repeat his famous victory over the Spanish there in 1639. First, however, he placed a squadron off the Longsands in the hope of ambushing a flotilla of armed merchantmen, commanded by Captain Harrison,

Sir George Ayscue, by Sir Peter Lely (National Maritime Museum, Greenwich, London)

which had been preparing to sail from the Thames estuary to reinforce Ayscue. On 7 July scouts sent by Ayscue to North Sands Head reported at least sixty Dutch ships approaching. Ayscue, who had gone ashore for medical treatment, sent a dispatch to order Harrison to hold his position before hastening back to his flagship, the *Rainbow*. All he could do in the face of such overwhelming odds was to draw his twenty ships together for all-round defence under the guns of Deal Castle and other shore forts which protected the Downs. He also ordered the installation of additional shore batteries which could pound the Dutch men-of-war as they drew closer to him. The Dutch fleet, which amounted to more than ninety sail, excluding fireships and dispatch vessels, seemed oddly hesitant to engage. According to Tromp having been first afflicted by calms, the northerly resumed on the evening of 8 July so strongly that several fireships separated from the fleet, and of those which remained three were in danger of sinking. By daybreak on the 11th the fleet was close to the North Foreland and in high hopes of entering the Downs and assaulting their enemy. Happily for Ayscue the wind suddenly dropped to a flat calm leaving the Dutch no alternative but to anchor. When the wind resumed it was from the south and Tromp immediately seized the opportunity to head north after Blake's fleet. It seemed that Ayscue's small command had enjoyed a narrow escape and that Tromp had lost a great opportunity. However, as a monarchist Tromp had many republican enemies and knew that his great reputation and his popularity with his men would not save him if he failed to save the convoys.

Throughout this alarming sequence of events Admiral Blake in his new flagship *Resolution* was leading his fleet up the Scottish coast in the face of the same adverse wind which had confined Tromp to the Narrow Seas. The southerly change of 11 July which allowed Tromp to pursue also favoured the English fleet and the 12th found him at his rendezvous off the Shetlands. He promptly detached Admiral William Penn's squadron to attack the naval escorts of the Dutch herring fleet. Penn's six smaller, faster frigates soon located their prey and after a sharp fight of about three hours the escorts were finally overwhelmed by superior fire-power when Penn's *Speaker*, 52, arrived to join the battle. Eleven escorts surrendered and a twelfth was captured the following day. Three were so shattered by the English broadsides that they were later scuttled, three others Blake sent to Inverness. The remainder he added to his fleet. More than 900 prisoners were randomly taken aboard Penn's ships while English crewmen were sent to man the prizes. This randomness alarmed Blake who ordered Penn to ensure that no ship was put at risk from being stripped of its crew nor from embarking too many prisoners. As for the fleet of more than 600 herring buses Blake chose to temper his masters' instructions with mercy. As early as 1 July he had ordered that the fishermen should be left unscathed.[11] Most of them had fled behind the screen of their escorts when the English frigates bore down. However, a Dutch account reports that one captured fisher captain, who was brought aboard the *Resolution* to meet the admiral, came from Schiedam, a port in which Blake had lived for several years as a young man. The two men exchanged reminiscences while the *Resolution*'s crew thronged the bulwarks to gaze in wonder at the fishermen below busily curing their herring. Leaving a gift of fish the Dutchman gratefully departed and like his compatriots headed home. This generous treatment hardly fulfilled Blake's directions to destroy the Dutch herring fleet but he had no intention of waging war on non-combatants, nor could his fleet have coped with the logistical problems presented by so large a number of prisoners.

Tromp had never been in a position to prevent the destruction of the fishing fleet's escorts but with just a modicum of luck he might reach the English fleet before the convoys encountered the enemy. Although the Dutch fleet of about 100 ships appeared dauntingly huge to the spectators who had watched it pass along the English coast it was not as formidable as it appeared. It was inadequately manned and so badly provisioned that if Tromp had possessed full crews they would have been hungry before they reached the Shetlands. Morale was low because Tromp had been compelled to cut the much-prized daily beer ration (eight pints per man), and because the month's supply of food they carried was of poor quality and had to be rationed because they might exhaust it unless provision ships found them at sea. Scurvy already haunted the fleet. Tromp's shortage of men led him to the extraordinary act of pressing the crews of English fishing boats and small coasters which the fleet captured as it moved up the East Coast, unwilling crewmen who put still more pressure on Tromp's inadequate stores. There was another weakness which might prove most damaging of all if Tromp and Blake met in battle. The East Coast fishing smacks, whether fleeing before the Dutch or run down and captured, contained sharp-eyed, knowing men. Blake might appear outnumbered by the Dutch host to awestruck landsmen but to these mariners it was obvious that the Dutch were not only under-manned: they were badly out-gunned. A Dover-based skipper, who had visited the *Brederode* in a vain attempt to persuade the admiral to return his pressed seamen, reported that she was an old East India ship of 56 guns, but the vice-admiral's ship carried at most 36 while there were not more than 'twenty sail in the whole fleet above 34 guns per ship'. The rest of the fleet were ships of only 20 to 30 guns.[12]

This hungry under-gunned fleet, still accompanied by several fireships which were barely capable of surviving a stiff breeze, now approached the same fateful rendezvous which Blake had selected: Fair Isle. Blake had calculated that incoming convoys would gather there either for mutual defence or to await naval escort. Tromp had realised that Blake would make that calculation. A battle seemed certain but as the fleets drew close together north of the Shetlands the wind dropped, fog came down and both rode the sluggish swell in mutual frustration. Late in the afternoon of 25 July the wind rose again, blowing briskly but erratically boxing the compass. As the sun set Tromp's lookouts spied the distant sails of English warships. The main body of Blake's fleet must be just below the horizon. During the night the wind settled into the north-west and at dawn the Dutch were surprised to find several West Indiamen sailing in their midst. Providentially, in the darkness they had fallen in with the Dutch, not the English fleet. For at least two of the newcomers, one of whom was the admiral of the convoy, their joy was premature for the wind suddenly strengthened into a ferocious gale. As one Dutch survivor later wrote:

The fleet being . . . buried by the sea in the most horrible abysses, rose out of them, only to be tossed up to the clouds; here the masts were beaten down into the sea, there the deck was overflowed . . . The tempest was so much the mistress . . . the ships could be governed no longer.[13]

With the Dutch drifting down on the Shetlands' menacing cliffs, it was every captain for himself and the fleet scattered. High on his lofty poop deck the anguished Tromp saw one of his ships engulfed. Ten of her crew were snatched from the sea by one of her consorts and one can only marvel at the seamanship such a feat would have demanded. Captains scarcely able to save their own ships, let alone come to the aid of lumbering merchantmen, saw two of the West Indiamen smashed on the cliffs. When the weather moderated on 27 July Tromp found his fleet of almost a hundred sail had declined to thirty-four. The fireships had been engulfed or wrecked. The English had seen ten Dutch warships cast away on the Shetlands and six more had foundered at sea. Several Dutch warships found themselves off Norway, fifty-one found precarious shelter in the western fiords of the Shetlands. On the whole the Dutch merchantmen had fared better. Although the convoys had been scattered several merchantmen had contrived to stay with Tromp's remaining ships and of the rest most would come safely home, although battered and much delayed. The English fleet had fared better than their opponents. Further from land at its height and so less menaced by a lee shore, they had found shelter in Bressay Sound on Shetland's east coast. Although none escaped some damage, and many were left unfit for action, at least the English could lick their wounds in a friendly anchorage. There was no such rest and recuperation for the Dutch. After the storm blew itself out Tromp cruised back and forth for two days vainly seeking to round up more ships as his fleet made hasty repairs in the lighter conditions. Finally he called a council of war on the *Brederode* of all his remaining captains. They knew that some of their ships had been wrecked with all or most of their crews drowned. They knew nothing of the fate of the rest and could only pray that they were still afloat and would manage to reach home. They took comfort from the fact that they had several valuable merchantmen in company which they could escort to safety, and from the fact that if the storm had robbed them of a chance to engage the enemy it had also frustrated the English. They all agreed to make the best of a bad situation and head for home. It was the correct decision.

The Dutch were scattered, the English were concentrated but licking their wounds. Both Blake and Tromp mourned the loss of a fleet action but their sorrow was misplaced. Paradoxically the gale had given the English some of the fruits of a victory while sparing Tromp from a probable defeat. The English were in a far better position to fight a prolonged fleet action than their opponents in terms of guns, men and provisions. This English advantage was not then fully understood by the Dutch although in the autumn they would learn a bitter lesson about their inferiority of armament. Blake might have believed the storm had robbed him of victory but that storm gave him its fruits because it inflicted heavy losses on the Dutch fleet with no losses to his own. Tromp had lost at least sixteen warships and several merchantmen without the firing of a shot. In a fleet action

Blake could not have hoped for so favourable a result with no loss to himself. At Blake's greatest victory the following year the Dutch would lose seventeen warships and thirty merchantmen but the battle would cost the English a ship and hundreds of casualties including some of their best captains. The Dutch knew they had suffered a disaster as their warships straggled home during the following weeks with many seamen injured, more struck down by scurvy, all half starving. Of the fifty-one stragglers none could be refitted in time to take part in the autumn campaign in the Channel. Unexpectedly there was to be another English gain. The disaster gave Tromp's republican enemies the opportunity to get rid of this staunch monarchist. His instructions had not only sent him out with inadequate provisions, they had forbidden him from returning to port for supplies or to repair his ships. He must supply himself from pursuing storeships which might not find him and effect all repairs at sea. Clearly these instructions were written by armchair strategists from a comfortable boardroom but their lack of realism did not prevent his enemies from making Tromp a scapegoat for the failure of the campaign. Tromp resigned before they could have him dismissed but his enemies had thrown away the services of the Netherlands' most experienced admiral and further undermined the fleet's morale. Unaware of the fate of his adversary Blake came south as soon as the bulk of his fleet had completed running repairs. He was off Southwold on the Suffolk coast on 9 August and a week later arrived safely in the Downs, where his ships could be repaired in a secure anchorage. There was need for speed because Blake had learned of a fresh Dutch sortie, this time down-Channel, and he wished to reinforce Sir George Ayscue in the hope of a decisive engagement.

As Tromp's strength had waned in the north Sir George Ayscue's had waxed in the south. He had been reinforced shortly after Tromp sailed north and although reports of his numbers vary he must have had between forty-five and fifty ships, two of which were of 60 guns, including the *George* to which he moved his flag, and the *Vanguard* which his Vice-Admiral, William Haddock, took over from Captain Harrison who had brought the reinforcements from the Thames estuary. Dutch observers considered that at least eight other ships mounted from 40 to 36 guns. This may well be an underestimate. Ayscue would need all the strength he could muster for he would soon be confronted by a new and dangerous opponent. Michiel Adrianszoon de Ruyter, the man of the future as Tromp was the man of the past, was to cut his teeth as an independent commander on Ayscue's squadron. Ayscue received instructions about 17 July that he must take his fleet westward to protect East India Company and West Indies ships coming into the Western Approaches. He was also to attack and take any Dutch warships or merchant ships he encountered. On 31 July he escorted five East Indiamen into Plymouth and then cruised off Land's End where he took four prizes, of which one was French, and returned with them to Plymouth.

The failure of Tromp to destroy Ayscue's command had meant that the Narrow Seas were unsafe for Dutch merchantmen coming up-Channel. The States General therefore sent de Ruyter to sea with the rank of commodore and a squadron of twenty men-of-war and four fireships. On 1 August de Ruyter had heard reports that the English had a squadron of forty-five ships off the Isle of Wight. By then

A Dutch East India merchantman and two men-of-war, by Wenceslas Hollar (Bibliothèque Nationale, Paris)

Ayscue was in fact further west but to know that would have given de Ruyter little comfort. His duty was to protect an expected merchant fleet which was bringing from Cadiz part of the annual supply of silver with which the Spanish paid for Dutch merchandise. The States General, equally concerned for the silver, hastened reinforcements after de Ruyter, nine more ships joining him off Dunkirk on 11 August. By the 16th he was just north of the Casquets, a series of rocky shoals north of Guernsey. He had about sixty merchant ships under his protection, some inward and some outward bound, when at two o'clock in the afternoon he saw a fleet of forty-five sail coming down on him from the north. It is not clear just how many warships de Ruyter had at hand. He had detached some ships for temporary convoy duty. Moreover the officers and crews (at least of the armed merchantmen) were sometimes of lamentable quality, which may explain a succession of collisions which had cost him one ship sunk and another sent home for repair with yet another to escort it. De Ruyter claimed that the English outnumbered him and he may have been correct.[14] However, Ayscue and his officers mistook the high-sterned West Indiamen with their numerous gun-ports for warships and considered themselves heavily outnumbered. Undaunted by his enemy's apparent strength Ayscue led his squadron into the Dutch in the old way, steering the *George* straight into the mass of Dutch men-of-war and assuming that his command would follow him and engage with the enemy. Some did so with enthusiasm, others hung back. These were probably armed merchantmen whose captains, as part-owners, feared the loss of their property more than the loss of their reputation for gallantry.[15]

We lack any official report from Ayscue as to the course of the battle while de Ruyter's account seems confused. He repeatedly says that the English had the wind, quite correctly for it was north-easterly and Ayscue was heading south. He laments that his fireships were to leeward so that they could not be employed and remained helpless spectators of the battle, claiming that with them he could have destroyed Ayscue's squadron. Yet he also claims that his ships 'twice . . . fought' their 'way through their fleet' by which he may have meant that his ships fired on Ayscue's ships as they twice broke through the Dutch line. An anonymous English reporter described Ayscue 'and six more charging through the whole body of the enemy's fleet' and after heavy fighting 'Sir George tacked about and charged them all again . . .'[16] A Dutch report of the battle written much later states that as Ayscue approached de Ruyter placed his three blocks of ships with himself in the centre and having the Vice-Commodore van der Broucke on the right and Rear-Commodore Verhaeff on the left.[17] De Ruyter reported that his ship, the *Neptunus*, found herself with six or seven other Dutch ships between 'the Admiral and Vice-Admiral', that is between Ayscue and Haddock who could be identified by their pennants waving above the gun-smoke. This suggests that the English forced their way in with a double thrust at the Dutch centre.

The battle was in fact a confused mêlée in which ships were firing at each other at such close range that both sides were certain to inflict considerable damage and many casualties among their crews. De Ruyter reported that the Dutch suffered between 90 and 110 casualties including 50 to 60 killed, not counting Vice-Commodore van der Broucke who died, probably of a heart attack, after the firing ceased. The English had 'divers slain and many wounded' (another report says 15 and 60 respectively) including Captain Packe, the Rear-Admiral, who had his leg shot off. The English reported that the Dutch fought 'very stoutly' and behaved themselves 'with great courage'. One who became a legendary hero among his fellow countrymen was the Frieslander Douwe Aukes, captain of the *Struisvogel*, an armed merchantman. Caught in the thick of the fight Aukes exchanged broadsides with two enemies on either quarter and when they drew off a third ship came crashing aboard. The crew lost heart and called on their captain to surrender. Aukes seized a linstock[18] with a lit fuse and, pointing it down the open hatch to the powder magazine, promised to blow up the ship if there was more talk of surrender. Frightened and shamed by his resolution the crew fought on but did not, as later legend embellished it, sink two English ships and drown 800 men with their broadsides. De Ruyter himself believed that the English vice-admiral (the *Vanguard*) had been sunk and another man-of-war left sinking. In fact, apart from a fireship, no English ship was sunk although the English came close to losing the *Bonaventure*, an armed merchantman. She was dismasted and in danger of capture when Captain Smithson ignited his fireship causing the enemy to scatter, while he and his crew escaped in the ship's boat. The *Bonaventure* was towed to safety, jury-rigged, and withdrew with the fleet in the growing darkness. The *George* and those which followed her into the thick of the fight suffered considerable damage to their masts and spars and some shot penetrated their hulls. Ayscue's cabin was torn apart and all three masts of the *Pelican*, 36, survived precariously with round-shot embedded in them. Had a gale got up several English ships would have been dismasted thanks to similar injuries and torn rigging. In general the Dutch damaged English rigging, the English damaged Dutch hulls, a phenomenon which would be frequently repeated. There were other precedents. The convoy escaped unscathed. The Dutch determination to protect their precious merchantmen was to be more often successful than the English determination to capture or sink them. The Dutch belief that they had severely damaged the English ships with their gunnery proved illusory. They needed repairs, particularly to their spars and rigging, but none were in danger of sinking. The English assault was made with great dash and courage by the state's ships, with caution and flinching by the armed merchantmen. This meant that Ayscue was outnumbered in the fierce fight in the centre and may have seriously diminished the advantage the English had in their heavy iron guns. It may also have given de Ruyter and his captains a false impression of Dutch equality in fire-power.

Both sides claimed victory but it was de Ruyter who kept the seas. The English reports claimed that they had hung around the following day to resume the fight but the Dutch had withdrawn towards France where the English dared not follow in their damaged state for fear of heavy weather. The Dutch claimed that the English retreated as night fell and that although in sight the following day made no effort to resume the contest. Indeed Ayscue seems to have lost little time in withdrawing to Plymouth Sound where he could make more thorough, long-term repairs than he could attempt at sea and with the enemy in the offing. An anonymous English participant justly wrote: 'The enemy stood off and we tacked about into Plymouth Sound to repair our ships for another dispute, the Dutch being resolved for another engagement.'[19] This resolve was more determined than the English realised. With his convoy safely on its way westward de Ruyter persuaded a council of war to launch a daring attack on Ayscue's squadron at its Plymouth anchorage. Why wait for the English to come out and fight on equal terms when they could be assaulted as they lay moored, their spars sent down, their decks probably already cluttered with fresh timber, ropes and blacksmith's tackle and so incapable of manoeuvre? It was a tempting prospect and it foreshadowed the exploit of fourteen years later on the Medway which made de Ruyter famous.[20] However, as the Dutch were approaching the entrance to the Sound a sudden change of wind frustrated de Ruyter who reluctantly withdrew. There is no evidence that Ayscue was aware that for the second time in a month a change of wind had saved him from disaster. Shortly afterwards Ayscue retired for no recorded reason but possibly he was troubled by the condition for which he had sought medical help in July, probably a fever caught during the West Indies expedition. As for de Ruyter, he was sailing with one eye over his shoulder for he knew that soon Blake must come down the Channel after him. In any event his days of independent command would shortly end for the Dutch fleet was preparing to sortie under Tromp's successor.

CHAPTER 4

From Triumph to Defeat

Above and beyond all the Lord of Hosts appeared in His power, putting terror in the hearts of our enemy, and a spirit of great cheerfulness and courage in our own.

Captain John Mildmay, 1 October 1652

I presume your Honours long for an account of what hath passed between us and the Dutch fleet and I hope you have hearts prepared to receive evil as well as good from the hands of God.

Robert Blake, 1 December 1652

De Ruyter had been prepared to take the bold course of pursuing the English into their own anchorage because he was eager to knock out Ayscue's squadron before Blake's larger fleet could reinforce it. For a few days de Ruyter cruised off the Lizard hoping that Ayscue would sortie to attack him before Blake arrived, in the meantime keeping watch for approaching Dutch merchantmen who would need a convoy home and especially the silver ships from Cadiz. Several of de Ruyter's ships had suffered heavy damage in the battle and he decided to escort his worst damaged ship to Brest for repairs. Meanwhile having sent some ships into the Thames for further repair on 18 August Blake headed down-Channel, tacking against the prevailing westerly. He was in that situation familiar to all sailing ship commanders: he was blinkered by the fog of war. He did not even know that Ayscue's squadron had met the enemy and had been compelled to refit in Plymouth. He knew nothing of Tromp's fall and had to assume that he would soon be putting to sea in his rear. He possessed no detailed knowledge of de Ruyter's movements in any detail and seemed oddly reluctant to employ fast-sailing scouts. Nevertheless he was determined at worst to reinforce Ayscue, at best to fight a fleet action. By 20 August a Dutch ship bound for Lubeck counted him seventy-two strong off Beachy Head, although this news did not reach de Ruyter for almost a fortnight. Blake had only reached the Isle of Wight when his masters in Whitehall Palace, who also expected Tromp to sortie, sent him word that the Dutch were about to emerge from the Maas with sixty warships. This intelligence was faulty. De With, Tromp's successor, was far from ready for sea. Nevertheless, having dispatched the *Convertine*, 44, *President*, 36, *Dragon*, 36, *Convert*, *Sampson* and *Golden Dove* to reinforce Sir George at Plymouth, Blake returned to the Downs to guard the Narrow Seas. His aborted voyage had not been fruitless for he had swept up several valuable prizes and driven another merchantman ashore near Dieppe.[1]

On 26 August Blake detached Vice-Admiral Penn and eleven frigates to intercept Dutch merchantmen and protect English merchantmen in the Channel. Penn was to patrol between Dungeness and the French coast but under no circumstances to wander further south-west where Blake might lose touch with him. Still expecting the Dutch main fleet to sortie, he wanted all his ships close at hand. On 28 August Blake once more heard that sixty Dutch men-of-war and armed merchantmen were preparing to sortie, this time from the Spanish commander anchored off Dunkirk which the Spanish were then besieging. In fact de With would not sail for a fortnight during which the English ships were not destined to lie idle. First Blake found himself launched against an unexpected opponent. The French had been cooperating with the Dutch in their operations against Captain Badiley's squadron in the Mediterranean and this strengthened the hand of the pro-Spanish party in the Council who on 12 August had asked Cardenas, the Spanish ambassador, to prepare an Anglo-Spanish commercial treaty. He set a draft of a treaty before them on 2 September but in the meantime he sought English help for the Spanish siege of Dunkirk. Cardenas had learned that the Duke de Vendôme was preparing to dispatch a French squadron from Le Havre to break the siege from the sea. Two days before the squadron sailed Cardenas obtained his wish: on 27 August the Council ordered Blake to intercept it.[2]

The French squadron consisted of eight warships and six fireships, and was commanded by Commodore de Menillet in the *Triton*. Blake sortied with the 100-gun *Sovereign* in the lead followed by his flagship, the *Resolution*, 88, and several other warships. De Menillet was at anchor off Calais when he saw the English approach at about 5 p.m. and hoisted his colours to show that his command was not Dutch. Blake advanced with pennants flapping and trumpets sounding, making it obvious that he intended to attack. De Menillet hastily ordered twelve shallops laden with supplies for Dunkirk to retreat northward. One French warship cut his cable and managed to escape. The opening English salvo contained 200 shot and these, with several more broadsides, severely damaged the French frigates, leaving one sinking. De Menillet, who had been given strict orders not to become embroiled in the Anglo-Dutch war and to retreat rather than fight if challenged by the English soon found himself overwhelmed. The *Gift of God*, a man-of-war chartered from the Knights of Malta was boarded and taken and soon after de Menillet's *Triton* and five other ships were captured along with three fireships. The shallops escaped to the shallow water off Dunkirk sands where the English men-of-war could not follow. The fleet returned triumphantly to Dover with its prizes where the *Sovereign*'s captain, perhaps over-elated because his ship bore the French king's standard, ordered a salute of all her guns, a deafening thunderclap which alarmed the townsfolk and spawned wild rumours. The French had lost 300 men killed and 500 wounded while 1,200 soldiers, reinforcements for the Dunkirk garrison, had been captured. All but de Menillet and his officers were repatriated to Dieppe on 14 September, to save the cost of feeding them. The ships remained in English hands despite the outraged protests of de Vendôme who unavailingly demanded Blake's dismissal. The Commonwealth government insisted that only restitution for all the wrongs done by the French to English shipping in the Mediterranean and elsewhere would earn their release. To add salt to the French wound the lack of relief compelled Dunkirk to surrender on 6 September.

In any event it was time for Blake to try to engage de Ruyter who was said to be cruising off Ushant in the hope of reinforcement or at least an opportunity to convoy Dutch merchantmen home. Here Blake faced a difficult choice. The obvious strategy would have been to wait in the Downs for de Ruyter to come home while Penn and his scouting squadron patrolled the Channel. However, there were problems even in this simple-sounding solution. The Dutch would have the advantage of the prevailing westerlies so that de Ruyter would be more able to manoeuvre and could run for the French and Flemish coasts. The rapidly shoaling water, while a hazardous refuge even for the shallow-draughted Dutch ships, would be much more dangerous for Blake's deep-draughted warships. Moreover, the proximity of de Ruyter to Dutch waters would surely bring out the Dutch main fleet, catching Blake between two fires. The alternative was to abandon the role of stopper in the bottle and head down-Channel to where the wide, deep waters between Devon and Brittany gave room for manoeuvre. He could there pick up Ayscue's squadron which he would need if de Ruyter and de With succeeded in combining. Here also there were disadvantages. The Dutch could pursue him down-Channel; de Ruyter would still have the weather gauge; the Channel's width might allow de Ruyter to slip past. Nevertheless Blake decided to head west. If there was a choice between action and inaction Blake would always choose action, at least at this stage of his naval career.[3] In hindsight it was the wrong choice but not a foolish one.

Blake's decision would not have surprised Michiel de Ruyter who had long expected it. Having spent a week recuperating and repairing in and off Brest, he was now cruising in heavy seas between Ushant and the Lizard. He had a few merchantmen under his wing whose captains were anxious to get home and his own ships were low on provisions and water. By now he knew that the Dutch main fleet would not join him and that Blake must soon be in his path so that he must hope good fortune would enable him to do by stealth what he would be powerless to do by force. However, the young commander was still pugnacious. When on 15 September off Start Point his lookouts cried that English topsails were appearing over the horizon he had no thought of flight. The sails belonged to Penn's squadron which Blake had sent ahead to seek de Ruyter. The main fleet had anchored in Torbay after a ten-day voyage beating against the wind. Penn immediately called a council of war declaring he would fight although outnumbered, to which his captains agreed. However, he appears to have at least feigned a retreat for de Ruyter writes of his pursuing Penn for some hours. Penn must have been trying to lure his opponent down on the main fleet to which he had sent a warning as soon as he sighted the Dutch. This ruse failed as a result of deteriorating weather which during the night became a heavy gale. In the morning Penn found ten ships in sight, sheltering in the lee of Start Point, but they were reinforcements sent by Blake. De Ruyter had given up the pursuit.

Sir William Penn, by Sir Peter Lely (National Maritime Museum, Greenwich, London)

Provisions and morale were low, his merchant captains were clamorous to get home. During the wild night de Ruyter turned south-east towards Guernsey and would soon be heading up-Channel. Penn cast about but failed to locate the Dutch. De Ruyter had overcome many difficulties. With out-gunned ships and inexperienced crews he had fought a heavy action with Ayscue which if indecisive had ended more in his favour than his enemy's. Autumn gales had worked on the damage inflicted by Ayscue's broadsides to the point that ten ships, including his flagship, were judged unfit for sea when he finally joined de With off Nieuport. Yet he had inflicted damage on the enemy and evaded Blake's lunge after him. He had perhaps been lucky at the end. His reckless pursuit of Penn could have proved disastrous if he had sailed into Blake's arms. Nevertheless it was a remarkable performance by a young, comparatively inexperienced commander. He would be a formidable enemy of the English in the following decade.

Blake returned to the Downs eager for the battle which he knew could not be long delayed. His fleet was united, well provisioned, had ample powder and shot, his men were in good heart and had complete confidence in him. Morale in the Dutch fleet was very poor. The fleet deeply resented the eclipse of Tromp especially since he had been replaced by Witte Cornelis de With, the Vice-Admiral of Holland, a commander with no skill at managing men. Hot tempered, intolerant, he rarely suffered fools gladly and the timorous never. His officers feared him for his vituperative tongue and savage punishments; his men unfairly blamed him for replacing the much-loved Tromp. He had no capacity to lead men by example, inspiration and persuasion. He declared characteristically that he would bring his fleet into the presence of the enemy and the Devil might bring them off by which he meant that there would be no retreat with him in command. To be fair to de With he was almost as aggressive in his dealings with his masters as he was with his men and he had a great deal to complain about. Bad beer, worse food, inexperienced and ill-paid men, low morale, battered and unseaworthy ships, all these were the serious problems facing de With and he had ruthlessly set about solving them so far as he could. He had one more deficiency which was not his fault: he had never encountered English men-of-war in battle and could not believe the tales he was told by veterans of the action off Dover or of the battle with Ayscue's squadron. Even de Ruyter counselled caution in vain. Had not de Ruyter worsted Ayscue? As for Dover the Dutch had been surprised by Blake's unprovoked, unexpected assault. Broadsides capable of smashing ships were nightmares brought on by cowardice.

After de Ruyter reinforced him on 2 October, de With commanded a fleet of sixty-two sail despite the loss of the ten from de Ruyter's squadron sent in for repair. Blake may have had a slight numerical advantage since he had about sixty-eight ships in company. More significantly he had ships which the Dutch could not match, including seven which by their size and armament must have been an alarming spectacle to the more impressionable of de With's seamen: Captain Nicholas Reed's *Sovereign*, 100, Blake's flagship *Resolution*, 88, Vice-Admiral Penn's *James*, 66, Benjamin Blake's *Triumph*, 62, Rear-Admiral Nehemiah Bourne's *Andrew*, 56, William Haddock's *Vanguard*, 56, and John Coppin's *Speaker*, 54. There were ten further men-of-war with 40 guns or more and six

Witte de With (Netherlands Maritime Museum, Amsterdam)

with between 32 and 38. These did not include several large converted merchantmen mounting between 30 and 40 guns. The Dutch inferiority in guns was once more manifest. Few of de With's ships could boast more than 40 guns and these were usually lighter than the English guns. Only one had more than 60 (62) and that was the heaviest-armed ship the Netherlands had ever sent to sea. Untroubled by such deficiencies de With sailed from his rendezvous off Nieuport on 25 September intending to beard Blake in his lair behind the Goodwin Sands but barely were the Downs in sight when adverse winds pushed him into the North Sea. Blake and his captains spied the enemy and were eager for battle but the day was almost spent and the wind rising. All through the 26th and 27th Blake's fleet remained at anchor, frustrated by the south-westerly gale. They were cheered by reports from look-outs on the North Foreland that the Dutch fleet could still be made out through the rain squalls to the northward, so it seemed that de With was determined on a battle and was struggling to remain at anchor.[4]

On the morning of the 28th the sea had moderated, the sun shone, the wind was now westerly. Blake's captains gleefully weighed anchor and poured out of the Downs in a confused rush like schoolboys hastening from school rather than a fleet going into action. There was no order or discipline and so ships which had been damaged by the gales tended to fall behind. Blake had divided his fleet into the customary three divisions with Penn commanding the vanguard, himself in the centre and Bourne the rearguard but their ships were scattered and mingled by the headlong advance. Blake himself, well in the lead, paused at noon and waited for the fleet to catch up. The enemy was in sight sailing westerly about 'six leagues' (roughly 18 miles) east of the North Foreland. The Dutch had been even more disorganised than their adversaries. All morning de With had struggled to organise his ships into their three divisions for they had dragged their anchors and had been scattered by the gale. His fleet amounted to fifty-nine because several ships had vanished and would take no part in the action. De With could not engage his enemy until he had gathered up his fleet. One of Blake's few companions at noon was Captain John Mildmay's *Nonsuch*, 40, of Penn's division but the remainder of that division still lay a mile or two behind, somewhat mingled with Blake's division, while the furthest ships, which must have been Nehemiah Bourne's division, were reported by Mildmay to be 'about two leagues' (6 miles) away from 'the Admiral'. The first substantial body of ships to arrive about two hours later was Penn's division. Penn steered his *James* under the *Resolution*'s stern and called across to Blake to suggest that he should attack with his division and that Blake should come on as soon as his division closed up. Blake replied that 'as soon as some more of our fleet come up we should [all] bear in amongst them'.[5] He could see that in any event the Dutch would be upon them within the hour for de With, who was just beyond the northern tip of the Kentish Knock shoal, was turning about to face the English, intending to come down on them sailing south-east with the wind abeam.

De With's qualities as a commander were demonstrated at their best and their worst during the battle and its aftermath. He saw at once that the dispersion of Blake's fleet over many miles of sea gave him an opportunity. His ships were by now gathered roughly into their three divisions with himself commanding the van

Michiel Adrianszoon de Ruyter, Lieutenant Admiral-General of the United Provinces, by Hendrik Berckman (National Maritime Museum, Greenwich, London)

although de Ruyter's ships were so close on de With's port side that de Ruyter would find himself heavily in action along with de With's division. De Wildt was to the rear ready to join the fight wherever he was most needed. The battle began badly for de With with a humiliation which he probably felt set the tone for what followed. Spotting that the *Brederode* had joined the fleet he decided to shift his flag to it but when his boat came alongside the crew, resenting Tromp's eclipse, mutinously refused to allow him aboard. The admiral, justifiably furious, had to shift to the 44-gun East Indiaman *Prins Willem*, which he later claimed was the worst sailer in the fleet. Moreover although it was heavily armed it had a crew who knew little about gunnery and nothing about working a ship in battle. The admiral found himself doing everything from giving sailing orders to laying the guns, for the few officers who were not drunk were no more experienced than their men.

When Blake and Penn launched their charge at about 4 p.m. Blake's intention was to keep the advantage of the south-west wind by sailing down the eastern edge of the Kentish Knock shoal. However, Penn, in making room for Blake and his ships on his starboard side felt himself ground on the shoal. The *Sovereign* was then sailing on his starboard side within 'musket-shot' in slightly deeper water but its massive bulk drew even more water and it also grounded. To Penn's frustration he had to struggle clear, with his division clustered close by, while broadside after broadside resounded to the northward as Blake's and de With's divisions exchanged fire as they passed. As Mildmay subsequently reported the English had and kept the weather gauge; 'it was most hot service, our General (Blake) giving and receiving broadsides and so ranged to the length of the Holland's fleet'.[6] By now Bourne's division was approaching the fight, seeing Penn's division mysteriously stationary and the Dutch fleet emerging from vast clouds of gun-smoke and bearing down upon them. Nothing daunted Bourne headed his *Andrew* into the Dutch firing on either hand. There was a confused mêlée in which several Dutch ships suffered damage and one of the English ships, captained by a gamecock named Badiley, became so closely surrounded that, as one observer reported, Badiley could have tossed ships' biscuits on to his enemies' decks.[7] Hard as he fought he was dismasted, shot several times through the hull, and in danger of being either sunk or captured, until the *Speaker*, *Diamond*, and *Greyhound* came to his rescue. The *Pelican* also did good service but she and the *Guinea*, who was also in the thick of the action, were both badly damaged. Despite massive damage above and below and sixty seamen killed, Badiley later managed to work his ship into Yarmouth under jury rig.

The Dutch situation was deteriorating because Blake was coming down into their rear, having turned as soon as his charge took him past the Dutch column, while Penn and Captain Reed, who had extricated the *James* and *Sovereign*, from the shoal, found themselves and the rest of Penn's squadron ideally placed to take the Dutch in the flank as they streamed past. 'We fell pat to receive them', Penn later commented with pardonable satisfaction, 'and so stayed by them until night caused our separation.'[8] Moreover those Dutch ships which were on the fringe of the action because they were in de Ruyter's division on the eastern side or in de Wildt's division to the rear had a tendency to edge further away from the

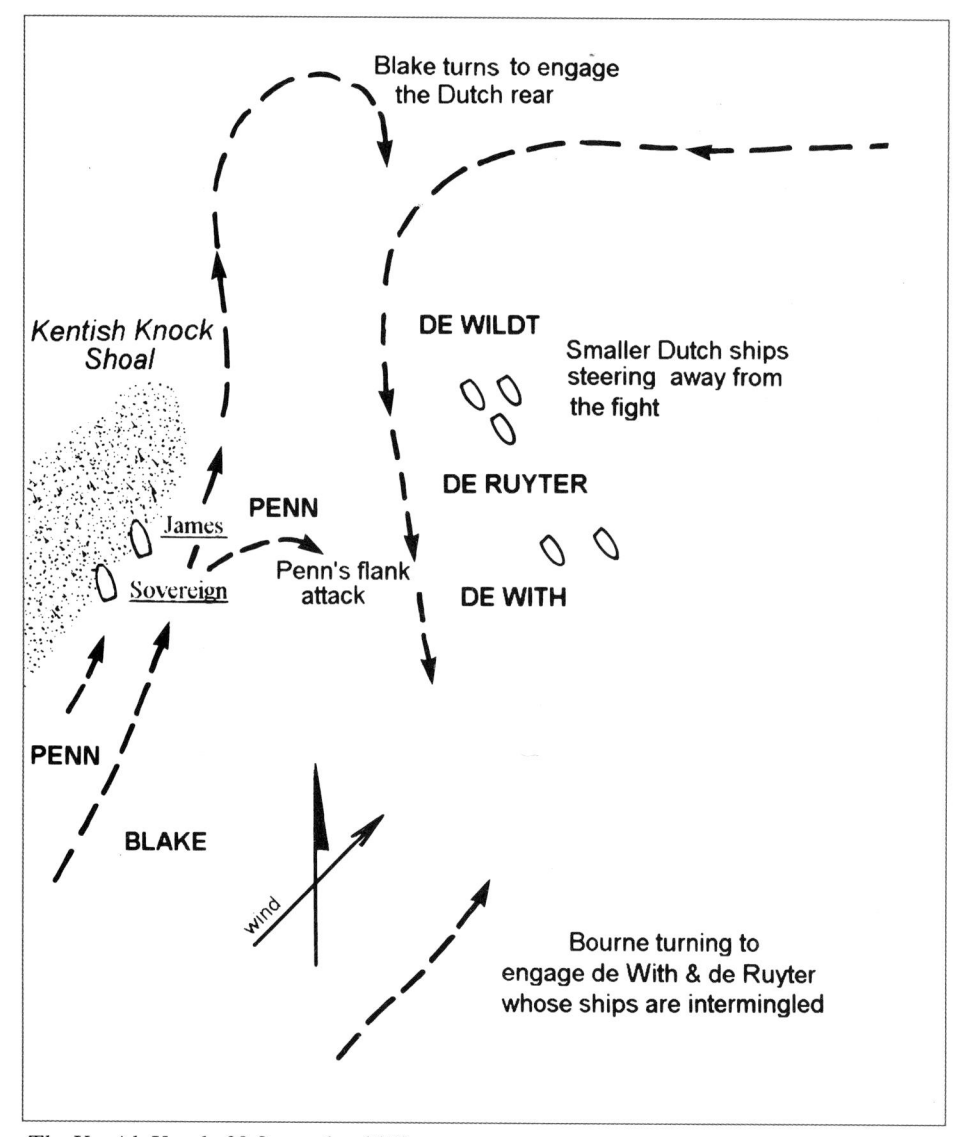

The Kentish Knock, 28 September 1652

broadsides which were smiting those closer to the centre. As the main mass of Dutch ships were sandwiched between Bourne's division to the south and Blake's and Penn's to the north and west one anonymous observer had a memorable glimpse through the smoke of the *Sovereign* – 'that great ship, a delicate frigate' (meaning 'as delicate as') gliding downwind 'as she sailed through . . . the Holland fleet'. Towering above the Dutch ships, its side appeared to burst into flame as it

The Sovereign *(National Maritime Museum, Greenwich, London)*

fired a broadside before disappearing behind the dense clouds of its own cannon-smoke. 'Blessed be the Lord she hath sustained no very great loss but in some of her tacklings and some shot in her, which her great bigness is not much prejudiced with.'[9] The fight went on until they 'could see to fight no longer'. The anonymous reporter claimed that a Dutch ship had sunk before their eyes and they had captured two others 'one of 30 guns and the other of 36 guns, neither of which did much oppose us after we boarded them'.[10]

This success was described by Captain Mildmay who was responsible for it.[11] About 7 p.m. Mildmay's *Nonsuch* emerged into a clearing amid the clouds of acrid smoke where it found the Dutch rear-admiral's flagship, dismasted and under tow by another Dutch ship, 'of about 500 tons' and thirty guns. The man-of-war cast off the tow and fled after the Dutch fleet. Mildmay fired on the cripple, ran aboard her and a boarding party quickly compelled its surrender. He then pursued the larger ship and after a half-hour's chase captured her. Leaving a prize crew on board he returned to the dismasted frigate and took off various officers which included the captain of the vice-admiral of Holland's ship who had taken refuge aboard it when his own ship had sunk. Mildmay lay by the cripple until midnight and then decided he could not risk his men on a ship which was apparently slowly sinking deck by deck. He removed the eighty survivors of her crew and abandoned her. Displaying the same remarkable ingenuity they had shown after the action off Dover, Dutch mariners boarded her the following morning and somehow salvaged her.[12]

De With had also been in the thickest part of the battle although less happily than Mildmay. When the Dutch fleet took the long tack which brought them past Blake and Penn and down on the briefly isolated division of Bourne they were following their admiral's lead. It was a bold stroke and deserved greater success and de With afterwards believed it would have succeeded if all his captains had shown as much resolution as himself. Since he was in the van his ship was repeatedly struck by broadsides from the enemy, initially from Blake and then from other English ships as they streamed behind their admiral. So badly damaged did the *Prins Willem* become that at the close of the battle de With had once more to shift his flag. He had been aggrieved to observe several ships sheltering behind their companions and firing at the enemy only as opportunity served, and even firing over and, worst of all, into Dutch ships in their eagerness to avoid exposing themselves. At best they fired very slowly, raggedly, each gun firing individually once it had reloaded. He could only admire the discipline of the English gunnery with broadsides fired from some ships only at a signal on the ship's bell, and only when the enemy was well within range. Admiral de Wildt's division at the rear suffered the worst for it was caught between the fires of Blake's and Penn's divisions and its ordeal was more prolonged. His own ship was taken and although he fled to another at the last moment that too fell into enemy hands and he was made prisoner. Another of his ships blew up and sank with great loss of life. De Ruyter had fought as bravely as any but his vessel also suffered heavy damage. Throughout the Dutch fleet ships were kept afloat only by heavy pumping and the remarkable skills in ship handling and repairing of their mariners. By contrast, apart from Badiley's vessel which at least made harbour, the English suffered little except damage to upper yards and rigging.

As the autumn evening deepened into night, folk on the Essex and Kentish coasts could hear the thunder of the cannon fade to a distant rumbling. The intervals between the flickers of orange light over the horizon, like flashes of summer lightning, grew longer until finally silence fell. The following day the two fleets found themselves still only 6 miles apart, both still sending up fresh spars, jury-rigging masts and repairing shot-torn sails and rigging. Blake assumed the presence of the enemy meant they were prepared to fight another round and he was certainly eager to oblige them. However, at first winds were too light, the fleets drifting slowly eastward. When the wind strengthened it blew northerly giving the Dutch the weather gauge. Blake hoped this would bring the enemy down on him and, as Captain Mildmay reported, he 'hauled on backstays a little to see if the Hollanders would bear up'. However, the Dutch were in no position to fight a battle. Nine Dutch ships had gone missing during the night, three more had been captured or sunk, three more were under tow. The Dutch fleet had shrunk to less than fifty and the majority of their captains were eager to head for home. De With erroneously believed that Blake had been reinforced, but his pugnacious spirit wished to resume the battle. Fortunately wiser views prevailed. De Ruyter was as courageous as his commander but he knew that to launch their remaining ships, many of them seriously damaged, their crews weakened by scurvy and their recent exertions, against Blake's larger, heavily gunned fleet would be to embrace destruction. So, breathing fire against timorous captains, de With reluctantly agreed to make for Goeree, the nearest Dutch haven.[13] It was certainly the sensible course. De Ruyter had reported after his fight with Ayscue that the English artillery made their fleet more powerful than their numbers had led him to expect. De With for all his pugnacity had learned the same lesson, reporting gloomily that the guns on their smallest frigates 'carry further than our heaviest cannon'. All through the afternoon the two fleets forged steadily northeast but the English were too slowed by damage aloft to bring the Dutch to battle. The faster English frigates finally came within range about 4 p.m., and several broadsides were exchanged during the following two hours. Even the *Sovereign* managed to bring its guns to bear as the light faded but (as Mildmay observed) the Dutch kept their largest East Indiamen to the rear to withstand the fire. English gunfire inflicted more damage and more casualties but it could not bring the enemy to bay and finally the Dutch vanished into the darkness.

Blake kept up the pursuit the next morning but in vain, for the Dutch were now entering dangerously shallow waters where the English dared not follow. Moreover Blake's ships, by now low on provisions, were approaching a lee shore at a dangerous time of year with holed ships, shot-torn rigging and 'maimed masts'. Reluctantly but sensibly Blake headed home where his mariners were welcomed as conquering heroes. However, the English were celebrating a victory which might have been more decisive than it was. Blake had not yet learned how to concentrate his forces, something which was very difficult when standardised signalling between flagship and fleet was scarcely born. Nevertheless when he emerged from the Downs he should have waited to gather in all his three divisions before advancing. Knowing nothing of de With he feared he might try to escape and so hurried forward to bring on a battle without waiting for his rearguard to catch up and with Penn's division and his own scattered confusedly. De With espied an opportunity which he was swift to embrace even though he was tacking against the wind. The grounding of Penn's flagship meant that Penn's division was delayed and so, as the enemy came down past it with Blake now in pursuit, both first and second divisions were reunited more by chance than design, and both engaged the enemy in the flank and rear as it made for Bourne's isolated division to the south and inflicted some loss on the enemy. De With had been more successful in gathering his fleet but once he made his lunge his fleet rapidly lost its concentration, thanks to the pusillanimity of so many of his captains who shunned the action and drifted off to the east. De With believed he could have won the battle if they had done their duty and stuck by him. However, ironically, their care for their ships or their lives may have robbed Blake of a decisive victory. The superior English gunnery did terrible damage to the ships which fought bravely and left undamaged those which shirked the fight. So the victory was indecisive and the Dutch fleet had survived despite its inferiority in guns, and with more resolute captains and better tactics might re-emerge as a formidable opponent. The Commonwealth government would display a dangerous lack of awareness of the limitations of the victory.

The English government's uninhibited joy in victory would not have mattered if this had not encouraged it to behave as if the war was all but won. The Dutch fleet had been worsted in an indecisive battle when it was under-manned, with too many private vessels and too few states' ships in its composition, when many of its crews were inexperienced in gunnery, many indeed landsmen or soldiers or ill-disciplined merchant seamen. It is incomprehensible that the Commonwealth government should have believed that this setback would compel the Dutch to make peace. The Puritans had long admired the way in which this people had survived defeats and vicissitudes for decades in the process of winning their independence from Spain. Nevertheless the Commonwealth prepared to launch a diplomatic offensive to reap the fruits of their victory, with all the more enthusiasm because in recent elections to the Council the peace faction, with Cromwell prominent among them, had gained seats. This expectation of a peace would not have mattered if the Commonwealth had kept its most important weapon sharp in case of failure. The fleet should have been ready for any eventuality but it was not. Ships needed repair above and below, all needed re-victualling, the sailors were growing mutinous because of their arrears of pay. Yet in the euphoria following the Kentish Knock the government failed to vote more money for the navy, which was already over budget by more than £400,000. Even more extraordinary, having already decided to spend £300,000 on new construction, the government neither voted the money to pay for it nor cancelled the programme. That autumn saw the warships *Kentish*, *Essex*, *Sussex* and *Hampshire* launched amid waving flags and cheering spectators, but these glittering occasions only deepened the naval deficit. Victualling and repairs slowed as naval contractors grew cautious; they were only prepared to give credit after the government had voted supply.

It might seem that there was no cause for alarm because Blake had the fleet which won the Kentish Knock to counter any Dutch sortie and the Dutch fleet itself must have been in disarray. In fact these advantages proved transient. Some ships which had played no part in the battle were in the dockyards undergoing refits. Ships damaged in the battle had to wait their turn and lack of funds was slowing the work. The fleet was further depleted by the urgent need to divert ships elsewhere. The King of Denmark, a most unfriendly neutral, was behaving as if he was a Dutch ally. A fleet of English merchantmen laden with timber, tar and hemp – all vitally needed supplies of war – were imprisoned on the wrong side of the Skaggerak by the king's refusal to allow them to pass out of the Baltic. A squadron of ships had been sent to remonstrate with the Danish government but, although it was permitted to repatriate the crews of the trapped ships, it was too feeble to impose its will on the defiant sovereign. When the squadron's flagship, the *Antelope* was cast away, the king even refused to restore its salvaged guns and other equipment. More ships must be gathered for a stronger naval expedition and though nothing would come of this and the trapped merchantmen

The battle of Leghorn, 4 March 1653, by Willem Hermansz van Diest (National Maritime Museum, Greenwich, London)

would continue to moulder at their anchorage until the war's end, in the short term Blake must surrender vital ships. In the Mediterranean matters were no better. A flotilla commanded by Richard Badiley which contained only two men-of-war and several Levant Company merchantmen he was escorting had been attacked by a large Dutch squadron commanded by van Galen, a redoubtable seaman. During a fierce fight of many hours Badiley's guns had inflicted serious damage on his Dutch attackers while the merchantmen fled to Elba, but he had been compelled to retire there also when the Dutch succeeded in capturing his consort, the *Phoenix*. Meanwhile a flotilla commanded by Henry Appleton, a man rendered lethargic by illness, was bottled up in Leghorn by van Galen enduring the unreliable hospitality of the Grand Duke of Tuscany. Badiley, on one of several furtive visits to Leghorn aboard neutral feluccas, succeeded in retaking the *Phoenix* which had come in for repair, and even more remarkably in sneaking her through the blockade. A still more ambitious plan to bring Appleton's flotilla out while Badiley attacked from the sea ended badly with Appleton's force overwhelmed while Badiley was down-wind and helpless to aid him. Appleton fought his ship for six hours during which the Dutch squadron suffered heavy damage and van Galen was mortally wounded. Nevertheless, it was a defeat which compelled Badiley to abandon the Mediterranean.[14] This gloomy conclusion was still unknown in England but the government knew that Badiley's position was desperate and planned to dispatch a fleet of at least twenty ships to his aid. These ships must come from Blake's fleet or from reinforcements intended for it. Blake, no grumbler, gave up twenty of his best ships on the government's promise that they would be replaced from the ships in the naval dockyards. There was an element of 'jam tomorrow but never jam today' about these assurances. Future reinforcements cannot fight battles which occur before they have arrived. Blake vainly protested as he saw his victorious fleet melt away. The government was complacent because the Dutch were assumed to be feeble. How valid was this assumption?

Certainly the Dutch fleet had had a melancholy homecoming. More than 2,000 wounded mariners and soldiers were disembarked. The number of the dead is unknown but must have been large. Several hundred had perished in the blowing up and sinking of just one ship and the heavy iron shot and the murderous splinters which they hurled like shrapnel though the crowded decks of those ships which faced the English broadsides – must have more than doubled that number. Among the officers mutual recrimination began early. Several found themselves in jail accused of cowardice while the government tried to find means by which they might be tried and punished. The jealously guarded autonomy of the competing admiralties ensured that little would come of this. The crews, when not actually in mutiny, fled the fleet at every opportunity and so opportunities had to be restricted. There was no leave for the hale who glared mutinously from ships moored well off shore. Then with astonishing obtuseness the States voted increased pay for new recruits for the navy but not for the battle-hardened sailors already on board.

This was the gloomy situation when Tromp resumed command on 27 October. He only accepted the call with reservations. He was determined not to suffer the humiliations to which he had been subjected on his return from the Northern Voyage. There must be no more querulous questioning about his decisions at sea nor blame for failures arising from matters beyond his control.[15] He had three major problems any one of which would have daunted a less indomitable man: crew, ships, and supplies. To restore discipline, especially among the ships' captains, he took with him to Helvoetsluys a public prosecutor empowered to try officers who failed in their duty. Furious to discover that the differing rates of pay for new and old seamen were driving his men to desert by the shipload he had the order rescinded, obtaining the increase for all seamen and this, together with his popularity, gradually brought back many seamen. In theory he had a fleet of seventy sail to escort the out-going convoys, once he had found crews for them, but their hulls were foul under water. He reminded his masters that his famous victories over the Spanish fleet had been achieved thanks to the superior sailing qualities of his ships. The *Brederode* was in dry dock and half a barrel of mussels had been torn from her rudder alone. He dreaded the fast-sailing English fourth- and fifth-rates getting among the Dutch convoys while his men-of-war lumbered ineffectually in their wake.[16]

One problem defeated him. During his temporary retirement Tromp had brooded over the effectiveness of England's 'big ship, big gun' strategy. His proposed remedy, to build ships capable of fighting their English opponents on equal terms, might seem obvious but it found many opponents. Tromp had recommended a building programme to the States General of thirty new ships comprising six of 150 feet in length, twelve of 140 feet in length and twelve of 134 feet in length which were respectively the equivalents of English first-, second- and third-rates. Had these been begun then the Dutch navy could have achieved by autumn 1653 something like parity with the English when going into battle although the English would still have had a larger number of big ships if they could mobilise them simultaneously. Of course, the Dutch would still have had to import enough heavy iron guns to arm them and recruit and train sufficient gun-crews to serve the guns. In any event the States General and the admiralties, while agreed that more ships were needed, would not accept a 'big ship, big gun' strategy for fear that such heavy ships would be unable to dock in some of their ports or navigate some of the estuaries leading to them. The state of Holland was particularly opposed. A committee debated the matter which included de With. He had recognised at the Kentish Knock the technological superiority of the English men-of-war and the need to match it and the committee's recommendations, despite some watering down, substantially supported Tromp's proposals. It was to no avail. Despite Rotterdam's support and unity among the admirals, the programme begun in February 1653 would include only one ship of 150 feet, ten of 136 feet and nineteen of 130 feet. All the nineteen would be light and built for speed. The Dutch navy would pay heavily for this blunder.

In the late autumn of 1652, however, these were distant considerations for Tromp who must get a fleet to sea with what resources he had. Somehow, within a month of his arrival at Helvoetsluys, he had assembled a fleet of eighty-eight ships with a further five fireships and eight smaller vessels. They were still badly under-manned because the States General, which had never authorised pressing merchant seamen, shrank from doing so now. However, Tromp, relying on his indispensability, waited until he was at sea and then raided his convoy for the seamen he needed. He had also triumphed over the bureaucratic nightmares associated with five jealously competing admiralties to victual his ships properly. By 24 November his fleet had emerged into the North Sea. He had originally been instructed to send part of his fleet with the convoy to the Isle de Rhé and employ the rest against Blake. Impatient with any plan which involved dividing his fleet in the face of the enemy he had insisted the instructions be changed. He would take his entire fleet and convoy to the Isle de Rhé and there the foulest ships would be careened before his return up-Channel escorting an inward convoy. First, however, he would seek out Blake. The large fleet was divided into four divisions, respectively commanded by Tromp, Cornelis Evertsen, Pieter Floriszoon and de Ruyter. De Ruyter received the fourth division because de With's pride would not allow him to serve in a position inferior to Evertsen's.

Facing this imposing fleet was the object of Dutch naval preoccupations, Blake's fleet in the Downs. This had by now contracted to no more than '52 large and small of which 42 were middle-sized ships' as Tromp accurately estimated.[17] The ten lesser ships were either fireships or scouts. Tromp gathered his fleet at 4 a.m. on 29 November in the Dover Straits where they anchored to hold station. The wind was then shifting between west-south-west and west-north-west. He espied Blake still in the Downs at dawn but Tromp did not sail until 11 a.m. at which time he saw the English ships streaming out of the south end of the Downs. With his convoy of merchantmen screened by his fleet Tromp sailed down Channel, tacking against a south-west wind in order to get to windward of his opponent. Blake had sortied as soon as the intentions of his opponent became clear for he was equally determined to fight but must gain the wind to have any hope of success against such heavy odds. He therefore battled down the Channel much closer to the shore in a race to win the weather gauge. Before the astonished gaze of watchers on the Downs, who could never have seen so many ships on one course, the fleets raced in parallel separated by shoals called the Rip Raps (now known as the Varne). This tacking race could not continued indefinitely because the probing point and shingle ridges of Dungeness loomed ahead. There Blake must either steer towards his enemy or fly before the wind and find a safer haven. The latter course might seem sensible if inglorious at odds of at least two to one, but Blake never hesitated and steered out to engage. Again he made no effort to concentrate his forces, simply hurling his ship and the few companions who had kept up into the Dutch. Those who perceived this headlong charge as foolhardy hung back while the slower ships arrived too late to take part. This doomed Blake's lunge. If he had managed to lead his forty-two ships at the Dutch in a compact mass the result might have been different. Tromp's numerical advantage would have proved difficult to exploit as his ships got in each other's way while those at the forefront of the action were facing the broadsides of the English warships.

As it was Tromp could not win a major victory in terms of numbers of ships sunk or taken. All that occurred was a number of hard-fought actions between individual ships of both sides in which the Dutch ability, through their numbers, to come to each other's aid gave them the advantage. After an exchange of broadsides between Tromp's *Brederode* and Blake's *Triumph* the second English ship, the *Garland*, 44, captained by Robert Batten, thrust between them and the *Brederode* collided with her so heavily that her bowsprit and beak to the waterline were wholly snapped off. The crew of the *Brederode* quickly grappled the *Garland* and tried to capture it. The *Anthony Bonaventure*, 36, an armed merchantman, boldly attacked the *Brederode* on her unoccupied side. For a heady moment it seemed as if the Dutch might lose their flagship as cutlass-wielding sailors from both English ships poured over the *Brederode*'s bulwarks. However, Evertsen, seeing his admiral so beset, steered alongside the *Anthony Bonaventure* which was compelled to surrender after the death of her captain, Hoxton, fighting at the head of his men. The *Garland* also succumbed, although her captain, Robert Batten, appears to have blown up the after part of his own ship. The explosion hurled the quarter deck and poop clear off the ship, impartially slaying Dutch boarders and English defenders. Of her 200 crew Batten and 60 officers and men were killed, many others seriously wounded and about 100 made prisoner. Tromp put a prize crew aboard the smouldering hulk. Tromp and Evertsen had taken two English ships but not without cost. Apart from the killed and wounded among their crews, both their ships were 'miserably torn' and Tromp observed that the *Brederode* apart from her lost beak-head and bowsprit had 'not a round spar whole in her' nor 'hardly a shroud on the masts' undamaged and she was leaking badly.[18]

Although close by Blake could not assist his beleaguered ships for the *Triumph* was heavily engaged by other Dutch warships, including that of de Ruyter, losing her mainstay and then her fore top-mast. She was assisted by the *Vanguard* and others, but the straggling English warships, whose captains had lacked confidence in this sortie from the start, only indecisively attacked the Dutch rear. The battle had not begun before 3 p.m. and the shortness of the winter afternoon saved the English from worse losses. When night fell the *Triumph* found herself almost alone and, as firing died away, she followed the rest of the fleet to anchor off Dover. A huge glare behind them marked where the ship of Captain Dirk Joynbol burned to the waterline and sank with the loss of her captain and some of her crew, although the remainder were plucked from the sea. The fire's cause was never established but came after exchanges of broadsides. This was the only Dutch ship lost to compensate for the loss of the *Garland* and *Anthony Bonaventure* and the *Hercules*, 36, which was caught coming up from Portsmouth to Chatham to be fitted out for the Mediterranean. Her crew of only eighty had run her ashore and escaped but, seizing the advantage of wind and tide, the Dutch managed to haul her off and bear her away triumphantly.

The following day Blake sought the dubious safety of the Downs knowing he must soon seek the greater security of the Thames. That day he wrote an urgent dispatch to the Admiralty Commissioners in which he grimly hoped that they had 'hearts prepared to receive evil as well as good from the hand of God'. He reported the death of Hoxton and the loss of his ship, *Garland*, but not the loss of the *Anthony Bonaventure*. He offered his resignation, remarking that they had recently added 'two able gentlemen' to shoulder the responsibility of command. He was referring to Lieutenant-General George Monck and Major-General Richard Deane who had both been summoned from Scotland to share the naval command. He also reported that several captains had failed to support him in the battle.[19] On the 4th he informed the Council that a council of war had decided to move the fleet into Margate Road the following day, if the wind served, or else to Long Sands Head, so as 'to have the river to friend if need should arise'. It was 'no way safe or warrantable' to put the fleet at hazard of an enemy 'so far too strong' for them commanded by one 'so well versed in the destructive ways of hostility'. The fleet sailed for Long Sands Head early on 5 December.[20]

Maarten Tromp and the battle of Dungeness (National Maritime Museum, Greenwich, London)

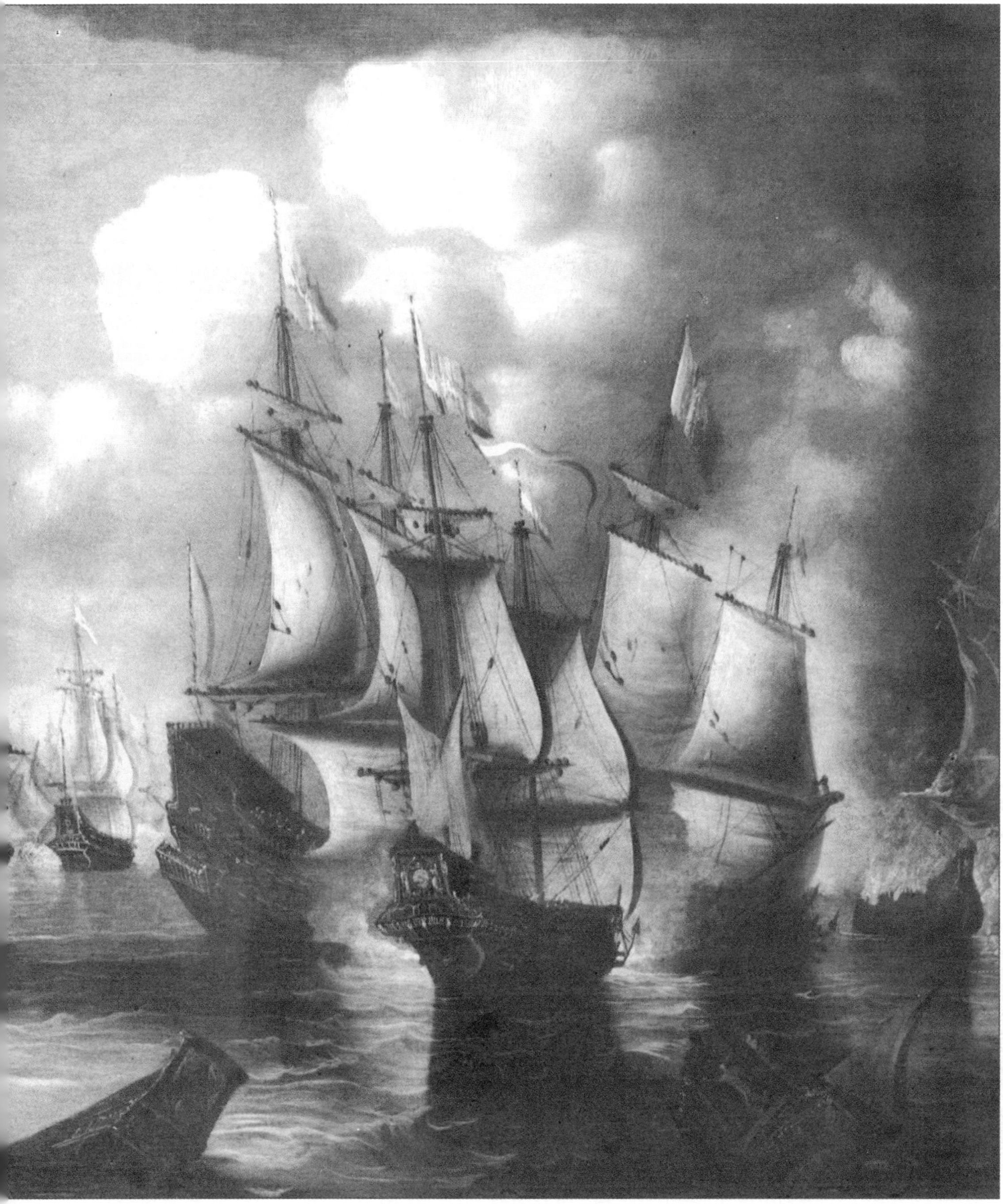

All night after the battle the Dutch had remained at anchor, those which had taken part in the fight desperately repairing their rigging and plugging the shot holes in their hulls. Tromp was eager to pursue but adverse weather frustrated him. On the 3rd he crossed the Channel to anchor off Boulogne trying to gather up his fleet which had been dispersed both by the battle and by the adverse weather on the 2nd. From there he assured the States General that he would pursue and defeat Blake as soon as his fleet was concentrated. He also sent them a summary obtained from garrulous captured officers, which explained why the English fleet had shrunk since the Kentish Knock. If the prisoners could be believed, Blake now commanded forty-two ships, ten more were cruising off Ushant, eighteen had sailed for the West Indies in two squadrons. In addition twenty frigates and six armed merchantmen were in the Thames preparing to sail for the Mediterranean; thirteen ships and frigates were at Portsmouth, a dozen more were fitting out at Chatham while the two first-rates, *Sovereign* and *Resolution*, were moored in the Thames.

For Tromp this was excellent. The Dutch fleet was concentrating, the great English fleet of late summer was dissipated to different ports or different theatres. He must, therefore, strike the decisive blow of which admirals so often dreamed but which circumstances rarely permitted them to achieve. However, he might have reflected that the news was not all good: Blake, as he learned from Evertsen while writing his dispatch, had already retired into the Thames. By doing so he was once more concentrating his fleet. The *Sovereign* and the *Resolution* were already there. Once made ready for battle they would be a powerful reinforcement. So would the dozen ships then fitting out if there was time to get them up to Blake's fleet. So also would the ships making ready for the Mediterranean. Blake had lost two ships at Dungeness and others, including his own, had suffered damage but it would not be long, if this intelligence was accurate, before he had a combined fleet of more than seventy sail. The question was whether Tromp would arrive before its individual units were made battle-ready and assembled. Tromp wasted no time. He had to take care of the 600 or more merchantmen which were anxiously awaiting convoy off the French coast. Floriszoon and a squadron were sent to convoy them to the Isle de Rhé. Then Tromp led his fleet north-east for North Sands Head and the Thames estuary. Alas for his hopes, his plan to beard the English in their lair ran aground on the reluctance of his pilots to guide him through the intricacies of the channels which led upstream from the mouth of the Thames. The fleet had many pilots who had navigated merchantmen up to London itself in peacetime but they were terrified by the prospect of piloting the heavier draught Dutch warships. They feared to bring them in and were even more daunted by the responsibility of bringing them out again. They talked of shoals so large that, although navigable at high water, they could not be crossed against an adverse wind or current before the ebbing tide would leave the warships stranded. After a council of war on the *Brederode* Tromp reluctantly abandoned his raid and crossed to the Dutch coast to gather up more merchantmen prior to sailing down-Channel to the Isle de Rhé. The immediate threat had passed but for English commerce the short-term consequences of the battle of Dungeness were humiliating and costly.

CHAPTER 5
Portland

> We have destroyed about seventeen of their men-of-war, and have not lost one ship, only one that was so torn it was not fit to keep the seas.
> *News of the Fleet*, 22 February 1653

With Tromp baulked by the perils, real or fancied, of the Thames estuary, Blake's slowly expanding fleet could lick its wounds in safety, but this scarcely consoled him or his government for the humiliations which had now to be borne. Never can so small a battle have had such infuriating consequences. The story that Tromp lashed a broom to his masthead as a symbol that he intended to sweep the Channel of English ships is apocryphal but certainly he swept up scores of prizes during the following weeks. Once he even put boat crews ashore to seize the cattle and sheep of bewildered farmers on Romney Marsh. At last he sailed off for the Biscay ports which were the rendezvous of Dutch merchantmen. This provided a welcome lull during which the navy could recover the strong position which folly had dissipated. While prodigious efforts were being made to accomplish this the Dutch government was behaving with even greater folly following their victory than had the Commonwealth government after the Kentish Knock. The Dutch had won sympathy throughout Europe by its championship of the rights of neutrals, while the English had been condemned for its bullying maritime policies. Now the Dutch forfeited that sympathy by treating neutrals even worse. Dutch warships and privateers now seized any neutral ship carrying naval stores from the Baltic and carried it off to the Netherlands. Worse, they seized ships which were not carrying war materials nor even bound for a British port, acts of simple piracy. The Netherlands government boasted that by these measures and by compelling the King of Denmark to close the Baltic to English trade, and by further victories at sea they would bring down the Regicide government. It seemed that for the Dutch also neither statecraft nor common sense could survive a victory at sea.

The Commonwealth government, both in Council and in parliament, displayed that capacity for effective action and decision which characterises revolutionary regimes confronted by crisis in war but which so often deserts them when they confront the problems of peace. Voices favouring peace with the Dutch fell silent for the government had no intention of negotiating in the aftermath of defeat. Meanwhile the English were not prostrate because their naval units had temporarily abandoned the Channel. A battle was being waged on several fronts to remedy past neglects of which the most important was the provision of money. Here parliament acted promptly, voting on 10 December that the monthly taxation assessment should be increased from £90,000 to £120,000 a month. In the past this taxation had gone to pay England's army of more than 40,000 men. Now it was agreed that sufficient soldiers would be disbanded so that the remainder could subsist on £80,000 a month, leaving £40,000 for the navy. Still further sums were sought by reviving the slumbering market in the lands of royalist delinquents and leasing former royal palaces. The allocation of funds from taxation immediately encouraged the contractors to provision the fleet and revived the labours of hundreds of craftsmen in naval dockyards from Chatham to Plymouth. Ships were repaired, ships newly launched were fitted out. The Danish decision to forbid the movement to England of masts, spars and tar from the Baltic was counteracted partly by employing neutral shipping, partly by purchases in Scotland and in Norway, and by looking to New England as an alternative source.

All this activity would dispatch a powerful fleet to sea only if crews could be found for the ships. To solve this problem the government increased pay from nineteen shillings to twenty-four shillings a month for ordinary seamen while increasing that of higher ranks proportionately. It also made a serious effort to reduce the arrears of its sailors. Shares of prize money were increased to compete with those offered by privateers. These reforms checked desertion and encouraged enlistment. Nevertheless these means could not provide sufficient mariners to crew the large fleet needed to regain command of the Channel so the government pressed men on an unprecedented scale taking seamen aged fifteen to fifty from coastal towns. Moreover Cromwell was required to provide 1,200 soldiers for the fleet to improve discipline and strengthen the crews, the foundation of the Marines. Blake's complaints about the lack of resolution of several captains was taken seriously. Even Benjamin Blake, the admiral's brother, was sacked, although he was guiltless of any offence. Several captains were summoned to London to answer for their conduct at Dungeness but none were tried, let alone convicted and not all were replaced. Possibly the Council abandoned any thought of courts martial because the defendants could advance the embarrassing excuse that their ships had too few men simultaneously to man the guns and work the ships. The French ambassador's comment that Blake was defeated more by the cowardice of his captains than by the valour of the Dutch is an exaggerated over-simplification although it probably reflected a view popular in the London taverns.[1] Robert Blake had unflinchingly accepted responsibility for the defeat but the Council firmly declined his resignation.

Blake and his colleagues told the Council that they were ready to tackle a ninety-sail fleet with only sixty of their own so long as the sixty were all men-of-war, of at least 26 guns and at least forty armed with 36 guns or more. Better a smaller fleet of heavily armed naval ships than a larger fleet which included uncommitted, unreliable armed merchantmen. The government now accepted that captain-owners, more concerned for the danger to their property than the fate of the battle, might not fight resolutely. Hired merchantmen could not be dispensed with immediately but would be gradually phased out as the government's shipbuilding programme reduced the need for 'armed auxiliaries'. Meanwhile civilian captains were replaced by naval officers, a practice increasingly applied also to subordinate officers. Unfortunately many naval captains were also unreliable, not because they were too cautious but because they were undisciplined individualists. They saw a battle as a free-for-all to which their admiral had invited them, in which their object was to batter an enemy ship into submission and then make a prize of it to the profit of themselves and their eager crews. Such men considered the race to Dungeness folly in view of the odds and had not wholeheartedly supported their commander. Individualism must be stamped out. In future the admiral's lead must be followed, his orders obeyed without question, once the council of war had dispersed. This was the principal motive for composing a set of Laws of War, most of which carried the death penalty, which was the basis of the later Articles of War. Some prescribed sober and reverent worship and proscribed lewdness and profanity. Others concerned embezzlement and the treatment of prisoners; five concerned treacherously aiding the enemy. Most of the rest stiffened discipline, and punished cowardice, negligence, and lack of zeal in battle. The Articles were taken very seriously. Promulgated on Christmas Day 1652 they were frequently read to the men and printed copies were nailed up in the steerage of all warships.[2]

The government also reformed the organisation of the fleet at sea and its administration ashore. The appointment of Monck and Deane coincided with a determined effort to maintain better order in battle. The command structure became more formal and elaborate with an admiral-in-chief (still called 'general') who also commanded one of the three squadrons (usually the Red) into which the fleet would be divided. He would have two deputies in case he was incapacitated, a vice-admiral who would command the White squadron and a rear-admiral who would command the Blue squadron. These three officers would be paid respectively £3, £2 and £1 per day. Each squadron would itself be divided into three divisions, the centre one of which would be commanded by one of those three senior officers, while the vanguard division would be commanded by a vice-admiral and the rear division in each would be commanded by a rear-admiral. The purpose of this elaborate hierarchy was to ensure that groups of ships would each have a commander to direct them in battle rather than have a fleet of eighty sail or more trying to follow the lead of a commander-in-chief whose ship might be obscured or even below the horizon from many of his captains. (Such a fleet could easily stretch over 10 miles if in line.) During the coming campaign the fleet would have three commanders-in-chief, Blake, Deane and Monck, although it was initially intended that Monck should remain ashore carrying out administrative duties while Deane sailed on Blake's flagship. This odd-sounding arrangement was not destined to cause problems. Ashore parliament replaced the Council's Admiralty Committee with a more professional body of six men, the Admiralty Commissioners, who would be responsible to parliament itself. The Commissioners included the experienced Sir Henry Vane the Younger, who had campaigned for this reform, with two of his parliamentary allies, the Fifth Monarchists John Carew and Richard Salwey, George Thomson, MP for Southwark and two London merchants. This committee proved dedicated and

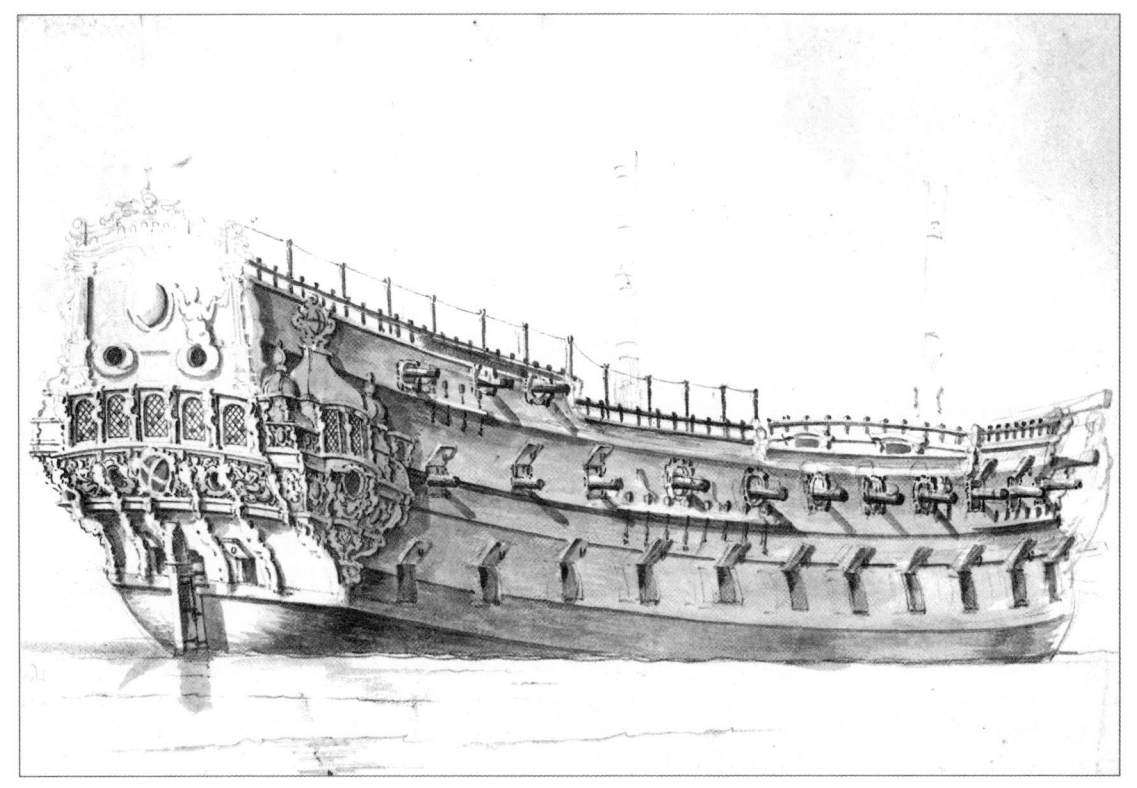

The Portland, *a fourth-rate built during the First Dutch War, by William van de Velde the Elder? (National Maritime Museum, Greenwich, London)*

efficient, sitting 'daily early and late' as Thomson later boasted. Since the parliamentary members were radicals fellow men with strong ideological commitments to Puritanism were likely to be preferred for naval appointments.[3]

These reforms and reorganisations were all in place when the three 'generals-at-sea', Blake, Deane and Monck, headed into the Channel on 10 February. General Monck, having no desire to navigate a desk while his colleagues saw all the action, sailed both as joint commander-in-chief and as admiral of the White squadron in the *Vanguard*, 56, a second-rate.[4] His captain was the redoubtable John Mildmay. The Blue squadron was commanded by Vice-Admiral Penn in the *Speaker*, 56, and the Red squadron by Blake and Deane, both of whom were aboard another second-rate, the *Triumph*, 62. John Lawson, a Baptist radical, had no squadron of his own because of Monck's appointment, but sailed as vice-admiral of the Red squadron in the *Fairfax*, 56. At least fifty-two ships had sailed from the Thames but by the time others had joined from the Downs, from Portsmouth and from Plymouth, the fleet amounted to about seventy sail. More significantly, a substantial proportion were second-rates and large third-rates. Besides the ships mentioned above, these included the commands of five rear- and vice-admirals of squadrons: Samuel Howett's *Laurel*, 48, James Peacock's *Rainbow*, 58, Lionel Lane's *Victory*, 60, and John Bourne's *Assistance*, 40.[5] There were thirty-two states ships with from 36 to 50 guns and four converted merchantmen with 38 guns or more. Although Blake picked up at Dover the 1,200 soldiers which Cromwell had allocated him, he was still complaining that he was not fully manned despite the government's efforts. Nevertheless he was probably as well off for men and as formidable in gunnery as he had been at the Kentish Knock even though he lacked the first-rates *Sovereign* and *Resolution*.[6]

Blake's priority was to find Tromp, defeat him and then turn on any convoy he might be escorting. In fact Tromp had gathered a convoy of more than 150 merchantmen at the Isle de Rhé. Although Blake formed a reasonably accurate picture of Tromp's movements from incoming neutral shipping he feared that Tromp might evade him, convoy and all, as de Ruyter had done earlier. He therefore sacrificed concentration as he repeatedly criss-crossed the Channel, the squadrons tending to separate as the Channel widened. He would have done better to employ his faster vessels as scouts and held his larger ships closed up. He also misread Tromp, thinking he would evade battle if possible whereas Tromp was as eager to attack as Blake himself, and he did not anticipate that Tromp would hug the English coast. When on 18 February the two fleets stumbled on each other some miles south of Portland Bill the eighty-ship Dutch fleet was well closed up screening the convoy which was even closer to the coast, whereas the three English squadrons were separated. Monck's squadron was reasonably compact but was now barely in sight to the south. Penn's Blue squadron was somewhat ahead of Blake and the Red squadron had divided during the night and a substantial portion commanded by Lawson lay several miles south-east. These separations would hardly have mattered if Blake had had the wind but he did not. It would take several hours before Monck could struggle up against the north-west wind whereas Tromp could swiftly descend downwind to engage. Lack of daylight would not prevent a full-scale battle because the fleets had sighted each other early in the morning.

Tromp, as eager for battle as his adversaries, bore down on Blake's Red squadron which had been reduced to about twenty ships by the unplanned separation of Lawson's rearguard. The Dutch charged in four squadrons commanded by Tromp, Floriszoon, Evertsen and de Ruyter. Tromp must have thought God had delivered Blake into his hands. He could smite with all his force at the English centre while the van (Penn's White squadron) was apparently sailing away on a long tack to the west and a dangerous gap had opened up between the centre and rear of Blake's own squadron. Best of all a large part of the English fleet was so far south that only the masthead lookouts could spy all its topsails above the horizon. Yet Tromp was sailing into what would be the worst defeat of his career (if one disregards his final battle in which he was slain before it was completed). This result must be explained although this reconstruction must be conjectural since the accounts of the commanders are confused and frustratingly incomplete.[7]

Immediately he sighted the enemy Blake ordered his captain to shorten sail, turned to the wind and hoisted his red battle flag. His squadron immediately followed his example, closing upon their commander in a compact group for mutual defence, cannon bristling all ways. There would be no flinching this time, although the sight of Tromp's eighty-ship fleet bearing down on Blake's twenty or so must have been an awe-inspiring sight. Blake could have turned his squadron and hastened south, with Penn and Lawson close on his heels, bringing the Dutch down on a fleet reunited with Monck's squadron. This would have had no appeal to the combative Blake. Not expecting his opponent's eagerness for battle he would have feared that Tromp would not follow, preferring to continue up-Channel protecting his valuable convoy. Indeed the previous evening Blake and his officers had worried that somehow Tromp's fleet had contrived to evade them and were ploughing up-Channel away from them. Once he had them in his grip Blake had no intention of letting go. Moreover he may have worried that his ships might not follow as at Dungeness. They might think he was really in flight and scatter to seek their own safety. Finally with naval signalling scarcely in its infancy he might have failed to make Penn and Lawson understand his intentions before Lawson's few ships and perhaps even Penn's squadron were separately overwhelmed. He preferred to turn at bay, expecting Penn and Lawson to come to his aid. This they did, but first Penn had to tack back to the north-east and then turn south-east with the wind before he could take the Dutch in the flank. Lawson was just as eager for battle but he was on a long tack which would take him behind Blake's bunched ships. He must follow it out and then, like Penn, turn on his starboard tack to gain the wind and force his way into the battle. Blake knew that while the morning phase of the battle raged around his ships Monck would be tacking up to him. Hopefully the best sailers of Monck's squadron would be entering the battle by noon. These tactical manoeuvres were successfully carried out and even Monck's ponderous *Vanguard* seems to have reached the battle shortly after midday.

Nevertheless Blake endured a fierce attack for the first hour or so of the battle as his squadron bore the full weight of the Dutch assault when Tromp and his subordinate admirals came down on him.[8] The Dutch met a hot reception when the fleets opened fire at about 9 a.m. The storm of gunfire must have been awesome both in its savage intensity and its sheer noise. In Portsmouth, on the Isle of Wight and along the English coast folk emerged from their houses and peered south in amazement as the thunderous roar came over the horizon. The cannonade was clearly heard on the deck of a privateersman off the Fairlight 150 miles away. Floriszoon in the *Monnikendam* attempted to interpose his squadron between Blake's forces and the oncoming flotilla of Lawson. Unhappily his subordinate captains either lacked his courage or were taken by surprise by his change of course. He found himself confronting alone a group of English frigates which met the *Monnikendam* with steady fire. Floriszoon ran down to leeward firing as he went but the *Monnikendam*'s main yard crashed to the deck and the mizzen yard quickly followed, both tearing down standing and running rigging. She drifted helplessly out of the battle as her crew struggled to repair the damage. She had lost eight killed and several wounded.[9] Tromp subsequently

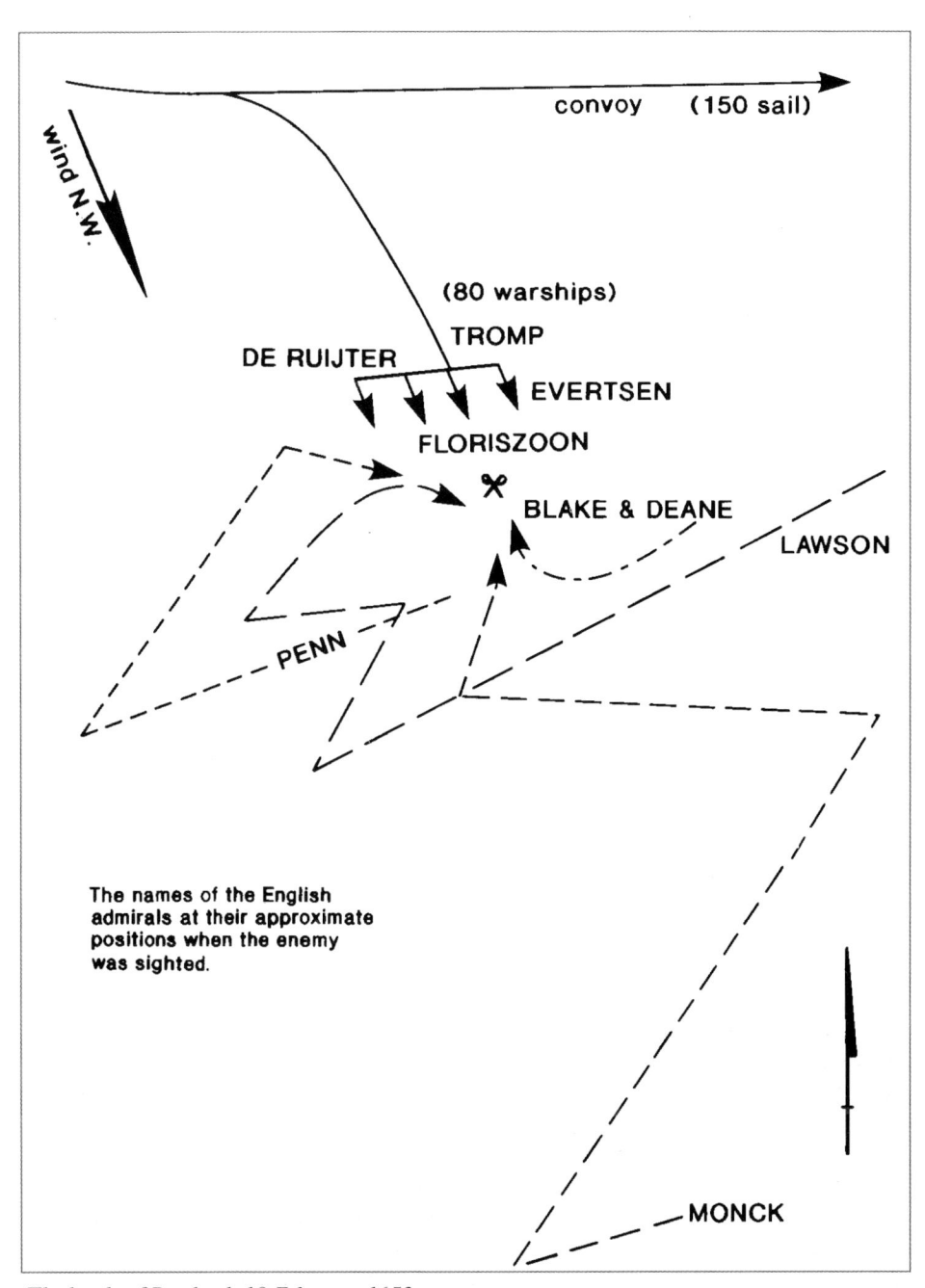

The battle of Portland, 18 February 1653

reprimanded Floriszoon for firing 'too much at random', really a rebuke for a rash lunge which had taken him out of the action.

Lawson's ships continued to work their way round the southern quarter of Blake's squadron to gain the wind for their attack as Admiral Penn, who had tacked as soon as his commander's intentions were clear, turned east to support him. Awaiting their arrival Blake's ships withstood Tromp's assault amid clouds of smoke which soon stretched away to the south-east like a hideously discoloured fog-bank. It was hot work for Blake and indeed for Penn as soon as he came into action, first against Evertsen and then against de Ruyter. Not, however, as hot as Tromp would have wished, for as he later observed 'divers of our captains were not as staunch as they ought to [have been]: they did not second myself and their other honest comrades as the English did'.[10] Tromp admired the way in which when he tried to attack the *Triumph* Blake's captains supported him: 'I had such a welcome from three or four of his ships that everything on board was on fire and Blake still unhurt'. In fact the *Brederode* was not in as alarming a situation as this implies although she lost her main and mizzen yards in the firefight. Moreover the *Triumph* had been hard beset with seven Dutch ships all seeking to attack her at once. She suffered damage to masts and yards and many killed. Blake's leg was gashed by a bar-iron shot and Captain Ball and Blake's secretary were both killed at his side. Blake insisted on remaining on his quarter deck for fear his men would be disheartened if they knew he was wounded. Reportedly the *Triumph*'s crew lost 100 out of 350. Evertsen later wrote that both Blake and Tromp saw their squadrons 'reduced to harmlessness'.[11] This was overstated although many ships were at least temporarily incapable of manoeuvring.

The fight was fierce with the English continuing to fire their broadsides at intervals determined by the time taken to reload all the tiers of guns. One anonymous Dutch observer reported they 'always shot at our round timbers and never fired in a hurry'; that is, they fired at the curve of the hull below the 'tumble-home' where the shot-holes would do most damage and held their fire until all were ready.[12] The Dutch ships still fired at their opponents' rigging and yards, still seeking to disable rather than sink, with the guns tending to fire as soon as they were reloaded with no overall control to produce a single broadside. Although damaged aloft the *Triumph* was so free of shot-holes that it never proved necessary to man the pumps during the battle. Nevertheless it was at first an unequal struggle and several English ships were threatened by the Dutch tactic of 'disable and board'.

De Ruyter attacked the *Prosperous*, 44, a large converted merchantman which met him with fire so heavy that he decided the best defence was to capture her. His boarding party met such a furious resistance that they were driven back over her bulwarks, but de Ruyter, more fearsome in his wrath than the enemy, drove his men to try again and this time they took the ship. De Ruyter carried off the unwounded among her crew, leaving a prize crew and her wounded crewmen including her captain, John Barker. The *Assistance*, one of Penn's ships, was so badly battered, her mainmast over the side and abandoned, that she limped off back to Portsmouth. Vice-Admiral John Bourne was among her wounded. The *Oak*, 32, John Edwin commanding, had her mainmast severely damaged and fell temporarily into the hands of the enemy. She was subsequently recaptured and reached Portsmouth the following day.

After his successful capture of the *Prosperous* five English ships surrounded de Ruyter's flagship and fired whenever they could make their guns bear. They were probably from Monck's squadron for the *Vanguard* was heavily engaged as soon as she arrived and lost thirty killed including Captain Mildmay. De Ruyter was rescued by Evertsen who forced his way through the press with ships commanded by among others Commodore Balck and Captain Ness. De Ruyter retreated, heavily damaged. His men on the *Prosperous* were captured when she was retaken by the *Martin*. This was after de Ruyter's departure, for as Tromp later reported: 'they did not know where the prize had got to with the people they had put on board'.[13] The *Prosperous* was sailed to Portsmouth with crew supplied by other ships. Other prizes captured by Dutch boarding parties were also rescued. It was now the Dutch who suffered heavy losses as ships were captured, sunk, burned or blown up. Ness survived broadsides from Lionel Lane's *Victory* only to be confronted by the broadsides of Vice-Admiral Peacock in the *Rainbow* which drove him out of the fight. The most dramatic incident involved John Day's *Advice*, 44. Her experience significantly illustrates the contrast between the Dutch tactic of 'disable and board' and the English tactic of 'smash and sink'. Five Dutch warships had assailed the *Advice*. Two of them, the ships of Captain Swers of Amsterdam and Captain Poort of Rotterdam, grappled her port and starboard bulwarks with a view to boarding from both sides. The other three were driven away by other English ships and one of the rescuers grappled onto the port side of Captain Swers's ship which was already grappled to the *Advice*'s port side. While Dutch and English fought across the *Advice*'s waist above she continued to fire into her tormentors from her gun-deck below – despite the danger that her gun flashes might ignite both her adversaries and thereby immolate herself. Finally Poort's ship was cut adrift, slid away and sank, her wounded captain still defiantly brandishing his sword. Probably none of her crew were saved. On the other side, caught between the hammer and the anvil of two English ships Swers's ship went down suddenly and only Swers and six of his crew managed to scramble to safety among their captors.[14] Tromp subsequently reported that the *Advice* also sank but this was wishful thinking. Battered and bleeding, with thirty-five of her crew killed and many more wounded, including her captain, she was slowly brought to safety in the Portsmouth dockyards. In the contest between 'smash' and 'grab' 'smash' had been overwhelmingly the victor. Meanwhile the powder magazine of another Dutch ship exploded spectacularly, which must have been as alarming for her assailants in such a confined action as it was fatal for ship and crew.

In the early afternoon several of the faster English frigates began to tack up toward the convoy. They were probably sent by Monck since it seems improbable that Blake would have been able to do so from the centre of the inferno. Tromp later used their sortie to explain his withdrawal. Although the safety of the convoy was his first priority he needed no excuse to withdraw. He had lost several warships sunk, captured and by fire and explosion. The English had lost only an armed merchantman, the *Sampson*, which had been so battered that she had to be scuttled. Blake had lost three or four ships which had withdrawn to Portsmouth for repair but his fleet was still almost whole, concentrated and full of fight. Tromp's fleet must have been dispirited by so many losses, was low on powder and shot and needed to try to redistribute what little munitions remained. Most Dutch ships had gangs of exhausted men either pumping their ships dry to improve their sailing qualities or, in the worst-damaged, to keep them afloat. The short winter afternoon was drawing in. Both sides were utterly spent. It was time to disengage. The battle could be resumed on the morrow.

Nevertheless Tromp must have retired with a heavy heart. He had seen his victory plain before him at 8 that morning. He had the wind. He had a large numerical advantage at the point of attack. He was confronted in Blake, Deane and Monck not by experienced naval officers who had learned the lore of the sea and of warfare as they climbed through the ranks, as had he and all his admirals, but by colonels and generals from Cromwell's army. Yet victory had mysteriously disappeared amidst the powder-smoke of the battle of Portland. He had found Blake on the defensive, with only a score of ships about him, apparently helpless before the charge of his four divisions. He did not know that he was attacking a man who was a master of defensive warfare. His defences were no longer the walls of stone and earth of the Civil War, but the hero of Lyme and Taunton was undaunted. Blake's walls might now be wooden but he commanded many hundred times the artillery he possessed when he had frustrated the royalist besiegers at Taunton for almost nine months. Blake knew he had only to hold out for an hour or so before Lawson and Penn would be coming to his relief. By noon he could look for reinforcement by another master of war, George Monck. If he had been confident he had reason to be.

Meanwhile on the 150 ships of the Dutch convoy men had all day peered at the smoke-clouded horizon, fearfully listening to a louder and longer cannonade than ever heard before in the history of naval warfare. At last they heard the thunder die away. They steered on into the darkness wondering whose topsails would be above the horizon behind them the next morning.

In fact it was Tromp, although the English were also in the offing and the Dutch at the rear of the convoy could already hear Monck's speedy fourth- and fifth-rates snapping at their flanks. Monck's frigates seized on any straggler and fired at all ships within range in the hope of rendering them helpless. However, there could be no general action on the 19th because Tromp, pinned by his responsibility to the convoy, and with his ships low on ammunition, could not turn at bay. Moreover the English could not force an action because that morning the wind was so light that they could not overtake the Dutch until well into the afternoon. The slow-sailing second-rates and even some of the third-rates barely came within range before dark. Tromp had performed prodigies of organisation during the night and early morning as his ships' crews repaired their ships and tried to redistribute the remaining powder, shot and cartridges. High on their ornamental sterns the lanterns had burned all night for with the English fleet looming behind them the fate of stragglers was certain. Nevertheless at dawn the hunters snapped up a prize indeed: the 1,200 ton *Struisvogel* (or *Ostrich*), an East

Robert Blake (1598–1657), General-at-Sea (National Maritime Museum, Greenwich, London)

Indiaman of 46 guns 'with 15 ports of a side on her lower tier' which towered above Tromp's ships. The victim of several broadsides from the *Lion* during the battle, when Floriszoon and de Wildt came alongside her at sunset her crew reported that her captain, all her officers and most of her crew were dead. De Wildt took off her wounded and towed her all night. Later he abandoned her. When asked by Tromp why he had done so he explained that the crew were so helplessly drunk they could not obey his orders.[15] More probably de Wildt simply wished to rid himself of a burden which would make his own capture almost inevitable. An English observer made no mention of drunken crew, but declared that she had more than a hundred corpses on board and that the few survivors reported that many wounded had already been removed. The Dutch also lost the *Holland* of Rotterdam, Captain de Munnick, which had lost her mainmast. Once captured her crew was taken off and she was fired and sunk.[16]

During the morning Tromp drew his more serviceable ships into a long half-moon between the convoy and the pursuing English with the *Brederode* at the centre of the arc, Evertsen on the left 'horn' and de Ruyter on the right. Meanwhile the Dutch continued to try to plug shot-holes, raised spare main yards to serve as jury-masts, repaired broken yards and sent up makeshift rigging. The crew of Floriszoon's *Monnikendam* raised new main and mizzen yards. The melancholy clanking of the pumps could be heard from ship after ship. The English frigates achieved several successes and Tromp reported that during the day 'Captains Jan le Sage of Zealand and Bruijn van Seelst of Amsterdam, with a few small merchantmen were cut off from the fleet.'[17] Moreover, there was action around the crescent during the afternoon by which time the convoy was off the Isle of Wight. After this firefight de Ruyter's ship, already heavily damaged aloft, had to be towed. The *Monnikendam*'s new main and mizzen yards were once more shot away and her crew were working continuous shifts at the pumps to keep their ship afloat. Captain Jan le Sage was killed and his ship taken by frigates and Captain van Seelst's ship was taken and burned. As the light fell the English fleet veered off for the night and seizing their opportunity several Dutch men-of-war sailed up to the *Brederode* complaining that they were almost depleted of powder and ball. Tromp ordered the storeship to distribute any remaining 8-pounder ball to those ships with that calibre of gun. It was all he could do in an increasingly desperate situation. So for the Dutch ended the second miserable day. The third would be worse.

> In the morning the English were a mile to the rear of us and then came sailing up. About ten o'clock the fight began. We were still [being towed] . . . The fighting was very fierce on some ships and some did their best to run. Towards evening the English made . . . in among the merchantmen and took some. . . . During the night it began to blow very hard and on the morning of the 21 February we [anchored].

De Ruyter's laconic entry conceals the desperation of Tromp and his commanders. They must have felt that Sunday, 20 February, would be disastrous. Their powder magazines were empty or almost exhausted. The convoy was half mutinous and ready to disperse in panic-stricken dashes to neutral French ports. Few Dutch sailors wished to be herded for refuge into Flemish ports controlled by the hated Spanish. Many would have preferred English captivity to Spanish hospitality. Several naval captains who had done little in the battle were ready to desert their commanders now that their ships were too damaged to pursue them. When the English cannonade opened at 9 a.m. several ships began to take flight. Tromp fired a signal-gun to recall them, ordered their captains to come on board and demanded to know if they would fly like knaves. When they protested they had nothing left with which to fight he ordered them to take position in the middle of the convoy where their presence would give heart to the merchantmen. Those ships which still possessed powder and shot would guard both them and the convoy. All morning the action raged with several ships captured or sunk from either the convoy or its escort, the Dutch warships resisting their tormentors as best they could. So they fled eastward with the English frigates, like so many wolves, barking and biting at the convoy's flank. At noon Blake drew off, to Tromp's intense relief for he believed that if the battle had continued another hour they would have been utterly destroyed for lack of ammunition.[18] It is likely that Blake himself was also conscious of emptying magazines. The wind was strengthening and many of his ships had masts and yards which were likely to fall at any moment.

By late afternoon convoy and escort were off the French coast. Both were much depleted from the fleet of more than seventy warships and about 150 merchantmen which had first sighted the English fleet on Friday morning but in defeat Tromp was still resolute. He would save as many merchantmen as he could and his remaining warships too if only he could find a loophole. The English fleet had the north-west wind behind them and loomed menacingly astern. The Dutch were approaching a lee shore with several ships barely afloat and others in a sorry state aloft. However, Tromp had been at sea since he was ten years old. As much master-mariner as warrior he could calculate the odds on what the soldiers who commanded his adversaries would consider a desperate gamble. At nightfall, with the English reluctant to approach this dangerous lee shore, Tromp gave the signal to anchor near the cliffs of Cap Gris Nez. Blake, observing this, ordered all lights lit to keep his fleet together during the night for he believed his enemy trapped, pinned by the north-west wind and the ebbing tide. In the growing dark Blake, Deane and their officers could see the loom of the Cape at the foot of which they believed were dangerous shoals and rock. Tromp could not remain where he was. At dawn he must steer out into the embrace of his enemies in order to double the cape which would give them their opportunity for one last assault. It was certainly time. Some of Blake's ships were pumping, all had suffered damage aloft. On many the topmasts whipped in crazy gyrations not anticipated by the ships' riggers as the heavy swell and keen wind put undue strain on jury rigs or on masts and spars which had been weakened by glancing strikes. Even a moderate gale would leave many dismasted and drifting helplessly down on an unfriendly coast. At first light the lookouts peered hopefully towards Cap Gris Nez but in vain. Their enemy had vanished. During the night Tromp had led his fleet through a deep-water channel close under the cliffs which was unknown to his adversaries.

Against all likelihood he had saved the bulk of his command. He was just in time. Snow flurries, a darkening sky, a stronger wind harping in the rigging warned both sides of severe weather building up. Dutch masts went overboard on the 21st (including the *Monnikendam*'s mainmast). More vessels came under tow as the fleet struggled through the shoaling water where their adversaries dared not follow. On 3 March they anchored off Dunkirk. By then fleet and convoy totalled only seventy vessels out of approximately 230 at the beginning of the action. Not all the missing were either sunk or captured. Many merchantmen had found refuge in neutral ports or were scattered about the Channel, mislaid by both sides.

The English wasted no time regretting the lost opportunity for a still more decisive victory. In London the news of Portland brought rejoicing both in the streets and in the corridors of Whitehall Palace – although with none of the over-optimism which had followed the Kentish Knock. At sea Blake, Deane and Monck were aware that King Winter could inflict a defeat on them more terrible than the one which they had inflicted on the Dutch. It was time to get their damaged ships off this dangerous shore and claw their way to the security of the Downs or the Thames estuary. They knew that despite Tromp's escape their victory had been devastating. Seventeen men-of-war and about sixty merchantmen they claimed as sunk or taken. The Dutch killed, wounded or captured cannot have been less than 3,000. The English lost only the scuttled *Sampson*, although some other ships were so badly damaged they would be out of action for weeks. They estimated their casualties at about 600. Their fleet once more commanded the Channel which meant that the Dutch must again order their convoys to take the longer northern route. There were other reasons for Dutch depression. The English had won without employing such first-rates as the *Sovereign* and *Resolution*, both of which had fought at the Kentish Knock. Despite the advantage of numbers and concentration, with the English squadrons dangerously separated on the first day, the best Dutch warships had been unable to overwhelm the English second-, third- and fourth-rates because of heavier guns better served by disciplined gun-crews. This had once more led some Dutch captains to flinch from the fight, not surprisingly. By contrast the English crews had fought with solid resolution because, like their commander, they did not believe that they could be beaten and it seemed that their confidence was well placed. Finally this victory over Dutch admirals who combined decades of sea experience, had been won, Penn aside, by generals and colonels on loan from the English army. It was a sombre picture.

CHAPTER 6

The Last Battles

How great and wonderful the Lord hath been unto this fleet hath plainly appeared by His mighty and glorious presence going along with us to the ruin of our enemies and preservation of his poor servants.

George Monck, Scheveningen[1]

I have run my course. Be of good courage.

Martinus Tromp, Scheveningen

The first half of 1653 demonstrated both the weakness and the strength of the Dutch republic. Her gravest weakness was the vulnerability of her commerce and the aftermath of Portland demonstrated this with merciless clarity. In a war with England if the Dutch could not win a major naval victory the Channel was almost useless as a trade route. All Dutch commerce from the Mediterranean, the East and West Indies and North America must come north around the Shetlands and then follow the North Sea route employed by Dutch traders to the Baltic and Norway. This simple-sounding solution was a cure with grievous side-effects. The distance from Finisterre to the Texel is approximately 1,000 miles (1,625 kilometres) but is 2,200 miles (3,450 kilometres) by the northerly route.[2] More provisions would be consumed, crew would demand more pay, wear and tear on ships would increase, insurance rates would climb because of the increased climatic hazards. Cost was vital because the Dutch had built a trading empire by transporting goods more cheaply than others could match. The aftermath of Portland proved dismal for Dutch trade. Once the news of Portland spread abroad merchantmen in foreign ports dared not clear for home. Those at home must lie at their moorings for Tromp had warned them that he lacked warships to escort them. It was claimed that grass grew amid the cobbles of the Amsterdam streets and that 3,000 houses stood empty. Unemployment was widespread. If the Dutch fleet could not even escort its merchant marine it could hardly sortie against the English fleet. The straits to which it was reduced was demonstrated in March when de With sortied with a flotilla which he was furious to discover contained only eighteen men-of-war instead of the forty he had been promised and that not one was large. Having no illusions about the capacity of small Dutch men-of-war to withstand English broadsides, he could only steer north to attack the Newcastle coal fleet. The colliers seeing his topsails rise over the southern horizon hastily took shelter under the guns of Scarborough Castle.

A brisk cannonade soon drove the Dutch out of range of their prey and de With's council of war wisely decided that to attack in the face of Cromwellian artillery would be suicidal. Bitter and frustrated, de With retired to Schoonvelt declaring that without bigger ships the Netherlands faced disaster.

Amidst all this gloom it might seem that the Dutch would have sought a negotiated settlement but although they made a diplomatic gesture they were as fearful as their opponents of negotiating after a defeat because the victors would demand unacceptable terms. Rather they now demonstrated their greatest strength: their capacity to rise swiftly from the ashes of defeat more tenacious and as determined as ever, a capacity the Spanish had experienced over decades of struggle. Nothing could more vividly demonstrate this remarkable resilience than that having seen their fleet encounter the worst disaster of their history in February a fleet of more than a hundred ships sortied in early May. Despite the bickerings and jealousies of the states, despite the divisions between competing admiralties, despite the divisions between republicans and monarchists, the Dutch had once more exhibited their capacity to produce fleets of warships and send them to sea.

The English had not been idle during the period of the Dutch recovery. There had been none of the complacency and assumption that the war would soon be over which had bedevilled the government's actions after the Kentish Knock. The English fleet had suffered heavy damage at Portland. It took almost as long to make the English fleet battle-worthy as it did the Dutch.[3] Moreover the fleet had been grappling with other problems. Although they had suffered far fewer dead and wounded than the Dutch many sailors had been wounded and contagious disease attacked the unwounded once the ships were in port. In their victory dispatch Blake and his colleagues had pleaded for relief for the 'widows and orphans' of the 'divers both of honesty and worth slain' and for the 'languishing estate' of the wounded. The commanders were moved by a desire to care for their men but they also knew that if great hardships befell the families of wounded and killed seamen recruitment would become even more difficult. Shortage of men, not shortage of ships or guns or even supplies, was the weakness the English navy had to contend with during this titanic struggle. Parliament needed no urging. They voted immediate payments to the recently widowed and pensions for the permanently disabled and in their care for the wounded sent to Portsmouth the most eminent physician in England, Dr Daniel Whistler.[4] Whistler quickly discovered that the wounded were only part of his problem. Disease was scourging the fleet. As Monck and Deane reported on 30 March: 'the sickness increaseth daily on ship and shore'. A man ahead of his time, Whistler condemned 'the thronging of weak men into poor stifling houses' and ordered the removal of the worst-wounded from such fetid atmospheres into hospitals and urged the government to commandeer Porchester Castle, then leased out, to use as a hospital. He also condemned the practice of quartering wounded in 'ordinaries' (taverns) where they would drink bad beer brewed with Portsmouth's brackish water which was particularly dangerous when newly made. Whistler sent the less seriously wounded back to their ships which he considered healthier quarters than those ashore. His chief patient was the wounded Admiral Blake who like many of his men had come down with a fever. 'General Blake mends but slowly, which detains me yet here' he reported on 16 March.[5]

Healing the wounded and the feverish, although vital, was not enough. The Dutch would not wait until they recovered. More crew had to be found and quickly. Monck and Deane had the foresight to suggest a system of continuous service which unfortunately would not be implemented for nearly two centuries. Ignoring their sage advice the government continued to press seamen where possible and landsmen when that failed. Homecoming merchantmen were plundered. Commodore Badiley's ships had barely arrived from the Mediterranean before the hungry press was swarming about his ships at their Thames moorings. Not all that were swept up were able-bodied and Nehemiah Bourne, to whose exertions the admirals owed much, had to cull many who would only be 'a burden to the service'. The collier fleet from Newcastle was eagerly awaited because of the men who could be stripped from it but these wily mariners proved adept at escaping while others violently resisted Bourne's press-gangs.

While the men were gathered from as far as the Isle of Man and the Channel Isles the ships they would crew were made ready. All naval yards were scenes of bustle and improvisation as badly damaged ships were made battle-worthy. Remembering past losses to Dutch boarding parties Blake ordered the construction of forecastles on the smaller frigates from which his crews would be better able to defend their ships against boarders pouring over the waist. On 25 April seven Swedish ships providentially arrived with masts, pitch and lead and the fleet eagerly devoured their contents. Slowly the squadrons became ready for war. Penn went to sea first in early April to convoy the Newcastle fleet, and having escorted them to the Thames estuary, lay off the Suffolk coast where he was reinforced by John Bourne commanding twenty armed merchantmen. They took their combined force through the Straits of Dover to unite with the main fleet off the Isle of Wight on 29 April. The twenty ships which the government had intended for the Mediterranean also joined the fleet when Blake and Monck urged that these ships would be more usefully employed in the Narrow Seas. The fleet had risen to eighty men-of-war, not counting fireships, and this imposing figure would soon climb to 105. This did not include a flotilla which Blake was assembling in the Thames and which would reinforce the fleet when it was ready. In the midst of these preparations the admirals learned that the Commonwealth government which they had loyally served since 1649 had been swept away by Oliver Cromwell and a file of infantry. England was about to embark on the experiment of the Nominated Parliament, an assembly commonly referred to by its scurrilous royalist nickname: the Barebones Parliament.[6] The commanders and their subordinates wisely ignored these political excitements and got on with their job.

When the English fleet sortied it would carry the new sailing and fighting *Instructions* which had been drawn up by Blake, Deane and Monck in March and from which some authorities date the tactic of steering into battle in line-ahead formation. This conclusion is based on a significant passage: when a commander was seen to engage the enemy or when he fired two signal guns and:

hoisted a red flag at his fore-topmast-head then each squadron shall take the best advantage they can to engage with the enemy next unto them, and in order hereunto *all the ships of every squadron shall endeavour to keep in line with their chief*, unless the chief of (a) squadron shall be either lamed or otherwise disabled (which God forbid) (if so) *every ship of the said squadron shall endeavour to get in a line with the admiral . . .*[7]

During the first year of the Dutch War the English fleet, like the Dutch, had tended to sail into action in the traditional way: 'charging' the enemy (a word often used by participants) in no distinct formation, and bringing under fire the first enemy ship which they encountered. Apart from the action off Dungeness, when the English were scattered and outnumbered, this had worked reasonably well. English guns and gunnery were effective enough to counter the Dutch tactic of disable and board although it had cost the English two ships at Dungeness and caused the temporary capture of several English ships at Portland. However, at Portland even though Dutch ships often contained soldiers as well as mariners, the Dutch crews – depleted by scurvy, many of them inexperienced in hand-to-hand fighting – had been unable to withstand the counter-attacks of the English crews who were better fed and in better health. Moreover Cromwell had sent several hundred soldiers to be distributed around the fleet. They knew nothing of seamanship but everything about the use of sword, pike and musket. However, it was obviously better for the English to prevent the Dutch from employing their tactics at all, not least because English resources of spars and rigging were severely strained by the closure of the Baltic. Fighting in line should enable the English to take advantage of their fire-power by standing off from the Dutch ships and battering them from a distance with a cannonade to which the smaller Dutch guns could only reply ineffectively. If the English fleet had the weather gauge the Dutch would be unable to close the range, still less grapple and board. It was persuasive on paper although the commanders must have known that at sea realities are rarely so neat. However, both Monck and Deane were experts in artillery and Blake had defended besieged towns. They naturally perceived their warships as mobile batteries and wished to employ tactics which would use them to best effect. All these considerations probably influenced the new sailing *Instructions* which provided for very primitive but more effective signals between ships, and for sailing and tacking in a more disciplined, structured formation.

On 5 May Tromp sortied from the Texel commanding at least seventy men-of-war and five fireships (he had asked for twenty-five and one of the five soon sank) and headed north escorting a convoy of 200 merchantmen to the Shetlands where they would set course for the East and West Indies. As vice-admirals he had with him de Ruyter and de With. Although his first priority was to escort his convoy out safely and to escort south ships which had been imprisoned in northern ports by his earlier defeat, Tromp was determined to seek Blake out and bring on a decisive fleet action. Despite his experiences of English fire-power, and despite the fact that the belated building programme of new warships could not reinforce him during 1653, Tromp was as determined on victory as ever. He resolved that on his return from the north he would pick up reinforcements commanded by Floriszoon and Evertsen and then seek the English fleet in the Downs. Failing that he would remain in the Narrow Seas until the English fleet appeared, watching for any Dutch merchantmen who had risked a dash up-Channel.

Having dispatched his convoys off the Shetlands Tromp briefly visited Bergen and then returned to the Texel where Floriszoon joined him with sixteen warships on 20 May and together they sailed on to the Maas to pick up Evertsen's squadron. Thus reinforced Tromp now commanded a fleet of ninety-two men-of-war, five fireships and six smaller vessels. He was full of fight but he could not locate his enemy and Monck and Deane were equally unable to locate him. They had pursued Tromp to Shetland but arrived two days too late and his Bergen visit ensured that they did not encounter him on the way back. After a vain search of the Texel and the Vlie they retired to pick up reinforcements from Yarmouth. Tromp had hoped to catch the English fleet in the Downs and envelop it in a pincer movement by entering the anchorage from the north and south entrances but when he arrived there his opponents were seeking him off the Dutch coast. Frustration led Tromp to make a serious blunder. He sailed on to Dover and wasted irreplaceable ammunition on a fruitless artillery duel with the guns of the castle and its outworks. Finally scouts brought him news of the English fleet and he hastily steered northward in the hope of bringing them to battle. The English, aware of Tromp's appearance off Dover, had ordered all warships between Long Sands Head and Orfordness to join them. Blake, although still ailing, probably from the attacks of the kidney stone which would soon send him into temporary retirement, had brought his squadron out of the Thames and was moving them to a secure anchorage in the Gunfleet. This was a deep channel south of Harwich and north-east of the mouth of the Thames protected by the Gunfleet shoal. At six in the morning of 1 June Monck and Deane sortied from Sole Bay with 105 ships mounting a formidable armament of 3,817 guns and Blake's squadron had yet to join them. Once again the fleet was commanded from a first-rate. The *Resolution*, 88, with both Monck and Deane aboard, led the Red squadron in the centre. Vice-Admiral William Penn commanded the right wing as admiral of the White in the *James*, 66, while Rear-Admiral Lawson commanded the left wing as admiral of the Blue in the *George*, 56.

At noon the Blue squadron's scouting frigates let fall their top-gallant sails which, under the new signalling instructions, meant they had spotted the enemy. The fleet immediately altered course towards the Dutch fleet, having the weather gauge, and soon the enemy's topsails could be seen from the crow's nest of Lawson's *George* 'about four leagues' (about 12 miles) to leeward. At 4 p.m. Lawson, whose wing was closest to the enemy, backed his topsails, his squadron following suit, so as to slow his advance and let the main body catch up. The fleet were then immediately to the south of the Gabbard shoal, which lies about 40 miles east of Harwich. There the fleet anchored as an increasingly misty summer evening closed in, the scouts soon losing sight of their quarry in the growing darkness. However, if invisible the Dutch were still on station, lying at anchor all night several miles to the south-east. Monck and Deane, confident in both their fire-power and their numbers, and with some hope that Blake might appear in the morning, looked forward to a decisive battle. However, Blake had yet to leave the Gunfleet. When he anchored there he still did not know precisely where the two fleets were. Once clear intelligence of the fleets' movements reached him he prepared to sortie. Hearing that his presence would be welcome, as he put it, and 'being desirous to put in for my share for the service of the Commonwealth in this present juncture', his ships weighed anchor but were not at sea until the early afternoon of 2 June.[8] However, before noon a distant thunder told him that the battle had already begun.

The battle off the Gabbard, fought over two days, would be very different from the action off Portland only four months earlier. The fleet was not divided with a third of it under Monck struggling upwind to get into the action. Here the hundred or so ships were well organised in their three squadrons and close together. This time the English fleet had the wind and its commanders possessed a control of the battle which Blake had been denied in February. The differences did not entirely favour the English. Tromp did not have a convoy to worry about and therefore could fight the battle without continually glancing over his shoulder. However, the great difference between the two battles, indeed between this battle and any earlier battles, lay in the tactics adopted by Monck and Deane in which the *Instructions* played a large part. Oddly we do not learn this from the very sketchy reports provided by both the English and Dutch commanders but rather from letters written in Holland. Both were based on conversations with Dutch participants; one was written by a royalist to Sir Edward Nicholas, Charles II's secretary, the other by one of John Thurloe's Dutch spies.[9]

It is clear from these reports supplemented by others that the English approached the enemy downwind with Blake and Deane's Red squadron in the centre and Lawson's Blue to port and Penn's White to starboard. This meant that when these three masses of ships turned to port to sail in line broadside to the enemy fleet Lawson was in the van and Penn to the rear. This sounds simple but it was far from simple for the captains of more than one hundred men-of-war – coordinated by a very primitive signalling system and a set of *Instructions* which the captains had not practised. They paused for a while at 'double cannon shot' while they organised themselves into a line. No doubt it was ragged enough by later standards in view of their inexperience and the size of the fleet. Nevertheless it was a distinct formation and owing to the light winds and comparatively smooth sea it held together so that Lawson's squadron could lead this long procession of ships to within 'half cannon' shot of the Dutch, that is, about 500 yards. Half cannon shot was well within range for the experienced English gunners but beyond the effective range of some of the lighter Dutch guns. It was well beyond the effective range of the musketeers who crowded the Dutch waists and tops and who were supposed to disable the mariners and so make their ships the helpless prey of boarders or fireships. The English warships, in stately procession, fired a slow, methodical sequence of broadsides at their opponents while the heavier Dutch ships returned their fire as well as they could. The order to fire was given about 11 a.m. and there was passage of perhaps two or three hours during which the English broadsides galled their opponents. In the very first exchange of fire by the *Resolution* a random shot crossed the quarter-deck and killed the unfortunate Deane. Monck, that extraordinary man of destiny, had a narrow escape for he was standing beside Deane at the time.[10] With his cloak he hastily covered Deane's body and had it carried below lest the crew be disheartened by this ill omen.

In fact Tromp had more cause to fear for morale as the bombardment continued. Thurloe's spy reported that the new tactic was 'so great a terror to most of the States' ships as few of them durst bear up or abide it'.[11] This is an exaggeration but some Dutch captains, unaccustomed to feeling like ducks in a shooting gallery, flinched from the barrage and seem to have played no further part in the action that day. Subsequently there was a shift of wind which permitted the Dutch vanguard, commanded by the ever-aggressive de Ruyter, to close the range with Lawson. Tromp also spotted an opportunity, for the light and variable wind had caused a gap to open up between the squadrons of Lawson and Monck. He brought his squadron into the gap to attack Lawson from the rear while de Ruyter was engaging him from the flank. There was briefly a mêlée and one report suggests that de Ruyter got his ship aboard the *Resolution* and his boarding party might have captured it but for the intervention of several English frigates. This colourful story can hardly be true. The *Resolution*, back in the Red squadron, would not have been a target for de Ruyter. Possibly this is a confusion for Lawson's *George* but no other report suggests the vice-admiral's ship was in danger and significantly de Ruyter's diary makes no reference to the incident. Certainly there was heavy firing for some time between the opposing forces at close range. One Dutch fireship was sunk by gunfire and another warship blew up with the loss of all but five of its crew, although more by accident than because of English gunfire. One English report claimed that two other Dutch ships were sunk but they may have been fireships. The Dutch were convinced quite erroneously that at least two English warships had gone to the bottom. Amid the clouds of acrid smoke it was impossible to form a true picture. The temporary shift of wind had given the Dutch a chance to employ their tactics of 'disable and board' but these failed in the face of the steady pounding of massed iron guns. Soon the wind shifted again restoring the English advantage, and, remarkably enough, the English squadrons succeeded in resuming their line-ahead formation, still firing steady broadsides at the Dutch who resumed their eastward course into the growing darkness.

The following morning found the two fleets becalmed only a mile apart. Both admirals called councils of war. The Dutch were gloomy, as well they might be. Several ships had stolen away in the night and there was much angry talk of cowardly captains who had flinched from the fight. In truth the Dutch captains were as brave as anyone but they knew themselves out-matched. It was one thing to fight from the lofty decks of the *Brederode* or other large states ships. It was quite another to withstand broadsides from vessels which the English would have hesitated to class as sixth-rates: low-waisted, lightly built, crowded with men and feebly armed. Rather than criticising their commanders Tromp and his vice-admirals should rather have criticised those who sent such ships into battle against such odds. There were more serious causes for anxiety aboard the

The Battle off the Gabbard, 1653, by Heerman Witmont (National Maritime Museum, Greenwich, London)

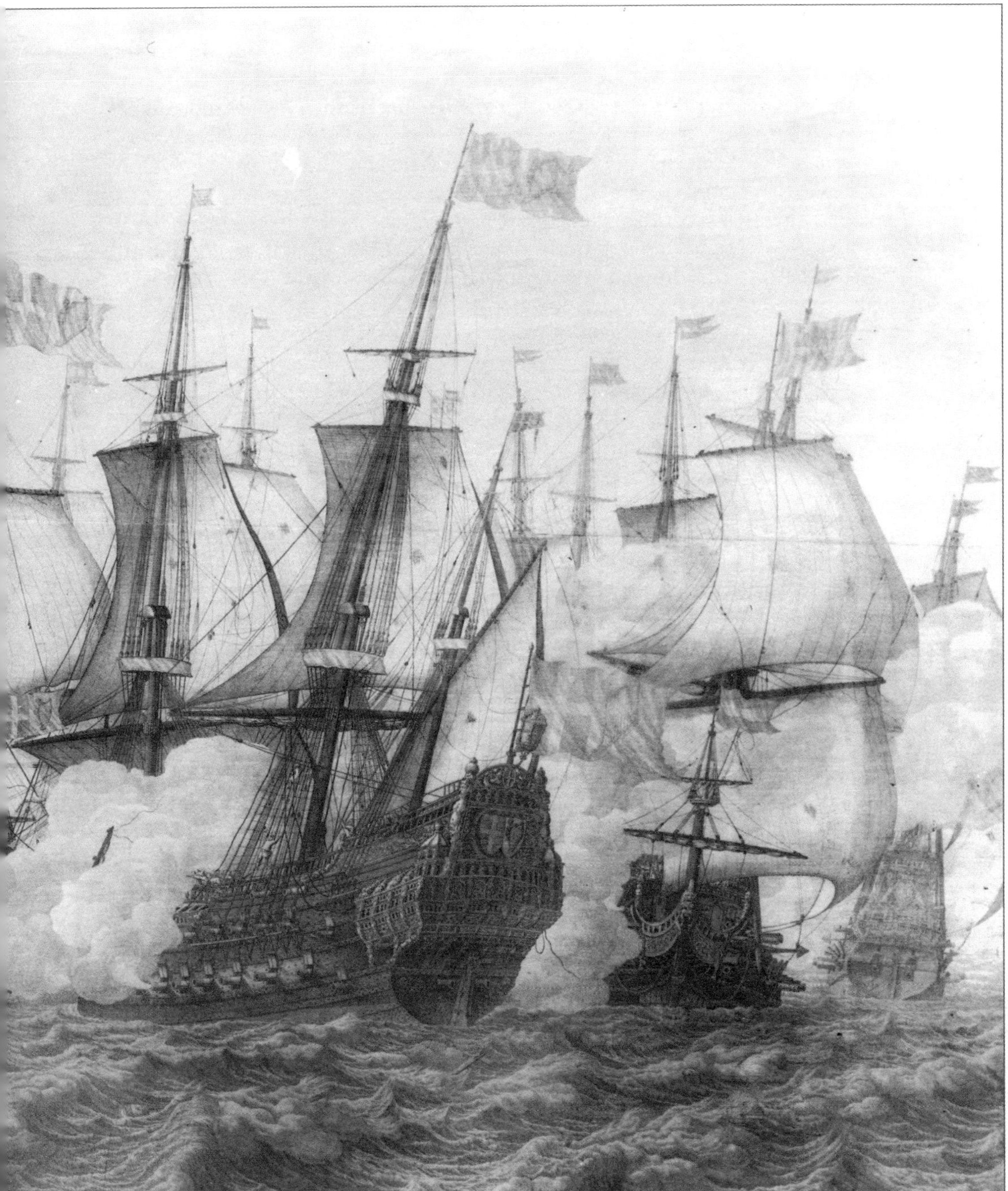

Brederode. The blunder off Dover had come home to roost: the ships were short of powder and ball. A prolonged assault on the English fleet could not be sustained. They might make one sharp attack if the wind changed but thereafter they must make a fighting withdrawal to the shelter of their own sandbanks.[12] Monck and his senior officers in the great cabin of the *Resolution* were also in a critical mood. They felt that the battle of the previous day should have been more decisive and that some of Lawson's squadron had displayed timorousness when they found themselves unaccustomedly isolated in the more open line-of-battle formation. As a result Monck determined that the three squadrons should sail abreast in the more traditional way (although the ships of the squadrons were probably intended to sail in line) and drive hard through the Dutch fleet and scatter them. He asked his officers 'to wipe out the past and do their best in the present'. For himself he undertook to pursue the Dutch as far as the shoals would permit. The English captains were all convinced that the Dutch headed for shoal water in the hope of luring the English ships to destruction. In fact they were simply removing themselves out of range and going home to land their wounded, acquire more crew if possible, and replenish their magazines. One English captain, who had probably served as a soldier in Scotland, expressed it best: 'the enemy will go where we cannot follow him, like the highlanders to the mountains'.[13]

There then began what proved to be for the Dutch a terrible second day of battle, although not as disastrous as it might have been thanks to the leadership of Tromp, and the disciplined support of de Ruyter and de With and their colleagues. Light winds prevented any resumption before noon but then the wind freshened and the two fleets drove after each other, the Dutch always downwind despite several attempts by Tromp to beat up to windward of his enemy. Finally, with all hope of an attack gone, Tromp steered for the Flemish coast. Throughout the afternoon the English vanguard was in range of the Dutch rearguard which included Tromp's largest warship. The broadsides from both sides could be heard as a distant thunder as far as London in the west and in the Dutch and Flemish and French towns to the east and south. It was a day in which, as one English observer happily wrote, 'we had the harvest and gleaning of the vintage and with less loss than ever before' as ship after ship sank under English gunfire or fell to English prize crews. At the height of the struggle with the *Brederode* still defiantly firing its rapidly depleting ammunition, Tromp saw with alarm that a fresh English flotilla of at least a dozen ships was bearing down on his port bow. It was Blake's squadron arriving at last with his nephew, Robert Blake the younger, leading in the *Hampshire*. The news that Blake was back was greeted with loud cheering in the English fleet and caused despondency, amounting to panic, among the sorely tried Dutch captains. Tromp's fighting withdrawal speedily turned to rout and in the confusion several Dutch ships fell foul of each other and were compelled to surrender to their pursuers.

Throughout the summer evening, as growing darkness slowed the firing, the Dutch streamed toward the safety of the Weilings at the entrance to the Scheldt estuary. Darkness and the Scheldt's fearsome shoals saved Tromp's fleet from destruction. Daylight would find Tromp licking his wounds but still defiantly demanding more ships, more men and more munitions. His indomitable spirit could not be quelled by defeat. Defeat, however, it was. When Tromp reached the Scheldt he had only seventy-four ships in company of more than a 100 ships with which he went into battle. A further eight were hastening toward the safety of the Texel. Of the rest seven or eight were on the bottom and eleven were in English hands including a 'vice-admiral of 1,200 tons and 14 guns in the tier'. This does not include Tromp's fireships all of which had burned without result. Nor does it include the ships which now had to be run ashore to prevent them from sinking, which for a time almost included the *Brederode* herself which had several feet of water in her hold despite hours of pumping. Most of those not in danger of sinking would need substantial repairs before they could be sent to sea.[14] As that normally aggressively confident admiral, Witte de With, told the States General in an angry outburst: 'Why should I keep silence longer? . . . I can say that the English are at present masters both of us and of the seas.'

De With was certainly correct, at least in the short term. Nothing could more clearly demonstrate the reality and scale of the defeat to the Dutch people than the fact that while their sorely damaged fleet had retired to the estuaries, the English fleet lay just off their coast snapping up prizes while it awaited any Dutch sortie. Thousands of civilians thronged the beaches and the long ridges of dykes, peering out at the hated enemy cruising along the coast. The States General issued statements minimising losses of warships and claiming heavy English losses at the Gabbard but it was propaganda without point.[15] In fact the English lost no ships, the dozen sent in for urgent repair were not large, and the report that only 126 men were killed and 236 wounded is credible. Only 16 were killed on the *Resolution* including the desperately unlucky Deane. Dutch trade had ground to a halt. Even the herring-sellers at the market had no wares and herrings were almost as important a component of the Dutch diet as potatoes would later become to the Irish. Herring buses at sea dared not return. Herring buses in port, by far the majority, dared not put to sea. The economic condition of the Netherlands grew rapidly worse. Banks remained closed. Merchants had empty warehouses and hungry creditors, or warehouses full of goods they could not send to market. Ships bulging with exports swung at anchor, unable to sail even if the English blockade suddenly disappeared because during the long delay their crews had consumed all their stores. The Dutch longed for peace, but their statesmen knew that although they had sent an emissary to London a treaty now would be a peace imposed by the victors on the vanquished. To prevent or at least postpone this dismal reward for their expenditure of blood and treasure they must break the English blockade. Blockade-running while Monck was temporarily absent picking up stores was not enough. The blockade must be ended permanently and the only way to achieve this was by gaining mastery at sea and this only a decisive naval victory could provide. It appears obvious today that the Dutch had as much chance of effecting this as their philosophers had of turning base metal into gold. However, for the States General to accept that bitter truth was to accept defeat. They would fight on. Certainly Tromp was as determined as ever to clear a passage for the vital convoys by defeating his English adversaries or die in the attempt. Despite his years (and a man of fifty-five in his era was advancing into old age) he scoured the Netherlands for men and munitions. Dry and wet docks were a forest of masts as artificers laboured to repair his damaged warships. The big ships which his masters had hesitated too long to lay down were now building and he repeatedly urged that they should be hastened to completion although their launch would come too late for his next sortie. The Dutch showed an astonishing capacity for building warships quickly but one vital element they lacked in 1653: heavy iron guns to match the batteries of their opponents. These they had to import and too often the ships bringing this crucial cargo fell into the hands of their enemy.

Once again the Dutch navy made a remarkable recovery, but they faced a problem. Their battle-fleet was divided. Tromp was fitting out in the Scheldt in the south while de With was fitting out his smaller but still substantial squadron in the Helder at the entrance to the Zuider Zee in the north. The two wings must unite before confronting the enemy. Yet they could only unite by putting to sea miles apart and with the enemy lying in wait between them. Naturally Monck and Blake were as aware of this situation and as determined to exploit it as their opponents were to overcome it. Fortunately for the Dutch it was a problem which could only be solved by seamanship, not by fire-power, and the Dutch commanders were as much masters of seamanship as Monck and Blake were masters of artillery. Meanwhile the English had their own problems. Maintaining blockade was difficult enough in the days of Nelson and Collingwood when the navy had behind it years of experience in keeping fleets at sea for months at a time. In the seventeenth century blockading was an activity at which officers and seamen were novices. The beer became so bad that the men preferred water, but water itself ran low. Sickness among the crews was the inevitable result. Frequent squalls or long periods of heavy weather hampered the transfer of provisions at sea from visiting stores ships. If they did not retire to Sole Bay to replace the sick and reprovision they would soon reach the point where the big warships would have insufficient crew to man the guns and work the ships simultaneously. Yet if the blockade was abandoned the Dutch would have won a victory without firing a shot and the Dutch convoys would soon be pouring northward along the German coast. Blake and Monck solved the problem by deception. They retired the main fleet to Sole Bay leaving behind fourth- and fifth-rates who busied themselves about the estuaries and off the beaches, occasionally raising and lowering flags as if signalling to larger units out at sea and keeping so tight a grip on the channel entrances that scouts could not get to sea to learn the true position. The frigates were so skilfully handled that Tromp never pierced their screen and did not learn that the main fleet had left until after Monck had brought it back at the end of July. Blake was not with him. He was now so ill with kidney stones that he was not expected to live. He retired to Bath where he slowly recovered but he had fought his last battle against the Dutch.

Blake was still convalescing when his old adversary sortied for the last time. Tromp put his faith in Dutch seamanship to solve the problem of uniting with de With. It did not let him down. At the beginning of August he sent orders to de With to move his squadron out of the Helder and station himself off its mouth. Tromp intended as soon as winds and tides would allow to emerge from the Scheldt and head north-east up the Dutch coast to confront the English fleet. Should the English main fleet move to assault de With's smaller squadron before Tromp could arrive then de With must withdraw once again within the shelter of the Helder. However, if, as Tromp hoped, Monck moved south-west along the Dutch coast to engage Tromp then de With could pursue Monck and engage his rear while Tromp engaged him from the front. On paper it sounds simple enough. In an era bereft of radio contact it was far from simple. At their moorings the only communication between the Dutch admirals was that which relays of horses could provide. Once at sea the admirals must rely on trust, their instincts and their knowledge of each other. These movements, so easy to envisage while contemplating a map, were at the mercy of unpredictable combinations of wind and tide. A wind which would be favourable for Tromp's advance up the Dutch coast (south or south-west) would be adverse for de With's attempt to move his squadron out of the Helder. That is why de With had to seize any favourable combination of wind and tide to move out of his refuge first. When news that de With was weighing anchor and making ready to disentangle his squadron from the Helder's channel reached him, Monck correctly interpreted de With's intentions and sailed north hopefully to defeat him or at least to shut him in. The English hovered off the Helder for the next few days until on 8 August the topsails of Tromp's advancing fleet rose over the southern horizon. Having no wish to divide his forces in the face of the enemy, Monck must abandon his blockade of de With and turn to face the main enemy fleet. The wind was westerly and Tromp headed off-shore to gain the weather gauge but to his chagrin the wind backed into the north to Monck's advantage. Tromp realised that the apparent disadvantage now provided an opportunity to draw his enemy 'off from the Texel shallows so that the warships there might have an opportunity of coming out and joining us'.[16] He turned the *Brederode* south and led his fleet back down the coast with the wind behind them, apparently retreating. Monck naturally pursued which allowed de With to bring his squadron to sea and in turn to pursue the English. De Witt was eager to engage the English rear whenever the battle opened but in fact firing began before he could come up because some of Tromp's ships were foul and slower than the English third- and fourth-rates who came up with them about 4 p.m. Heavy firing broke out as Tromp backed his topsails to concentrate his fleet so as to protect his reargaurd. The firing continued until about 8.30 p.m., as Tromp reported, 'without their getting any sensible advantage of us, or we of them, as far as we could see'. The English great ships came up about 6 p.m. or 7 p.m. and immediately brought their heavy guns into action. Monck's flagship, *Resolution*, was so hotly involved that she lost 17 killed and 25 wounded.

   Darkness fell with the fleets holding their station and the wind still north-westerly so the English would retain the advantage of the wind in the morning. This was not a situation Tromp was prepared to accept and he still wanted to unite with de With. The latter could be relied on to steer for the sound of the guns and he could not be far away. All night the English drifted downwind,

George Monck, 1st Duke of Albemarle, by Sir Peter Lely (National Maritime Museum, Greenwich, London)

hastily making repairs to running and standing rigging and replacing broken spars. As they did so Tromp managed to get his ships on to a northerly course and to tack past his unsuspecting enemies who imagined the Dutch were still drifting down to leeward. How Tromp managed to lead his fleet into this complicated tacking manoeuvre in the dark is not clear. He probably sent orders to his captains by boats, but we can only admire both the audacity of the commander and the seamanship of his captains. The following morning saw Tromp and de With triumphantly united into a fleet which had a slight numerical superiority in warships: 107 men-of-war and nine fireships to Monck's 104 men-of-war and sixteen smaller vessels. Unfortunately the morning also brought gale-force winds and a heavy swell. The Dutch coast with its long beaches and shallow waters was dangerously close. Neither fleet would consider going into action. They were too busy trying to gain sea room against the force of the wind and yet keep their fleets from scattering. During the night of the 9th the weather moderated and the largest action of the war resumed quite early on the 10th.

The two fleets had changed places once again during the long struggle against the westerlies throughout the 9th. The Dutch were once more south and slightly east of the English but they had not lost the weather gauge because the wind had shifted southerly. Tromp had his fleet in a ragged line and at 7 a.m. turned his ships toward the enemy, sailing in line abreast, and surged toward them downwind. Monck, as keen to get into battle as his adversary, tacked upwind to meet him, but seems to have had his three squadrons in the new line ahead formation in accord with the new *Fighting Instructions* first employed at the Gabbard. Monck had been bested by Tromp in the arts of seamanship. For this Monck, a successful soldier with no sea experience before he set off for the battle of Portland, could hardly be blamed. Tromp had commanded fleets for half a lifetime. Monck had failed to prevent Tromp from uniting with de With and during twenty-four hours had twice lost the advantage of the wind. Tromp now intended to come down on Monck with the wind and crush him. However, Monck refused to dance to the Dutchman's measure. Instead of awaiting the enemy in defensive posture as Blake had done at Portland, he resolved to tack up to Tromp and crash through his line and thereby regain the wind as he turned on the enemy. As Monck later wrote, the *Resolution* and *Worcester* led the fleet 'in a desperate charge through the whole Dutch fleet', the English firing broadsides, ship by ship, as their lines broke through. Once they were through Tromp hastily put about and tacked after his enemy presumably to prevent Monck from turning before the wind. Now both fleets were tacking against the wind and there ensued a tacking duel of the kind familiar to yachtsmen, but one involving horrors unknown to the America's Cup. Each time the English crossed they fired broadsides into their opponents. The Dutch replied with what weight of shot they could but as before the contest was unequal. With both sides bound in their formations it must have been more difficult for the captains of the frailer Dutch ships to flinch from the encounter. As Captain Cubitt of the *Tulip* observed:

> In passing through we lamed several ships and sunk some; as soon as we had passed them we tacked again upon them and they on us; [we] passed by each

other very near; we did very good execution . . . Some of their ships which had all their masts gone . . . put out a white handkerchief on a staff and hauled in all their guns.[17]

Cubitt's men gazed with hungry eyes at these symbols of surrender but he refused to send prize crews to seize them. The new *Instructions* insisted that ships must hold their place in the line and forbear from taking prizes or the formation's advantages would be lost as it disintegrated in a general mêlée. So the *Tulip* and her colleagues continued to fire broadsides on each leg of their tack as the fleets crossed. The fleets passed through each other on four occasions, doing 'great execution upon each', as the ships bombarded each other so close as to be 'almost at push of pike'. When two Dutch ships engaged Monck's *Resolution* Cubitt reports that the 'very heavens were obscured by smoke, the air rent with the thundering noise, the sea all in a breach with the shot that fell, the ships even trembling and we hearing everywhere messengers of death flying.' The journal of the *Vanguard* reported that 'many of their ships' masts were shot by the board, others sunk to the number of twenty. At last God gave us the wind.'[18]

In fact the English had the wind because now their enemies were fleeing before it. Most of the Dutch captains had had enough and turned with the wind and headed north-east for the shelter of the Texel with the English turning in pursuit. The retreating ships included the survivors of Tromp and Floriszoon's squadrons and some of de With's. De With, characteristically reluctant to accept defeat, indignantly signalled their recall but in vain and he sensibly grouped his remaining ships into a rearguard to slow the English pursuit. Some ships of Evertsen's squadron had been unable to work their way around the English fleet to follow their colleagues. Evertsen, his ship leaking badly and creaking ominously in every timber, led them westward. Fifty of his crew were dead or badly wounded. Among his ships was de Ruyter's once more under tow. It had lost its foremast and its main topmast and had seventy-eight crew dead or dying. Tromp was spared the knowledge that his fleet had been defeated yet again, for a musket ball from the *Tulip* felled him during the first pass. Carried below, his dying words to the anguished officers clustered about his bunk were characteristically stoic: 'I have run my course. Have good courage.' His pennant still flew above the *Brederode*, because his officers had no wish to further dishearten the fleet nor to encourage the enemy. All the long summer evening the English pursued, catching and sinking the disabled or taking prizes, until the failing light and the shoaling water forced them to draw off into the darkness.

It had been the fiercest action of the war. It is not clear how many Dutch ships were sunk although most accounts claim twenty sunk by gunfire or burned. Captain Cubitt tried to draw up an accurate account, which would discount those ships which were fired on by two captains and so claimed twice, and he was certain of fourteen but had not then interviewed all the captains which might have added more. Penn, not given to extravagant claims, estimated their loss at thirty. Dutch killed, wounded and prisoners must have amounted to at least 3,000. The precise English casualties are no clearer. They are sometimes said to have been 900 because Monck asked for that number of replacements after the battle, but this figure would have included losses to sickness while on blockade. The English fleet had not escaped unscathed although they only lost the *Oak*, 32, a third-rate, set on fire on the first pass, and a fireship, the *Hunter*. Their delight at recapturing the *Garland* and the *Bonaventure*, taken by Tromp off Dungeness, was qualified because they had been so battered they had to be scuttled. At least the Dutch could claim to have broken the blockade because the English were compelled to retire to Southwold to off-load the sick, embark replacements and carry out repairs. They also had to replenish badly depleted magazines. The fierceness of the English bombardment at what became known as the battle of Scheveningen (or the battle of the Texel) may be judged from the fact that this required 1,000 barrels of gunpowder and eighty tons of shot.

England rejoiced in victory with the first Protectorate parliament rewarding both Blake and Monck and their vice-admirals with gold chains and medals, while more medals were struck for their junior officers. Across the sea the Dutch buried Tromp with the pomp and ceremony appropriate to his long and devoted service.

CHAPTER 7

The Peacemakers

Behold how good and how pleasant it is for brethren to dwell together in unity.

123rd Psalm

Scheveningen was to be the last battle of the First Dutch War but not, unfortunately, the last disaster for the Dutch navy. The repairs and replenishment of Monck's fleet after the battle took time because the Navy Commissioners were desperate for money, men and new masts and spars. This gave the Dutch a lull which they were quick to exploit. While the States General claimed a victory for both domestic and foreign consumption, minimising or concealing their own losses and magnifying those of their enemy, the Dutch hastily cobbled together a squadron. It was entrusted to de With who was not grateful because it was too weak to engage the enemy or, he believed, even for the limited convoy duty for which it was intended. Nevertheless he was ordered to take a convoy to sea, some ships bound for the Baltic, others for the Indies, as early as it could be assembled. Monck sent Lawson to Dutch waters with a squadron and then sailed to reinforce him on 29 August. Two days later de With evaded all blockaders during bad weather and when Monck discovered this he did not order a pursuit, preferring to return to Southwold. This was wise. With weakened masts and spars and inadequately patched shot-holes a voyage north into the gales which regularly smote the North Sea in autumn would probably have proved disastrous. In any event he preferred to leave blockade duty to his fourth- and fifth-rates, having a soundly based dislike of subjecting his great ships to heavy weather on a lee shore. Meanwhile in the north de Witt hastily gathered up more than 400 merchantmen and hastened home. He did not wait for all ships to reach him which needed escort because he had been sent to sea inadequately provisioned. His crews were hungry, dispirited and growing mutinous. While returning he was reinforced by two squadrons so that his fleet amounted to 70 sail. Off the Texel he found himself refused leave to follow the convoy in to safety despite his pleas and protests, arrangements being made for provisioning at sea. His masters were anxious for him to gather up more valuable cargoes and also probably feared his crews would desert if the ships made port. It was a bad decision which cost many lives for as he had feared de With was caught by a terrible storm on 30 October which sank fifteen ships and dismasted twenty-four others, including his own. From some ships all crew were lost, from another half, while from another only 14 men were saved. It was a heavier blow for the Dutch navy than any inflicted by Blake or Monck and it ensured that the survivors would retire to winter quarters until the spring.[1] By then, although Blake had gone back to sea and was snapping up prizes in the Channel, the first Anglo-Dutch naval war was drawing to an end. It was only left for the two republics to agree terms.

Peace might have come sooner but for a path strewn with obstacles. By the end of 1653 Oliver Cromwell had been inducted as Protector and he had never looked on the war with favour. The successful naval battles may have given him pause. If God did not wish to chasten the Dutch why should he give victories to Blake and Monck? Nevertheless he believed in the duty of Protestant states to stand together. War should not divide them. However, as others have, he found war more difficult to stop than it had been to start. His own countrymen, even those who could be ranked among the 'godly', were bitterly divided. Some merchants wanted peace because war never really advanced their interest, especially if it was prolonged. Others were happy to increase their ships cheaply by purchasing the hundreds of prizes which the war brought to London and to profit from the unceasing supply of prize goods. On the other hand the East India Company was dismally conscious that war had given the Dutch virtual suzerainty over the spice trade. The Levant Company had suffered because Dutch naval success and the government's strategy had compelled the navy's withdrawal from the Mediterranean. A good peace might win concessions in the east. Any peace would enable Blake to sail for the Straits. The Commonwealth had been swept away by Cromwell and in its place, under his patronage, had appeared the Nominated Parliament. This experiment in godly government had perished of its own internal divisions, much to Cromwell's disappointment, but while it lasted the chances of peace withdrew even further as fanatics in and out of parliament called for a Holy War against the Dutch whom God wished the godly to smite because of their worship of Mammon, because of their being tainted by devotion to the House of Orange – that is, monarchism – and because of the Dutch Reformed Church's 'Presbyterian' opposition to toleration. Moreover a conquered Netherlands would provide a splendid springboard from which to assault the Catholic powers and finally march on Rome to overthrow Antichrist. When they heard London preachers extol these ambitious undertakings Dutch negotiators, who had been sent to England in search of peace, were naturally horrified. They need not have disturbed themselves. The man who would have had to lead the Ironsides to Europe to accomplish these wonders would have nothing to do with schemes more appropriate to Bedlam than his military headquarters. However, there were men who believed such lunacies not only in the Nominated Parliament but in its Council of State, and even in the Army Council – thanks to the presence of Major-General Harrison, a Fifth Monarchist with an uncertain grip on reality – and this did not make peacemaking easy. Even after the fall of the Nominated Parliament and the establishment of the Protectorate, Cromwell was not free to follow his inclination too rapidly. He did not wish his new regime to appear to have thrown away the fruits of victories by accepting what his fellow-countrymen would consider unfavourable terms.

Across the North Sea divisions similarly frustrated the peacemakers. Since

Oliver Cromwell, miniature by Samuel Cooper. (By courtesy of the Buccleuch Collection, Drumlanrig Castle, Scotland)

Holland owned 90 per cent of the Netherlands' shipowning and overseas trade, and almost as high a percentage of its manufactures, the States of Holland were even more anxious for peace than was Cromwell. The other states, with their strong Orange parties, were happy to see the war continue even if unfavourably since defeats were likely to turn the country to the House of Orange. During 1653 the fall of the Purged Parliament and the rise and fall (in December) of the Nominated Parliament were all encouraging signs for the Orangists. Political instability in England encouraged their hopes of a Dutch–Royalist combination in alliance with France to restore Charles II and win the war. This scheme, nightmarish both to the republicans of Holland and the English revolutionaries, increased de Witt's determination to end the war for it was clear that the Orangist dream would bring war with Spain as the price of French intervention. This would be even more ruinous to Holland's trade than the war with England.

With Cromwell ensconced as Protector a new year and a new era dawned together. Surely an agreement could be reached. Gradually it became clear to the Dutch ambassadors that Cromwell, despite endless talk which concealed rather than revealed his intentions, despite dismaying apparent changes of heart, despite frequent tears and exhortations to prayer – idiosyncratic methods of diplomacy of which he was a master – genuinely sought peace if England's security from an Orange Party–Royalist conspiracy could be achieved.[2] Since Cromwell's new position owed nothing to either millenarian Puritans or pro-war London merchants he could disregard their concerns. The demand for a 'union' receded early in 1654. Instead it was provided that all Dutch office holders should take an oath to accept the treaty which was being currently hammered out and that treaty would contain a clause prohibiting either government from supporting internal rebels against the other, while enemies of each country would be excluded from the other's borders. This would keep Charles Stuart at a distance from Orange friends. There were indeed no specific references to either the House of Orange or the House of Stuart but the implications were clear. Although Cromwell wanted more precise security than this could provide, the negotiators had reached an important stage because this formula was the most that the other Dutch states could be persuaded to accept and thus get the treaty through the States General. In order to get it past Cromwell and his Protectorate Council de Witt had to promise the Protector something more specific which would remove all threat to his country from any future Prince of Orange. Cromwell was well aware that an undertaking given by Holland alone could give him the security he needed because, however much the other states might resent that undertaking, Holland's weight would prevail. De Witt, whose capacity for political manipulation and duplicity can be matched by few modern statesmen, first succeeded in getting the basic treaty through the States General. He then in deepest secrecy persuaded the States of Holland to pass an Act of Exclusion which provided that William III (and his descendants) should never hold the stadtholderate of Holland nor (it followed) the positions of captain and admiral-general. This gave Cromwell the security he sought from an invasion by Charles II assisted by the only fleet in Europe capable of launching such an assault.[3] The remainder of the official treaty was largely (from the English standpoint) sauce without much substance. The

Dutch agreed to salute the flag but did not officially acknowledge the claim to 'sovereignty of the seas' nor yield the principle of neutrality covering cargoes. Since the maritime war with France was soon to end this did England little short-term harm. No dues would be exacted for Dutch fishing in 'English' seas. Arbitrators would decide compensation for losses in the East Indies (including the 'massacre' of Amboyna), and the now largely worthless nutmeg island of Pulo Run would be restored to the East India Company. The Dutch, rather than the Danes, would pay compensation for the losses of shipowners whose ships had been trapped in the Baltic during the war and Cromwell withdrew his demand that the King of Denmark should be excluded from the benefits of the treaty. The Dutch withdrew their rather arrogant demand that the Navigation Act of 1651 be repealed. Inevitably there was intense controversy and indignation in the other Dutch states when Holland's secret agreement for an Act of Seclusion stood revealed. However, de Witt had an unanswerable argument: the Protectorate would resume the war if the States of Holland repealed the act and it was not only Holland which was weary of the war. On 27 April the Dutch ambassadors banqueted at the Protector's court and when feasting was done he and his guests withdrew to a music room where, after other music had been played, the Protector presented them with a metrical version of the 123rd Psalm. 'We have', he told them, 'exchanged many papers but I think this is the best of them.'[4] They then settled back in a post-prandial glow of good fellowship and heard it sung by four voices: 'Behold how good and pleasant it is for brethren to dwell together in unity.'

Book Two

The Later Wars

CHAPTER 8

The Uneasy Peace

Ten years would pass before the peace achieved by Cromwell and de Witt was broken. They were eventful years for both countries but particularly for Britain. Space will not permit a description of the steep decline of the military power in Britain after Cromwell's death and the Restoration to which it led. Suffice to say that the great apparent power wielded by Britain under the Protectorate was shown to have little foundation other than the abilities and the personality of the Protector himself. Once he had been removed by death in the late summer of 1658 the edifice soon lay in ruins. His personal and political heir, Richard Cromwell, although a man of considerable ability and more common sense and integrity than his enemies, was unable to prevent a combination of soldiers and radical politicians from overthrowing him and restoring the old Purged Parliament. This institution, as bankrupt of any sense of reality as of prestige, was eventually removed by the Army Council, and then late in 1659 restored once more to power. Its third appearance coincided with a march on London from Scotland by the regiments of George Monck, led by the former general-at-sea who had spent the intervening years governing Scotland on the Protector's behalf. Monck it was who skilfully navigated the political shoals of the winter of 1659–60, masking his intentions not only from the politicians but even from his own soldiers, until he was able to readmit the purged members and so reconstitute the Long Parliament. From here it was a simpler step to call a general election for a convention parliament which in turn (as Monck had known it would) led to the invitation to Charles II to return to his throne. In all these great events the navy had played only a minor role. Admiral Lawson, the officer commanding the Channel fleet intervened only negatively: he did nothing to prevent it. Admiral Montagu had brought his squadron home from the Baltic during the crisis and it fell to this former parliamentary soldier, former Cromwellian admiral (and former colleague of the now dead Blake) to cross to Scheveningen to bring home the exiled king. For this he was rewarded with an earldom (Sandwich), but the greatest honours fell to the victor of the Gabbard and Scheveningen. George Monck, who had mysteriously contrived to employ the Cromwellian Ironsides to restore their old enemy to his throne, was made Duke of Albemarle by his grateful monarch. The navy was still magnificent, its numbers of ships of all sizes greater even than at the height of the Dutch War. The problem was that the state groaned under a burden of debt with an army and navy the royal government could not afford, yet could not disband until its arrears were paid.

In the United Provinces a great period of material, cultural and maritime achievement opened with the conclusion of peace with England in 1654. In this expansive period of success and development the navy was not forgotten. The Dutch had learned from past errors. The navy was not sold off after the Treaty of Westminster as after the Peace of Munster six years earlier. Indeed far from being reduced it was expanded and the lessons of the late war had at last been taken to heart. Warships were built which were larger than any warships the Dutch had built before, and they were more heavily armed in number of guns if not always in calibre. The mainspring of this expansion was the Grand Pensionary of Holland, Jan de Witt. De Witt had been only twenty-eight when he succeeded Pauw in 1653 but he was chosen from a slate of ten candidates by a unanimous vote. He soon became the most influential and important civil servant in the republic. He had already a distinguished career in government and politics by 1653. Born in Dordrecht in 1625, the son of one of the leading local regents, he was appointed city pensionary in 1651, represented his city in the States of Holland (the state legislature) and was chosen to represent his state in the States General. Here he gained valuable experience of the working of both institutions. We have already observed him successfully negotiating with Cromwell in 1654 and have witnessed the skill with which he manoeuvred to obtain a peace which the Estates General could accept in combination with the secret Act of Exclusion from the States of Holland on which Cromwell insisted. Soon afterwards he developed an almost obsessive interest in naval affairs which lasted throughout the rest of his life and devoted much time and effort to reforming and improving the administration, the manning, the appointment of officers, and the upgrading of ships. All this was singular because his duties, which were supposedly purely administrative, were not supposed to concern the navy at all. However, the disappearance of the stadtholder as Admiral-General left a vacuum which the Grand Pensionary could fill.[1]

De Witt began by suggesting ways of better controlling the admiralties, of which he had gained a detailed knowledge while the war still raged. In return for increased income the admiralties lost some of their independence to de Witt's centralising policies. De Witt was responsible for most policy decisions and the States General regularly agreed to his proposals. All of which made naval administration speedier and more efficient than it had ever been before. This explains the speed with which de Witt contrived to get the second major building programme through the state and national legislatures. When Tromp was killed de Ruyter was still only a commodore but de Witt presciently offered the young master-mariner, most of whose years at sea had been spent in the merchant marine, the prestigious post of Lieutenant Admiral. Here de Witt was baulked, for de Ruyter firmly declined, and so the former, recalling the successes of such English soldiers-turned-admirals as Blake and Monck, appointed Jacob van Wassenaer, Lord of Obdam, an aristocratic soldier. It was a reasonable choice but one which de Witt would deeply regret. In 1654 peace found the navy possessed of sixty-four warships armed with from 40 to 60 guns. These de Witt laid up and kept well maintained. In addition there were between eighty and ninety ships of smaller size and with fewer and lighter guns, which were designed as escort vessels for convoys and which during the First Dutch War were asked to perform tasks in battle for which they were largely unsuitable. Thereafter these fast, manoeuvrable ships were frequently employed escorting convoys through waters which other countries' quarrels had rendered dangerous. This navy largely saw the republic through the period of peace and increasing prosperity of the late 1650s and the war with Portugal from 1657 to 1661, during which Obdam blockaded Lisbon. In 1656 Obdam took a fleet to the Baltic which without firing a shot compelled the King of Sweden to abandon his attempt to seize Danzig. A dangerous situation developed in which the Dutch were supporting Denmark against the ambition of the King of Sweden to defeat Denmark and Poland and turn the Baltic into a Swedish lake. In 1658 Charles X invaded Denmark and besieged Copenhagen. Obdam returned to the Baltic with a fleet of thirty-five ships carrying 4,000 troops to reinforce Copenhagen. At the battle of the Sound the Dutch defeated a larger Swedish fleet under Admiral Wrangel, who lost five ships taken or sunk. The ageing *Brederode* ran aground and was destroyed and her commander, Admiral Witte de With, combative to the last, was killed. In spring 1659 Montagu took a squadron to the Baltic to assist the Swedes, but a potentially dangerous situation between the two republics was averted by the withdrawal of Montagu's squadron in August while the death of Charles X the following February restored peace to the region.

 The restoration of Charles II, sudden, unexpected, and improbably brought about by the Cromwellian army, not by royalists, burst on the Dutch republic like a thunder-clap.[2] The Orange Party was overjoyed, sure that Charles would intervene to promote the claims on the stadtholderate of his ten-year-old nephew, William III. De Witt and the republicans of Holland were downcast, particularly as even in republican Holland the House of Orange had many friends, and two provincial towns made no secret of their desire to revoke the Act of Exclusion. Amsterdam also was riddled with anti-republicanism, or at least with a desire to cultivate good relations with the House of Orange which, it was assumed, would in turn lead to better relations with post-Restoration England. To help this along Amsterdam organised and partly financed a rich gift for Charles II from the States General, which comprised paintings (including a Titian and a Tintoretto), Graeco-Roman antiquities and three contemporary paintings of the Dutch 'school' together with other valuable objects and a Dutch yacht, the *Mary*. All this, it was hoped, would encourage England's new government to look more kindly on the Dutch, to at last accept the Dutch principle that 'the flag covered the cargo' and to cease seizing Dutch vessels carrying 'contraband', a violation of Dutch neutrality revived during Cromwell's war with Spain (begun in 1655 and only finally concluded in 1660), and even to repeal the odious Navigation Act. The king enthusiastically accepted the gift at the Banqueting House, and talked of his willingness to enter an alliance with the republic. Positive benefits from that cold-eyed, cynical voluptuary were slower to appear. In fact the writing was plain on the wall. Far from repealing the Navigation Act of 1651 Charles's government had reinforced it during 1660 with a version even more damaging to Dutch interests. Although less sweeping than that of 1651 since now only designated goods were required to arrive in English ships, these included all the principal Baltic imports, and all the chief Mediterranean wares – about half the value of all imports. Since the Dutch had been ingenious since 1651 in continuing to import into England by using dummy English 'owners' and other devices, a register of ships was to be established while the master and three-quarters

King Charles II, by Sir Peter Lely (National Maritime Museum, Greenwich, London)

of the crew must be English. As the colonial trade had been rapidly increasing in value since mid-century this was tightened up even more with all colonial produce to be first imported into England whatever its ultimate destination and all foreign factors or merchants were to be excluded from the colonies. Requests for free trade from the Dutch had been met instead by an act to exclude Dutch shipping from English ports which would really work and which progressively excluded Dutch merchants and shipowners from English commercial life.[3]

Meanwhile Charles's sister, Princess Mary, was moving to advance her son's interest, seeking his appointment to a cluster of high if largely ceremonial offices in the seven states. When Leiden and Haarlem moved that William should be designated for the stadtholderate, de Witt realised that the Act of Exclusion was becoming a dead letter. (No other state had copied it since 1654.) In September 1660 the Act of Exclusion was repealed. De Witt then contrived to shelve the stadtholderate issue by persuading Princess Mary to agree that William should only be designated a 'child of the state' who would be trained and educated for high office by the States of Holland. This aroused intense indignation among Orangists, particularly when it was found that de Witt and other republicans, not Orangists, would supervise the prince's education. However, de Witt's solution, which at least gave the United Provinces some political stability, was overthrown by Mary's sudden death from smallpox in January 1661. The princess had nominated Charles as her son's guardian and this legacy would give a foreign monarch great influence in Dutch politics for years to come. Moreover this unwelcome development came at a time when relations between England and the United Provinces were deteriorating rapidly. Apart from the revised Navigation Act, the incessant quarrels between the rival East India companies were worsening, while there were new tensions over the West African trade, the Caribbean and the colony of New Netherlands which sat like an cuckoo in the nest between the Chesapeake and New England colonies and illegally traded with both. All Dutch fishing ports from West Friesland to Zeeland were alarmed by a bill before parliament which threatened to create a zone ten miles from the English coast reserved for English fishermen; fortunately it was not enacted. That little could be hoped from the new royal government was made ominously clear when Sir George Downing returned to the Hague as envoy. Downing, who as a child had been part of the Puritan diaspora of the 1630s and was the second graduate of Harvard College, was a former Ironside. (He had been Cromwell's Scoutmaster-General in Scotland in 1650.) He had been a leading proponent of the movement to make Cromwell king and had served in two Protectorate parliaments. Sent by Cromwell to complain to Louis XIV about the massacres of the Vaudois, he had served twice at the Hague in 1657 and 1659 and had conceived a virulent dislike of the Dutch. Clarendon described him as 'a proud and insolent spirit who would add to any imperious command somewhat of the bitterness of his own spirit.' Colbert described him more succinctly as the most quarrelsome diplomat of his time.[4] His appointment was significant. It reflected Charles II's loathing for republicans. He bore the Orangists no ill will, but it was the republicans who controlled the affairs of Holland, the mercantile heart of the Netherlands, the source of English discontent and prime focus of English jealousy.

The battles of the Second and Third Dutch Wars

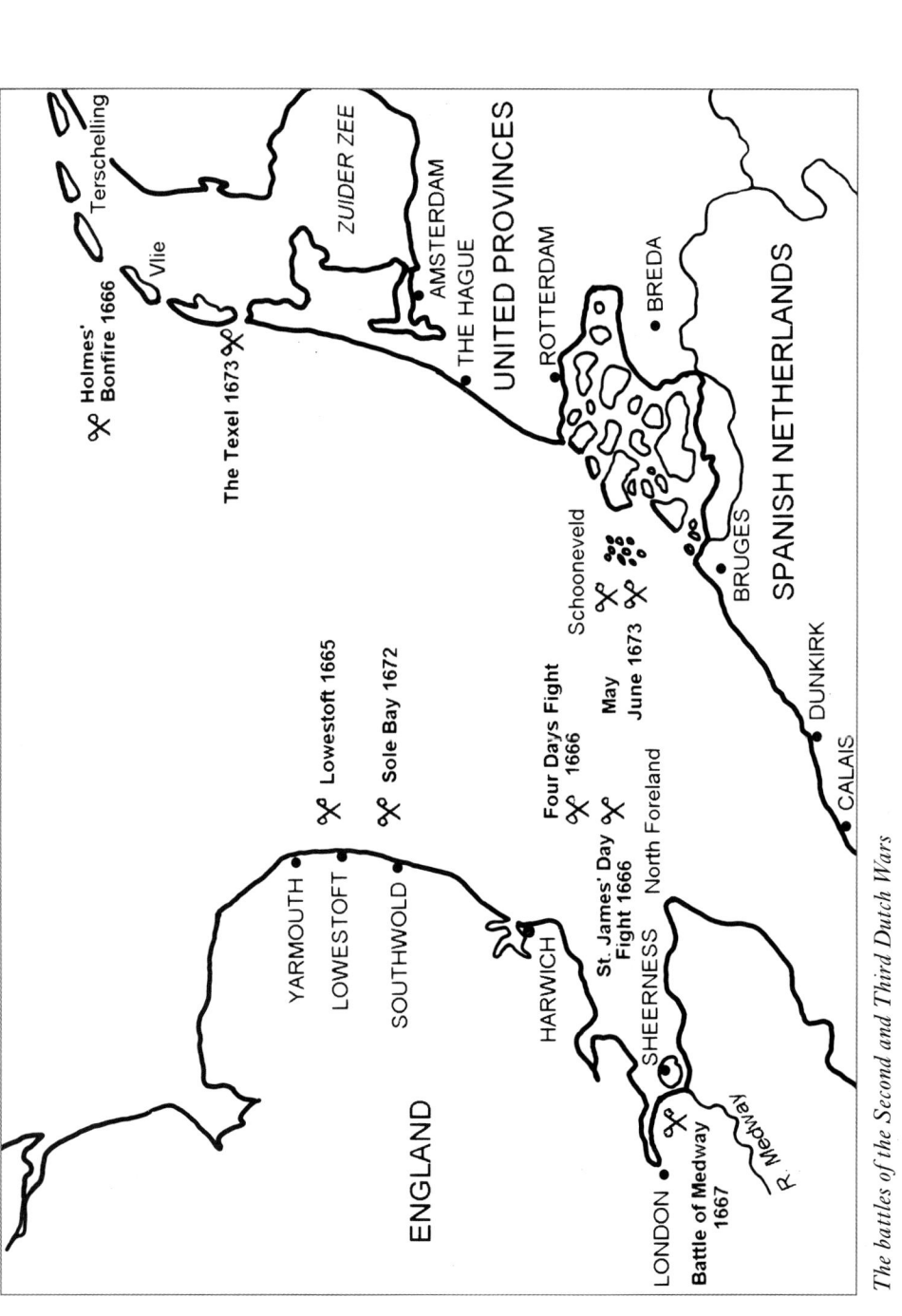

CHAPTER 9
A New War: Lowestoft

> ... the worst of peace is better than the best war.
>
> Anon.

The new regime in England contained many men eager for adventures which might line their pockets, might increase their status by the gift of honours from a king who was always generous in ways which would not empty his treasury. Former Cromwellians, carrying a lifelong taint of republicanism, could not afford to be backward in any proposed assault on the Dutch empire. To outraged English observers the Dutch superiority in international commerce seemed as great as ever and Dutch gains in trade must mean English losses. Although the Dutch demanded freedom of the seas for herself, they wanted no competition along the coast of Africa and in the East Indies, where relations between the Dutch and English East India companies resembled war even in peacetime. In 1662 the Dutch agreed to hand back the nutmeg island of Pulo Run in the Moluccas but somehow promises made in the Hague never translated into action in the East Indies. Few questioned the dictum that only force could curb the Dutch. They must be made to concede through tariffs and prohibitions or it must be plucked from them by naval might. As Monck said with brutal frankness, 'What matters this or that reason? What we want is more of the trade the Dutch now have.' Not only merchants and courtiers were infected with the anti-Dutch fever. The 500 or so members of the Cavalier Parliament, predominantly local gentry or younger sons or other connections of the aristocracy, were little better. They came from a section of society which was usually hostile to war because it was their taxes which would have to pay for it. Nevertheless their experiences during the Great Rebellion had confirmed their old view that religious toleration leads to political instability. They wanted a monarchy based on a strong parliament and a national Church to which all should conform, if only to expose nonconformists for they were bound to be political subversives. To them the famous toleration and republicanism of Holland (particularly) were alike anathema not least because they were bad examples to their old enemies and the new generation which was growing up. It would be unusually easy to persuade them to vote war subsidies when the time came. Meanwhile Grub Street had been mobilised. Pamphlets, broadsheets and ballads outdid one another in their depiction of the Dutch as cruel and rapacious, or as perfidious as papists: indeed they were linked to papists in their sinfulness, 'tied together like Samson's foxes by their tails, carrying the same firebrands of covetousness & ambition, to put all into a combustion wherever they come'.[1] Such sentiments were only strengthened when the Dutch signed a defensive treaty with Catholic France in 1662, committing Louis XIV to assist the United Provinces if attacked, and even guaranteeing Dutch fishing rights in 'English' waters – the North Sea.

An atmosphere conducive to war was growing during the first four years of Charles's rule. However, an explosion needs a fuse. It was largely supplied by a group of men eager for war who gathered around the Duke of York. The king's brother and Lord High Admiral, York naturally attracted ambitious courtiers, up-and-coming politicians, restive Cavaliers who had been too long in the shadows, and former Cromwellian soldiers, hard-faced men who had done well out of the Protectorate and hoped to do even better out of the monarchy. Some of these had already begun to gratify their thirst for adventure and hostility to the Dutch by investing in a new corporate venture: the Africa Company. First formed in 1660 as a trading venture to the Guinea coast, re-chartered in 1661, it attracted men willing to invest in the lucrative slave trade and in the hope of West African gold. However, the shareholders early included the Duke of York and his cousin Prince Rupert, and such courtiers as the Duke of Buckingham and the Secretary of State, Sir Henry Bennet.[2] By 1664 the company had become more ambitious, and much more of a challenge to the Dutch West India Company which had dominated African trade since they ousted the Portuguese in the 1630s. The Dutch had no intention of being usurped in turn so the Africa Company could only establish itself with naval backing. In 1661 five small men-of-war, commanded by Captain Robert Holmes, escorted the company's first expedition. When in 1664 the company decided to send a more aggressive expedition Holmes accompanied it in the frigate *Jersey*, 60 guns, with instructions to take or sink any Dutch ships which opposed him and to seize the Dutch forts. Holmes was a natural choice for a piratical venture. He had first served as Rupert's page in the French army, then learned sea-fighting in the royalist fleet during the Civil War and spent the years of exile privateering along the African coasts. 'A man of understanding fit to make a war, and courage to make it good; in the latter few go beyond him; in the former few come short' in Sir William Coventry's shrewd assessment.[3] He swept the coast with a swashbuckling bravura, snapping up Dutch ships and taking forts virtually unopposed, and negotiating and trading with native chiefs. The Dutch could not accept this outrage and were soon preparing their riposte.

Although Holmes, despite royal patronage, had led a private venture, the government had simultaneously demonstrated its own anti-Dutch agenda. The Dutch settlers of New Netherlands from their port of New Amsterdam (the future city of New York) and the New England colonists, no friends to the restored monarchy, had been colluding to contravene the Navigation Acts. This provided an excellent excuse to appeal to the old principle 'no peace west of the line' normally employed against Spain's American empire. Charles first granted New Netherlands (to be named the colony of New York) to his brother as a personal fief, the first of many interesting revivals of feudalism which America experienced during Charles's reign. Major Robert Nicolls then led an expedition

Sir Robert Holmes, detail from a painting of Sir Frescheville Holles and Sir Robert Holmes by Sir Peter Lely (National Maritime Museum, Greenwich, London)

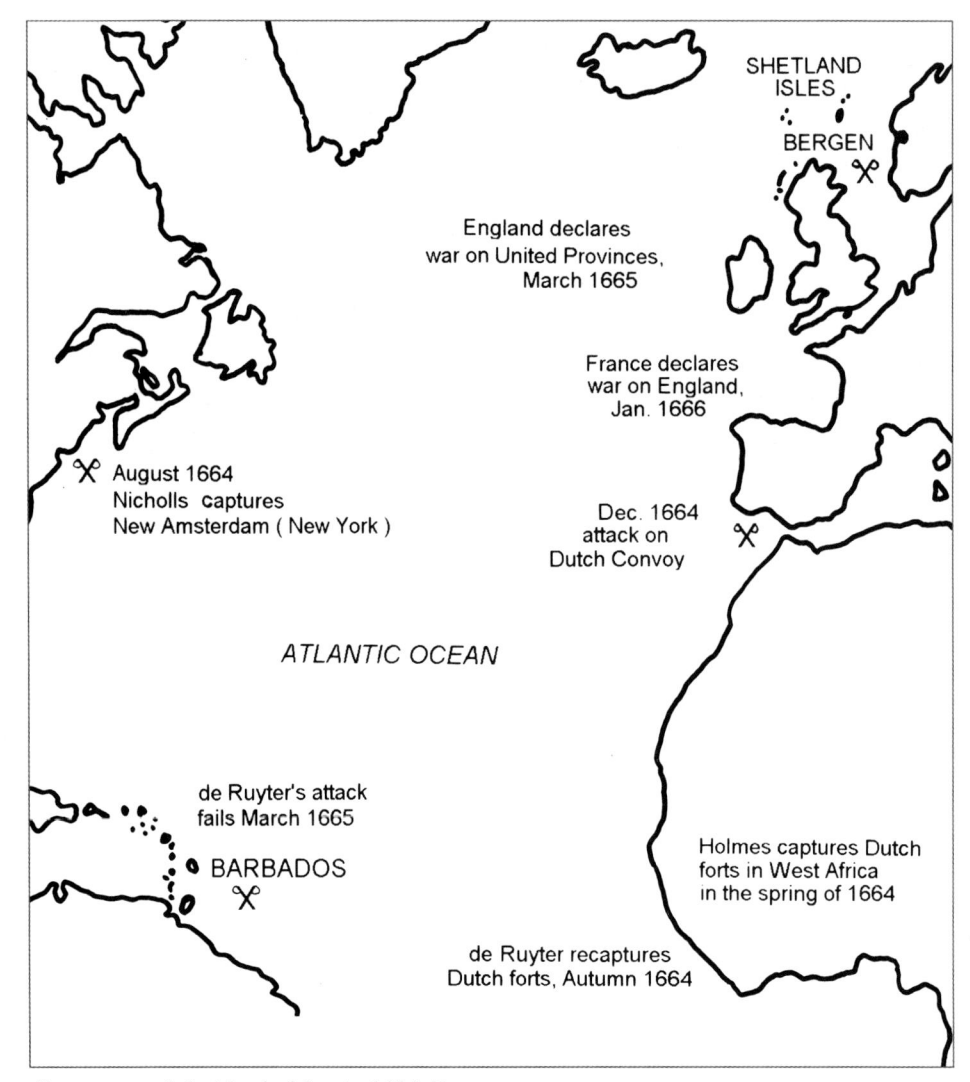

Events around the North Atlantic, 1664–5

to enforce the royal gift and 'to reduce that people to an entire submission'. On 26 August 1664 Nicolls anchored in Nyack Bay off Coney Island and demanded the surrender of Manhattan. The governor, Peter Stuyvesant, with few defences, surrendered without a shot. Nicolls then sent a secondary force to the Dutch settlements on the Delaware under Sir Robert Carr. Here, the governor refused to submit and Carr took and looted the fort.[4]

Meanwhile in London during that summer there were other symptoms of war. MPs with close court connections and allied to the pro-war faction exploited a

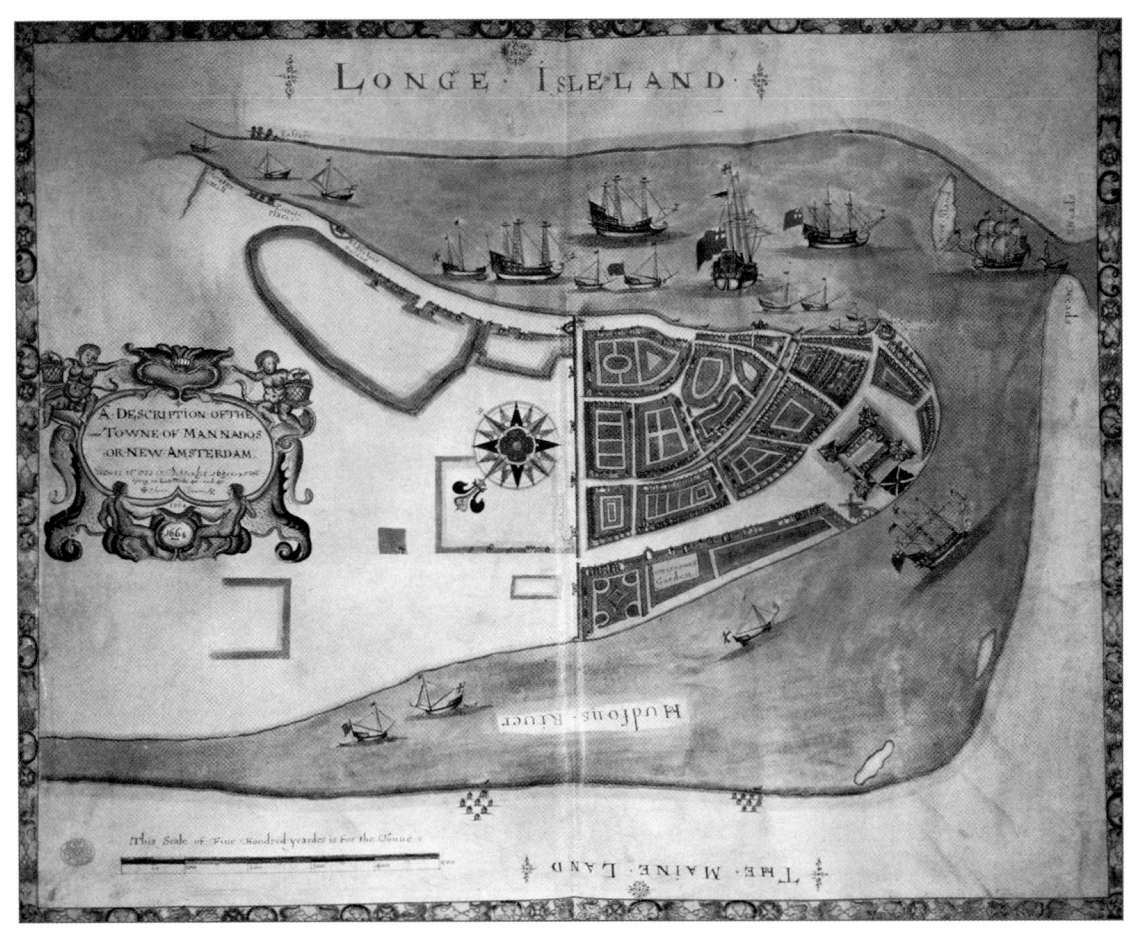

New York: plan of Manhattan, Long Island, the Hudson River and New Amsterdam, 1664 (British Library/Bridgeman Art Library, London)

Commons committee charged with examining 'the general decay of trade'. Adroitly managed by that great Dutch-hater, Sir Thomas Clifford, the committee encouraged merchants to contribute a long list of overblown complaints against the Dutch. Despite their grumbles the merchants were not calling for war for they knew that '. . . the worst of peace is better than the best war'.[5] War would devour their ships and erode their profits. However, the committee did produce a resounding resolution urging Charles to redress their complaints. Another bellicose influence was Sir George Downing, who argued for a strong stand against the Dutch particularly in the West African disputes. He did not believe that this would make war inevitable because he was confident that the inland states would not support the more vigorous policies of Holland as far as a formal declaration of war. However, Jan de Witt was just as insistent that granting concessions would only feed the English appetite for more. Both parties miscalculated: the English that the Dutch would not fight, and that if they did, they would be trounced in a single campaign; de Witt that the English parliament would never grant Charles enough funds to fight a war. For not all England was afire for war. The king himself did not underestimate the strength of Dutch naval power, and his chancellor, the Earl of Clarendon, described himself as passionately and obstinately against it for the damage it would do to trade and the fragile stability of the new regime. Samuel Pepys, one of four principal officers of the Navy Board, and who knew better than most how far the navy was really prepared for war, reflected 'We all seem to desire it, as thinking ourselves to have advantage at present over them; but for my part I dread it.'[6]

In September the news of Holmes's African exploits convulsed London with jubilant celebrations. Charles's popularity soared, as it seemed that the glories of the 1650s were to be repeated. The euphoria was short-lived, for the Dutch under the direction of de Witt were able to reverse the victories in a way which particularly galled Downing. Downing had established an efficient network of agents and spies, especially among the Orangist sympathisers. (He later boasted that he could have the keys taken out of de Witt's pocket while he slept, his closet opened, his papers delivered up to Downing for perusal, then returned, along with the keys.)[7] Any decision made by the States General would become known to Downing at once, almost before their own ears had heard it. De Witt adroitly manoeuvred his way past this leaky ship of state by simply moving a resolution to fit out twelve warships to send to the Guinea coast. This was passed on to the much smaller (and more tightly caulked) seven-member committee of the States General to consider. It secretly agreed to use de Ruyter's Mediterranean squadron, taking care to return its decision for ratification in terms so confused and incoherent that even those who heard it would have difficulty in making sense of it. Moreover, de Witt organised diversionary tactics when it was read – and passed.[8]

The orders which reached de Ruyter were plain enough. His squadron of twelve ships was to sail at once for the Guinea coast and restore Dutch supremacy, masking his intent by giving out that he was sailing to fight corsairs off the Barbary coast. Though he encountered the English Mediterranean fleet along the coast of Spain, and though its admiral, Sir John Lawson, had by now heard rumours that de Ruyter had received an urgent dispatch, the tale of Barbary corsairs allayed suspicion. No information seeped out to Downing. By the end of October, de Ruyter began working his way along Holmes's trail, recapturing forts and trading posts, releasing the captured Dutch ships, seizing goods in reprisal, and rehoisting the Dutch flag. By late December Pepys and all London knew of 'our being beaten to dirt at Guinea'.[9]

Meanwhile in England, parliament in November voted Charles £2,500,000 to furnish a fleet to safeguard English trade, the greatest supply ever voted to an English monarch, and so remained until the next century. In December when news of de Ruyter's reprisals came home, a special committee of the Privy Council gave all English ships licence to prey on the Dutch where they were most vulnerable: in the Narrow Seas, where their homeward bound convoys sailed through the Channel, and in the North Sea. This was war without formal

Samuel Pepys, by Sir Godfrey Kneller (National Maritime Museum, Greenwich, London)

declaration, as Sagredo, the ambassador for that once great sea empire, Venice, observed from France, 'a kind of war and the seed of it'.[10] The ratchet of escalation wound tighter as Thomas Allin, who had taken over command of the Mediterranean fleet, carried out his secret orders and attacked a Dutch convoy returning from Smyrna in rough and blustery December weather. The Dutch admiral began the usual courtesies by firing five guns as a salute. Allin replied with salutes of a different kind. 'After Captain Seale, being to leeward of the men-of-war, had given the Admiral what guns he could, and Captain Mohun he gave them his guns, being also to leeward, and I got to windward and gave him all my upper tier and 2 demi-cannon in the gun room, and charged for his vice admiral and rear admiral and gave them all we could . . .' Yet though Allin had the force of surprise and eight warships, he managed to capture only two merchantmen and sink another. Most of his own ships ran aground through poor handling and bad piloting in the worsening weather, or became so leaky they could scarcely make way.[11] Charles could not now avoid war even if he wished to but he made one last attempt to coax the French from their defensive alliance with the Dutch by trying to paint England as the victim rather than an aggressor. Robert Holmes found himself a prisoner in the Tower almost as soon as he set foot in England in January, to give some credence to this pretence. Holmes had nothing to fear. The Dutch declared war on 22 February and shortly afterwards Charles gave Holmes command of the *Revenge*.

Charles had inherited a powerful navy at his Restoration. Its fighting heart lay in the three first-rates of 80 to 100 guns, twelve second-rates of 60 to 80 guns and fifteen third-rates of 54 to 64 guns.[12] Though a fighting ship could outlast three generations of its men, it needed extensive repairs and major refitting to survive this long. The fifty-year-old *Prince Royal*, the *Resolution* since 1649, regained her former name and was extensively refitted in 1663 with a lengthened keel of 132 feet and 92 guns. The 100-gun *Sovereign* had seen little service since she fought at the Kentish Knock. She now became the *Royal Sovereign*, with major rebuilding in 1660. Pepys gives some idea of her size, by indicating the measurements of the great stern lantern in less than nautical terms: '. . . down we went to see the *Sovereign*, . . . and, among other pleasures, I put my Lady [Sandwich], Mrs Turner, Mrs Hempson, and the two Mrs Allens into the lanthorn and I went in and kissed them, demanding it as a fee due to a principal officer, with all which we were exceeding merry . . .'[13] The Dutch were to call her 'The Golden Devil'. Some more recently built ships needed only a name change: the 80-gun *Naseby*, built for Cromwell in 1655, became the *Royal Charles*, the 64-gun *Dunbar* became the *Henry*. But along with such ships, the new regime had inherited a massive debt and it was not until the autumn of 1664, with war almost upon them, that the Privy Council's Committee for the Navy turned serious attention to building new ships. It commissioned six two-deckers, after the style of the successful Commonwealth frigate, the 60-gun *Speaker* (now the *Mary*), though all turned out to be somewhat larger than this prototype, as the plans were amended to give extra breadth and depth to make them more stable.

Throughout the winter, the woods of Aliceholt, Waltham Forest, Bere Forest and New Forest yielded up a harvest of trees, for a second-rate man-of-war devoured over 2,000 oak and elm trees. However, only two second-rates, the *Royal Katherine* and the *Royal Oak*, which had been ordered in 1661, were ready for the first campaign.[14] In March 1665, the 80-gun *London*, coming out of the dockyard at Chatham to be delivered to Sir John Lawson as his flagship, exploded and sank, killing 300 people. Her replacement, the *Loyal London*, paid for by the city of London, cost over £4,300 and was not ready until June the following year. The government preferred to pay the timber contractors with promises rather than cash, and by May unpaid promises had dramatically thinned out the amount of timber coming in. The numbers were made up by hiring merchant ships, the old, unsatisfactory expedient.

The chief problems, as with the Commonwealth and Protectorate navies, lay in manning and provisioning. Unlike the Protector Charles II did not have an army of more than 40,000 men competing with the navy for crew. Nevertheless Charles was no better than his father at paying his sailors, and manning for such an extensive fleet of large, heavily armed ships demanded good pay regularly paid. Provisions were equally important in obtaining crew – and keeping them. 'Englishmen, and more especially seamen, love their bellies above anything else . . . to make any abatement from them in the quantity or agreeableness of the victuals is to discourage and provoke them in the tenderest point', admonished Pepys with hindsight, but throughout these wars the fleet all too often went to sea ill-provisioned, with stinking beer and mouldy biscuits.[15] In 1664 the navy had 16,000 men in pay. The fleet now being assembled would need 30,000. The navy still had to depend on pressing to fill its ships. Local ports were compelled to draw up lists of eligible seamen but the men ran away at the first hint of the press-gang, and those caught were often those too feeble or drunk to escape; men 'fitter to keep sheep than to sail in such great ships'. However well guarded they still absconded in droves, driving Navy Commissioner Sir William Coventry to conclude, 'Nothing but hanging will man the fleet.'[16]

For officers and administrators, Charles could draw upon those who had served with him in the last years of the Civil War or since as privateers; royalists such as Robert Holmes, Sir Thomas Allin, Sir Edward Spragge and Sir William Berkeley. Neither his brother nor cousin had experience of naval warfare between large fleets but York was battle-hardened from the wars of France and Spain and Rupert had been at sea on privateering raids. Sir George Carteret, a vice-admiral and Comptroller of the Navy for Charles I became Navy Treasurer, Sir William Coventry, younger son of a former Lord Keeper, became Secretary to York as Lord High Admiral while Sir William Batten, who had attempted to keep the fleet out of the Civil War, was appointed Surveyor of the Navy. Charles had also inherited a core of capable and experienced men who had served the republican navy and he could not man his own without them. Some Charles had renamed at his restoration, as he had done the ships. Edward Montagu became the Earl of Sandwich. George Monck, now the Duke of Albermarle, returned as the Duke of York's deputy as Admiral of the Kingdom. Many came from diverse social groups, and some of them, nicknamed the 'tarpaulins', had learned their seamanship as warrant officers or masters of merchant ships, promoted for skill and bravery rather than for gentility or by patronage. This group included men of

DEN E. MANHAFTEN ZEE-HELD IAN EVERTSZ. RIDDER, VICE ADMIR.L VAN ZEELANDT. &

Jan Evertsen, seen in a Dutch print engraved by Jan van Houten after a painting by Hendrik Berckman (National Maritime Museum, Greenwich, London)

the calibre of William Penn, John Harman, Thomas Teddiman, Christopher Myngs and John Lawson, the former Baptist radical; all to be knighted in the early years of the Restoration. However, these were men who had fought for parliament against a king, and in moments of heat the accusations would fly about, in spite of Charles's insistence that former differences be not recounted, and that he would punish any expression of past divisions.[17]

In order to strengthen the royalist element, James began to commission young men from the gentry class as 'gentlemen commanders', and not surprisingly the jealousy and friction between the tarpaulins and the gentlemen became intense and bitter in the tussle for appointments and promotion. The rivalries between the competing factions centring on Rupert and Monck became particularly savage. Sandwich believed the younger men should be encouraged, if only to temper their jealousy, 'but he says that certainly things will go to rack if ever the old captains should be wholly out, and the new ones only command'. Numbers of ambitious young aristocrats also came as volunteers, as Henry Brouncker, Charles Sackville, John Sheffield and John Wilmot did; though the seamen grumbled at the luxury of space and victuals 'the landmen' demanded, especially their tendency to fill up any vacant spot with their hen coops.[18] Sandwich was not certain that even an old one such as himself would be given a command. He had been joint commander with Blake in 1656 and in 1659 commanded the Baltic expeditions, but had no experience of actual sea battles. The Duke of York was outwardly friendly, but the negotiations over his appointment were conducted through intermediaries, which Sandwich found insulting, and only bore with it because he understood the reason. Although he had retired as a parliamentary general because of his detestation of the Regicide, he had come out of retirement to serve Cromwell and had later urged him to assume the title of king.

The fleet was structured as under the republic: a Red squadron (York), a White squadron (Rupert) and a Blue squadron (Sandwich). Each was itself subdivided into three with a vice-admiral and rear-admiral as before. These were all former Cromwellians whose names Penn had supplied to the duke: Penn himself, Lawson, Myngs, Robert Sansum, George Ayscue and Thomas Teddiman. The king jested to the French ambassador in front of them, 'they had all had the plague, but that they were perfectly cured, and less susceptible of infection than the others'. Clarendon looked at the list with less jocularity and accused Penn of conferring commands on those who gave the most money for a commission, though he admitted that Lawson, Penn and Ayscue served the king faithfully.[19]

On 20 April, James called a council of war of all the captains to give them instructions and the order of battle. The series of *Fighting Instructions* issued by Sandwich and the Duke of York, from late November to May 1665 are very like those issued by Blake and Monck in 1653, but with one marked change of emphasis. The earlier orders instructed the captains merely 'to keep in the line'; now each captain was to endeavour to keep fighting in one line throughout the battle and moreover keep station according to an order determined before battle began. The earlier order that a ship must not fall out of line to pursue or capture a disabled enemy ship unless commanded by a flag officer was reiterated. The unity of the line was to be preserved against the temptation of turning a battle into

James, Duke of York, the Lord High Admiral, by Henri Gascard (National Maritime Museum, Greenwich, London)

individual duels by captains bent on taking prizes or gaining glory at the expense of overall strategy. Second- and third-rates were spaced at intervals among the lesser ships, to spread the weight and expertise, though the commander-in-chief's division did have a higher proportion of the bigger ships. Disabled ships not in immediate danger of sinking or capture were to fall to the rear of the fleet for assistance, rather than look to succour from the nearest ship. James also now established signals for falling into line of battle, or for other squadrons to make more sail though he himself had shortened sail, with provision for other squadron commanders to relay the signals: a necessary foresight, for a fleet of seventy-five ships might stretch 7 to 10 miles.[20]

In April the English fleet sailed out from the Gunfleet and stood over towards the Dutch coast, the weather calm and foggy, but turning later to a fresh south-westerly gale. On the 23rd the Duke of York summoned the first in a series of councils of war to deliberate the strategy for the coming campaign. At this meeting they decided to lie at anchor 12 leagues (48 miles) north-west by north of the Texel, a position where they could expect to intercept Dutch convoys returning through the North Sea, and to meet the Dutch fleet as it sortied to protect their homecoming. After a few days at anchor, James grew restive and summoned another council to urge standing much closer to the shore to alarm the Dutch or at least provoke their fleet out. Lawson and Penn he persuaded. 'I submit to better judgements', Sandwich wrote in his journal, 'but would not of my own choice have done it.' Bringing their great ships so close to shore in uncertain winds was too dangerous, and being so close in would leave other channels unguarded. Besides, the Dutch squadrons were still scattered among their ports, and it was not likely that one alone would emerge to confront the entire English fleet. However, the English sailed so close to shore that Sandwich could see through his telescope the individual admirals' flags on their ships.[21]

Soon a hard north wind forced them off-shore again, and again the duke's standard hung in the mizzen shrouds summoned another meeting: the fleet would now stay well out to cover all the approaches. This time something did swim into their net. Their faster frigates spotted, chased and caught eight merchantmen from Bordeaux and Lisbon, though two men-of-war escaped when an English captain stopped his pursuit to take a merchantman instead. On Friday 5 May the council met again. With no sign of the Dutch coming out, could the English not force their way in? But their coastline protected the Dutch. The broadest channel, the Spaniard's Gate was thought too shallow for the larger English ships, and the other channel, the Land's Deep was too narrow, 'of entrance not above a ship's length', so that ships larger than a fourth-rate could only go in one at a time. Besides, using a good flood tide, the shallow-draughted Dutch could get out over the shoals and then during the ebb release their fireships onto the English who could not escape to sea against the tide. The English carried too precious a cargo to risk it, the Duke of York himself. Under his command, any such attempt was thought too dangerous. Nor could they any longer hope for rich convoys. The expected convoy had slipped past somehow, the Smyrna fleet was not stirring from Cadiz, de Ruyter not expected back from Guinea until late June, the East India fleet not due until June or July. To keep the entire fleet out for meagre pickings was insupportable. If they lingered in the hope that the Dutch would emerge the English fleet would face battle dangerously low in water and victuals. Far better to return to the Gunfleet, put aboard supplies, and be ready again to meet the East Indiamen, the Smyrna ships or de Ruyter. The English might have won the race to be first at sea, but poor victualling had lost them any advantage.

They spent the next several weeks at the Gunfleet, taking on supplies, entertaining one another to dinner on board ship, the young and enthusiastic volunteers boasting of what they would do in the battle to come. Thomas Ross aboard the *Royal Charles* promised a friend the first Dutchman's ears for an umbrella to shade the south windows of his lodgings; for if their thickness would not shelter him from the sun, he did not know what would.[22] Across the Channel, the Dutch assembled their squadrons from the Texel, the Maas and Zeeland. They had 109 sail made up of twenty-one ships of 60 guns or more, fifty-eight of 40–50 guns, and thirty smaller, but their slight superiority in numbers of ships and guns was offset by the heavier ordnance carried by the English ships.[23] The Dutch two-deckers, the equivalent of the English second-rates, for example, had lower tiers consisting chiefly of 24-pounders with one or two 36-pounders each side against the uniform 32-pounders of the large English ships.[24] However, their lower gun-ports were at least a foot higher above the water line, an advantage over their rivals in heavy seas or as a ship heeled over when tacking. Moreover their wider beam provided a more stable gun platform than the narrower English ships. Just as the English continued to bolster their numbers with merchant ships, so too did the Dutch, using the great Indiamen. But the Dutch had built swiftly and well and as the Venetian secretary reported, 'one may say with truth that the least of them is larger than the finest of all those which [the Dutch] employed in the time of the Protector'.[25]

The Dutch had not yet adopted the tactic of fighting in line. They still trained their guns high, often using chain shot – two balls linked by a short chain – to cripple a ship by shredding her rigging. The instructions issued to the senior commanders just before the outbreak of war stress this. They sought to turn their lighter weight and ease of handling to advantage, by striving to gain the weather gauge and then using the wind to move in groups against a great English ship and seize her by boarding, or to launch fireships against those crippled or caught downwind. The English strategy of fighting in line provided some protection against this, especially if the line had the wind. The damaged ship could fall out and make running repairs. As each pass took approximately three hours, repairs could also be effected in the intermission between passing and returning to pass again and most accounts of the battles record these welcome respites.

The Dutch too had rivalries and jealousies concerning the commanders. Jacob van Wassenaer, Lord of Obdam, appointed commander of the fleet after Tromp's death, remained as such for political reasons, partly for his impeccable republicanism, partly to appease the nobility who otherwise had little share in government; but the men did not rally to him as they did to the more charismatic Cornelis Tromp, son of the great admiral. Jan de Witt as Grand Pensionary divided the fleet into seven squadrons, which partly reflects the Dutch emphasis of fighting in groups, but also because it seemed the only way of stemming the bitter provincial rivalries, particularly between Friesland, Zeeland and Holland. De Witt, too, had a Hollander determination not to let Jan Evertsen, a Zeelander and an Orangist, gain command. If Obdam should die it would cause them some trouble, Downing reported, 'for I perceive by some Zeelanders that John Evertsen would hardly submit to be commanded by Cortenaer, and on the other hand these of Holland will hardly consent that the chief command should be given to any of another province'.[26] Further subdividing each into three divisions spawned twenty-one flag officers. De Witt left the Hague and arrived at the Texel on 21 April to oversee the preparations, but both Obdam and Tromp, his second in command, resented the chivvying. Obdam at least had sympathy with de Witt's republican views, but Tromp, like his father, a stalwart for the House of Orange, did not even have a common political bond. Downing noticed with satisfaction the heated exchanges, that de Witt had made himself admiral and general but understood nothing of either, that an exasperated Tromp would not even get out of bed to speak to him.[27]

William van de Velde the elder sat in his galliot in the midst of the ships and their men, drawing board on his knees, making sketches as they prepared for the fight. One shows the cutters towing the ships into position, on another he wrote the words 'naer de partij' – off to the battle. The battle of Lowestoft would begin early the next morning.[28] Downing's spy network, working efficiently again, had already sent over a copy of the Dutch fleet list and fighting instructions, and now gave warning that Obdam had orders to seek out the English, even to the mouth of the Thames. With the news came confirmation. Obdam had already caught some English merchantmen coming from Hamburg, with the cargo of timber and pitch the English so badly needed. The council of war agreed to shift at once to Sole Bay to continue provisioning with open sea close at hand and no danger of being trapped among sands. A passing Newcastle collier fleet, just escaped from the jaws of the Dutch, now provided fuel of a different kind for the man-hungry fleet. Though they carried the king's own order protecting them Sandwich pressed their crews.

At the last council of war on the eve of battle, Sandwich turned to the old problem of the merchant ships, twenty-four in a fleet of just over a hundred. He wanted them placed together in a rear squadron, so that the ships of the line would not be impeded by their slow sailing capacity or their master-owners' reluctance to engage in battle. Taking them out of the line would also reduce its length by nearly 3 miles, and concentrate the fleet more efficiently, leaving fewer points of weakness. Although Lawson had liked it the day before when Sandwich first mooted it, it was agreed to continue the former order of battle. The council of war probably feared that a separate squadron of armed merchantmen would have provided too easy a target for the Dutch.

Captain Lambert on the *Happy Return* spotted the Dutch first as they moved in with the north-easterly in their favour. He signalled the fleet by firing a gun and letting his topgallant sheets fly as a warning, a warning signalled on in turn by Rupert in the *Royal James*. The Duke of York shifted position at once to get further off-shore and gain manoeuvring room, standing out to sea in a south-

The Eendracht *and other Dutch ships assembled for a council of war in 1665 (detail), by William van de Velde the Elder (Maritiem Museum 'Prins Hendrik', Rotterdam)*

Jacob van Wassenaer, Lord of Obdam, an engraving by Theodore Matham after a picture by A. Hanneman (National Maritime Museum, Greenwich, London)

easterly direction until the flood tide at about four o'clock, when they anchored, the crews stripping the decks ready for battle, knocking down the temporary cabins and heaving the boards into the sea. They were now about 40 miles southeast of Lowestoft. Obdam had vowed before battle to return covered with laurel – or cypress.[29] With fair weather, the English would have optimum use of their heaviest fire-power, the great cannon of the lowest tier. Later that evening they sailed with the turning tide, to try and close the enemy. The north-easterly gave Obdam the weather gauge, and the English were puzzled by his failure to attack: 'God Almighty took away the skill of our Commander in Chief, or never gave him any', remarked one of his captains. An English report conjectured that perhaps the Dutch had superstitiously avoided battle on the anniversary of the English victory twelve years before at the Gabbard.[30] However, Obdam made no use of it the next day, either, and by the evening with the Dutch to the east and about 10 miles off, the wind began to shift. A Dutch fireship accidentally exploded, to English eyes a good omen for the fight to come.

By first light on 3 June, with the wind veering to south-west the English had worked into a position where they could now weather the Dutch. Only then did Obdam change course to the west, trying to hang on to the advantage he had frittered away, but the new day had also brought the English 'a fine chasing gale'. They had the weather gauge of the enemy. As the Dutch fleet tacked to come up, Prince Rupert in the van with Vice-Admiral Myngs led the pass. The Duke of York was in the centre and Sandwich to the rear. Then, with 'the bloody flag' hoisted, the fleets passed each other on opposite tacks, firing their broadsides, but still at too great a distance to make much impact. Though the English fleet began in line ahead, the Dutch squadron commanders from the first moved across pell-mell in haste to run with the glory, leaving their slower sailers well behind in a leaderless mêlée. During this first pass, Sandwich noted, the English ships too had bunched into ranks '3, 4 or 5 broad, and divers out of reach of the enemy fired over us and several into us and did us hurt', much as some Dutch captains had done at the Kentish Knock. After the pass came the usual lull: 'There was for a considerable time a perfect quiet without shooting one gun.'

Rupert again led the second pass made about 6 a.m. He tacked north-westerly to bring his ships up to the Dutch, matched by Obdam tacking to the south-south-east, trying to regain the weather gauge. The Duke of York, in the centre, with the experienced Penn at his side, recognised that the Dutch could weather the English fleet if it continued to tack in line after Rupert's squadron. He tacked at once to head them off, signalling Sandwich and his squadron to stand after him. Sandwich managed this despite the great crowd of ships close to colliding and both fleets surged past one another, in so narrow a space that Cornelis Tromp in the *Liefde* and Jan Evertsen in the *Zeeland* actually ploughed between Sandwich in the *Royal Prince* and two of his frigates close enough for their musket shot to wound Sandwich and his captain. After this pass, the English tacked again to the south-east, to close again and the two fleets, now sailing roughly parallel, 'knocked it out' with one another. The Dutch to the leeward could not use their fireships or their preferred tactic of using the wind to bear down in a body on the English flagships.

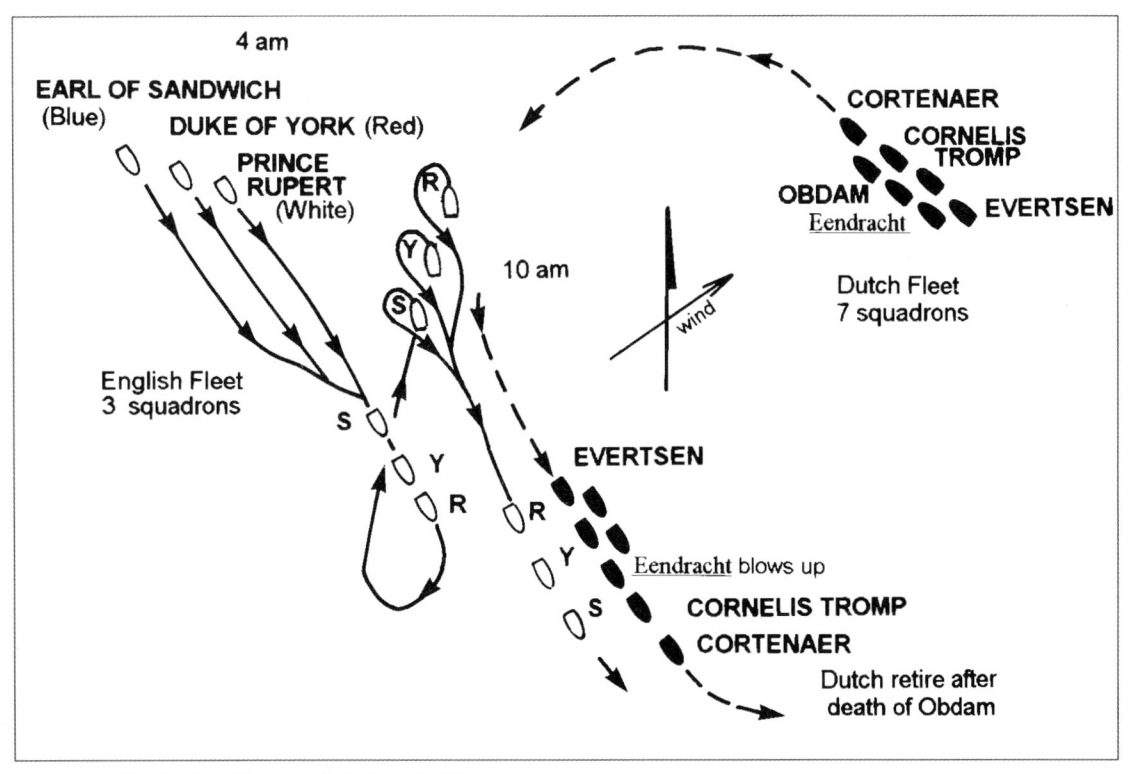

The battle of Lowestoft, 3 June 1665

At this point the billowing smoke so obscured the scene that the English commanders could not see what the Dutch were doing but relied on observing the actions of other English ships. When the Duke of York saw Sir John Lawson in the *Royal Oak* slightly ahead of him first bear towards the Dutch, then, almost at once edge off again to windward, he concluded that Lawson could see an attempt by some Dutch ships to gain the wind again. To prevent this, James himself kept near the wind, which in turn was a guide to the whole fleet to follow suit. In fact Lawson was wounded, and his master killed. The ship was drifting leaderless until Captain Jordan from the *George* crossed over to take command.

By now the pounding of the guns could be heard in London. John Dryden described the alarm as men first heard the sound, everyone trying to find a quiet place in the park or across the river, others down river, 'all seeking the noise in the depth of silence'. He with some friends hired a barge, making haste to shoot the bridge and get clear from the sound of surging water. Once away from the press of other craft choking the river, 'they ordered the watermen to let fall their oars more gently; and then everyone favouring his own curiosity with a strict silence, it was not long ere they perceived the air to break about them like the noise of distant thunder, or of swallows in a chimney: those little undulations of sound,

The battle of Lowestoft, 3 June 1665, by Hendrik van Minderhout (National Maritime Museum, Greenwich, London)

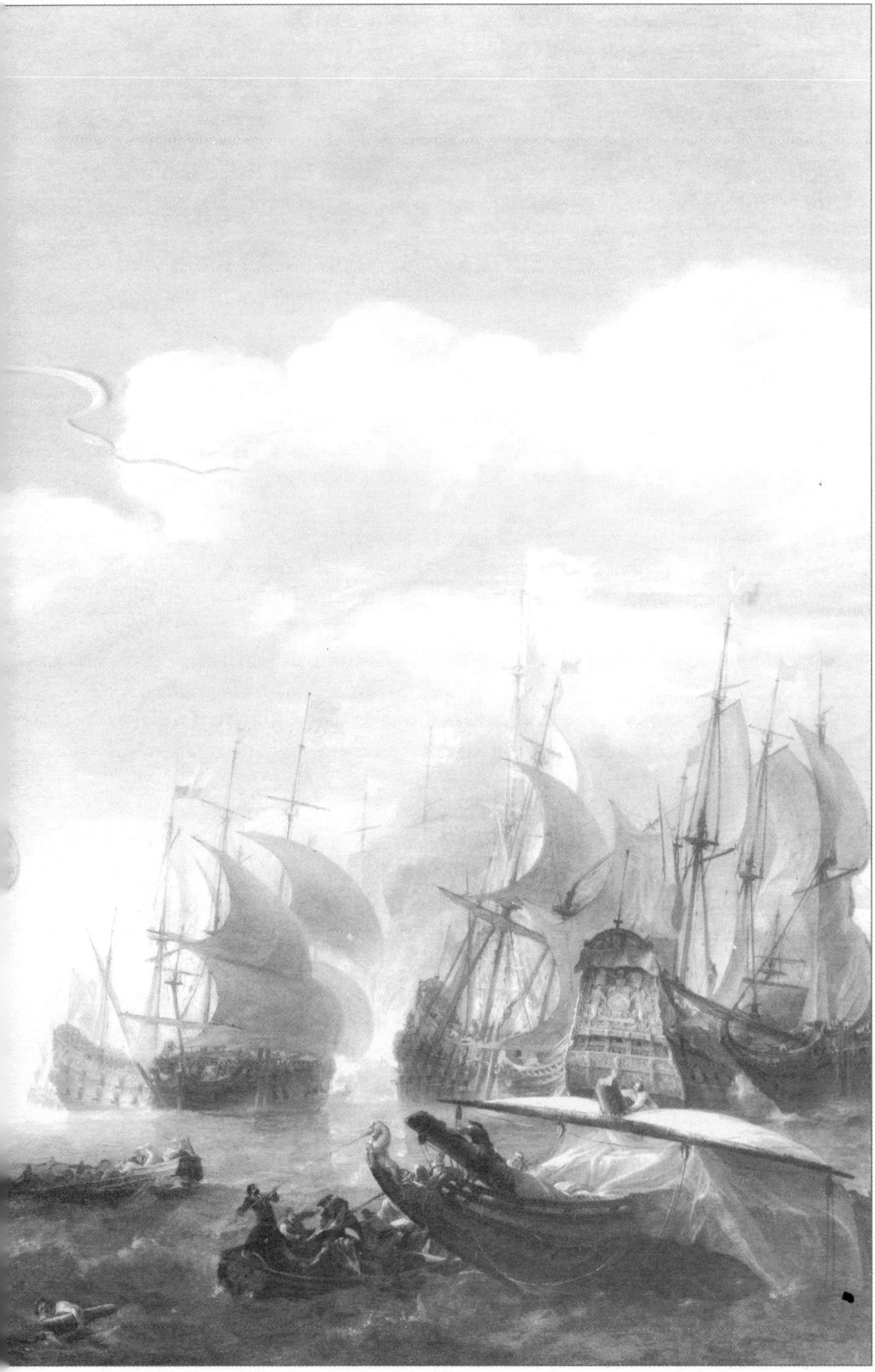

though almost vanishing before they reached them, yet seeming to retain somewhat of their first horror which they had betwixt the fleets . . .'[31] Across the Channel, meanwhile, with the guns booming, Sir George Downing did not stir out of his house in the Hague, staying close to the pile of great stones and barrels of earth he had put at the top of the stairs, ready to tumble down upon any who tried to come up; though he afterwards had the grace to admit that there had not been so much as an ill word spoken to him, nor were any stones cast at his windows.[32]

By midday, the main fury of fighting centred around Sandwich, in the *Prince*, who, supported only by one ship, had been slugging it out against Obdam and his mighty flagship, the 84-gun *Eendracht*, backed by the *Oranje*, a 76-gun East Indiaman, and several others of their great ships. The Duke of York in the *Royal Charles* closed in to help. Spurred on by the reinforcements, Sandwich let fall his mainsail and flying the blue flag on the mizzen peak to signal his squadron to follow suit pressed up hard against the Dutch to punch through the gap which had opened in their line. In the confusion four of their ships tangled together, helpless in the face of the English broadsides. The Duke of York unleashed a fireship to destroy them if they would not yield, and of the thousand men reckoned by Sandwich to be on board only a hundred were plucked from the sea. One of the trapped ships exploded with such force that she tore out the mast and rigging of the neighbour she was locked to, but this at least freed the latter from the death struggles of the other three, and some smaller Dutch ships managed to tow her to safety. Under the guns of the *Royal Charles*, the *Eendracht* suddenly erupted in a volcano of flames, as her powder magazine exploded, slaying Obdam and 400 of his crew. The *Oranje* while trying to lay close enough to board the *Royal Charles*, was set on by first the *Mary*, then the *Royal Katherine* and the *Essex*, 'until', Sandwich reported, 'she was scarcely able to swim'. Her men surrendering, she was set on fire. However, the *Mary* lost nearly a third of her crew.

The heavier fire-power of the great English three-deckers engaging at close range had inflicted a savage toll. With Obdam dead, the Dutch fleet now began to break up in confusion. Cortenaer, who should have succeeded him, had been killed earlier in the day. When his ship the *Hollandia*, now under a junior officer, began to retreat, the admiral's flag was left flying. The fleet took it as a signal for a general retreat. The young apprentice seaman, Edward Barlow, fighting on board the *Monck* in Rupert's squadron remembered how they 'seeing their Admiral and General lost, began to turn their arses and run'. They cut loose their boats, and set their studding sails to fly before the wind; dividing still further as Tromp and Evertsen each claimed the right of hoisting the flag as commander-in-chief, Evertsen and his followers heading for the Maas, Tromp with his followers to the Texel. With the Dutch coast 70 miles away and many crippled ships to shelter, the English could still bite sharply. In a rearguard tussle with Sandwich a Dutch ship forced to bear round sheered up against two of his fellows and all stuck fast, struck their colours and ceased firing. Sandwich, to keep up the chase, left them for the ships in the rear to secure but, to his horror, a fireship from Rupert's squadron burned them before the men were taken out. 'This cruel fact was much detested by us as not beseeming Christians . . .'

Sandwich fell astern in the night pursuit, forced to replace his main topsail which had been shot away, and the Duke of York took over the lead. With the duke asleep in his cabin, his gentleman-in-waiting, the volunteer aristocrat Henry Brouncker, ordered the captain to shorten sail. The captain obeyed, believing the order came from the duke himself. The pursuit lagged and by daybreak the Dutch were safely among their own shoals. By the afternoon they had slipped into the Texel on the flood tide. Though Rupert and Sandwich between them were able to pick off six or seven stragglers, the chance to annihilate the Dutch navy foundered on a wife's anxiety for her husband, for as Clarendon later explained, the duchess had given a strict charge to all the duke's servants to hinder him from engaging closely. She may have thought herself vindicated when news of the dead came to England: Vice-Admiral Sir John Lawson dying from a wound turned gangrenous, Rear-Admiral Robert Sansum, the Earl of Marlborough, Captain Robert Kirby and Captain James Ableson all killed; and closest of all, three aristocratic volunteers, Charles Berkeley, newly created Earl of Falmouth; Lord Muskerry; and the second son of the Earl of Burlington, Roger Boyle, all three killed by a single chain shot as they stood on deck next to her husband, 'Their blood and brains flying in the Duke's face – and the head of Mr Boyle striking down the Duke, as some say.' Charles wept at his great friend Berkeley's death, but Clarendon cynically observed that for others, Berkeley's death was a considerable part of the victory. All together, the English lost about 800 men killed and wounded.[33]

Of ships, apart from fireships, the English lost only the *Charity*, a merchant prize from the last war, cut off from the fleet in the first pass of the day, then shot 'as full of holes as a honeycomb'.[34] It took some days for the scale of the English victory to become known: 'great news, at last newly come . . . that we have totally routed the Dutch', Pepys crowed on 8 June, before going off to celebrate at a great bonfire, 'and mighty merry'. The Dutch lost seventeen ships, including three large flagships. The five thousand killed, wounded or taken prisoner included the three flag officers, Stillingwerf, Cortenaer and Obdam. Nor could the Dutch credit the loss of the *Eendracht* to enemy cannon, but insisted that an English sailor had got on board and fired the magazine.

The Deputies begged Tromp to continue the fight but he refused, 'saying that he would not expose himself with a cowardly rabble which was capable of making him lose his honour with his life and the fleet as well'. The Indiamen in particular had not fought well, their guns were lighter and their officers and crew had not been trained for open sea battles on this scale. Republican admirals blamed their monarchist colleagues, Jan Evertsen and Cornelis Tromp. The latter came close to arrest in June as rumours spread that he had been agitating for the fifteen-year-old Prince of Orange to replace de Ruyter. While the English roistered in triumph, the furious citizens of Brielle seized Jan Evertsen, the Lieutenant-Admiral of the Zeeland squadron, and threw him into the river. A garrison of troops rescued him from certain death for the enraged pack were pelting him with rocks. In the immediate aftermath, many had branded Evertsen as cowardly and a

Cornelis Tromp, Lieutenant-Admiral of the United Provinces (1629–91), by Sir Peter Lely (National Maritime Museum, Greenwich, London)

runaway, but at the inquiry which followed, the officers of the fleet testified to his bravery. When an investigating party examined his ship, they counted the 115 cannon shot hits, thirty of them below the water line. Others were found guilty of desertion and cowardice and the States General, at the insistence of de Witt, exacted retribution: three captains shot, three others disgraced with their swords broken by the executioner, a master forced to watch the executions with a rope around his neck. Although exonerated, Jan Evertsen resigned and went into retirement; his brother Cornelis was appointed to replace him as Vice-Admiral of Zeeland.[35]

With Obdam dead and de Ruyter still somewhere in the Atlantic, it was Tromp who hoisted the great flag with pendant below as commander-in-chief. To contain his imprudence and temper his monarchist fervour the States General agreed to de Witt's proposal, made prior to Lowestoft, to appoint three deputies with plenipotentiary powers to sail with the fleet and enforce discipline. It was after the Roman fashion, thought Sagredo, watching developments from France, but the consuls of Rome had known how to direct and command the forces, while these were men 'who have never been seen to handle a musket'.[36]

The English fleet dispersed between Hollesley Bay, the Buoy of the Nore, Harwich, the Rolling Grounds and Chatham, to be repaired and refitted, the men to the taverns and bawds, the captains and commanders to swagger in the victory, and compete for promotion. Jeremy Smith was knighted for his bravery, but others did less well in the fallout of temper and ambition and the fight for honours. 'It is strange to see how the people do already slight Sir William Berkely . . . who three months since was the delight of the court', mused Pepys.[37] Accusations that former republican officers had been battle-shy or had plans to switch to the Dutch side flew about and many must have found these battles on land more treacherous and uncertain than any they fought at sea. Certainly numbers of them were 'turned out'. Henry Brouncker's part in the lamentable conclusion to an otherwise stellar victory did not become public until late 1667, hushed up by his closeness to the Duke of York. The winds of faction and tides of favouritism lifted some up high and stranded others among the shoals. Rupert recommended Robert Holmes for the flag left vacant by Sansum's death, but the Duke of York handed it instead to his own protégé and flag captain John Harman. Holmes, 'like a rash, proud coxcomb' resigned in rage, claiming there were too many who sought to block his career.[38] He did not stay out for long. By early 1666, he had made his peace with the duke and taken command of a new frigate, *Defiance*, of 64 guns which was launched on the same day that the king knighted Holmes.

Others cemented connections of a gentler kind. Sandwich, the old Cromwellian, busied himself with negotiations for the marriage of his daughter Jemimah to the eldest son of the old royalist, and now Treasurer of the Navy Board, Sir George Carteret. It was a match between two families who had become fast friends across the divide of former hostility. And Sandwich needed friends and supporters, as he mulled over the slights to his reputation as the first printed accounts of the battle appeared which gave him scant mention. Both Sir William Coventry, who had been present throughout the battle, and the Duke of York praised the earl's bravery, yet the printed reports barely mentioned him. Sandwich grumbled too that in all the crying up of Rupert's courage his ship had scarcely been damaged. His own was holed like a colander.[39]

To most Englishmen heaven itself had passed sentence on the Grand Quarrel. The balladists mocked that with so many Dutch drowned, now the very herrings would be their own sailors – they would meet their admirals as 'Butter'd Fish'.[40] However, for all their rejoicing in victory, the English were doing little with it. Unlike Monck's fleet after the Gabbard they were not blockading the Dutch estuaries.

CHAPTER 10
The Four-Day Fight

> Let the enemy feel that though our fleet be divided our spirit is entire. To be overcome is the fortune of war, but to fly is the fashion of a coward.
>
> George Monck, Duke of Albemarle

Charles now decided that James, the heir to the throne, should not again risk his life in battle, but Rupert flatly refused the king's plan to keep the balance between Cavaliers and former Cromwellians by giving command jointly to Rupert and Sandwich, since a joint command would be no command at all. Sandwich became commander-in-chief and admiral of the Red, Sir Thomas Allin, who had been knighted in June, was appointed as vice-admiral of the Blue and Sir William Penn as rear-admiral of the White. Before the question of overall command had been settled the Duke of York ordered Penn to sail as soon as possible to intercept either de Ruyter or the East India fleet. Penn left precipitantly, and when Sandwich caught him up off the Texel he was dismayed to discover that Penn's squadron was dangerously under-provisioned and over 2,000 sailors short. It would be haste paid for dearly.

The East India fleet was expected to creep down the Norwegian coast where it could shelter from either storms or the English in the port of Bergen. Downing, who had sent warnings from the Hague of the fury of the Dutch and the speed of their preparations for revenge, had been arguing that the best way to undermine de Witt's republican-dominated government was by damaging the merchant interest. Sir Gilbert Talbot, the English envoy in Copenhagen, had reported that the King of Denmark was willing to break his treaty with the Dutch if it could be done to his advantage. He was prepared to help the English capture the Indies fleet while it was sheltering in his port in return for half the loot. If he did, Talbot argued, he could not avoid war with the Dutch which would close the Baltic to their ships.[1] This was the situation Sandwich was sent to exploit. Once off the Texel he delayed his northern sortie with Penn until Allin arrived from Sole Bay on 17 July with his squadron of twenty ships. Councils of war planned the strike as they sailed north, as Sandwich gleaned scraps of intelligence from a Greenland skipper, some Danish pilots, a ship recently at Bergen, about the movements of the merchantmen and of the anticipated homecoming of de Ruyter. As he was able to hug the coast more closely than the English and was sheltered by mist off the north-east of Heligoland, de Ruyter was able to evade the English fleet. On 30 July Sandwich learned that the merchantmen were now tucked away in Bergen

Sir Edward Montagu, 1st Earl of Sandwich, by Sir Peter Lely (National Maritime Museum, Greenwich, London)

harbour with gold and jewels, spices, silks and carpets, 'scarce at any time in one place so great a mass of wealth was ever heaped together'.[2] The young aristocratic volunteers aboard began in their mind's eye to share out the loot, 'some for diamonds, some for spices, others for rich silks', remembered John Wilmot, the Earl of Rochester, adding with disarming candour 'and I for shirts and gold which I had most need of'.[3] With beer and water running low, they needed to strike quickly. Sandwich had no illusions about the difficulty of the exercise, but the expectation of Danish assistance balanced the danger. The council of war resolved to detach twenty-two ships and two fireships under the command of Sir Thomas Teddiman to make the strike accompanied by Sir Thomas Clifford as negotiator. However, Clifford was soon baffled because the governor of Bergen, Claus von Ahlefeldt, denied all knowledge of the Danish king's agreement and refused to allow more than five ships to enter the narrow harbour. Talbot's easy assurance to Sandwich, that he should not be surprised if the governor seemed initially hostile for it would be merely 'in show to amuse the Hollanders and excuse himself outwardly to the world', now seemed overly optimistic.[4]

The Dutch positioned four of their largest ships across the constricted entrance and put men and weapons ashore to fortify the garrison. Inside the castle, Clifford and his attendant negotiators spent a fruitless night of proposal and counter-proposal. Outside in a dark night with driving rain and in the teeth of an off-shore wind, Teddiman's men warped their ships up to the harbour; eight in line with broadsides trained on the Dutch ships, and the other seven aiming at the castle. At dawn Teddiman lost patience, hoisted his fighting colours and opened fire on the Dutch. The castle guns raked his ships in return. The offshore wind prevented Teddiman from using his fireships and cannon fire cut the cables holding the ships steady so that they began to foul one another. He called off an attack he should never have begun and withdrew from the harbour, helped in this at least by the wind. If he had attacked as soon as he had arrived, rather than waiting to negotiate, he might have seized his prey because most of the Dutch crews were ashore and drunk.[5]

Sandwich meanwhile had been pushed further and further north by violent southerlies, his hungry men on short rations, and anchored to take on water in Bressay Sound in the Shetlands. As they sailed out a week later they received news of the Bergen repulse. 'Our ships are much tattered and torn. We have lost six captains . . . There is killed and wounded in our squadron upwards of 400 men.'[6] This against Dutch losses of 29 killed and 70 wounded. Of his attempt to mount an attack against the wind Teddiman says nothing. That he was a former Cromwellian officer did not later go unremarked. Clifford bitterly reported the aftermath. Dispatches arrived from the King of Denmark instructing Ahlefeldt to connive with the attack but the squadron was so battered and the loss of men so heavy that they dared not make a second attempt unless the Danes intervened decisively on their behalf. This they declined to do. On 10 August Teddiman abandoned the Norwegian coast and met up with the homeward-bound Sandwich. The two squadrons came into Sole Bay on 21 August, empty of victuals, laden with near-starving, sick men; and once again nothing to show, with the Baltic still closed to English merchant ships. Sandwich reflected on the

Sir Thomas Teddiman, by Sir Peter Lely (National Maritime Museum, Greenwich, London)

mistakes which had led to this dismal finale to the victory of June, when England appeared undisputed masters of the sea. If Penn had stayed even two days before sailing he would have been better supplied, it would have given Allin's squadron time to join and instead of waiting for him off the Texel as Sandwich had done, the united fleet could have sailed north at once, and had a better chance of encountering de Ruyter or of catching the Indies fleet in the open sea.[7]

In the Netherlands de Witt was once more demonstrating his devotion to the navy.[8] At the beginning of the war he had the States General appoint himself and some other members to the Texel anchorage as supervisors. There he could oversee the fitting out of the contributions to the fleet of the Amsterdam, North Quarter and Friesland admiralties. In order to keep his finger on the pulse at Flushing, Helvoetsluys and the Hague he devised a practical coastal signalling system. His interventions might have sometimes appeared a little eccentric for the chief minister of a state, as when he set out in a cockboat with a leadsman and proved that the Spaniard's Gate was deep enough to take their largest ships against the denial of the pilots and flag officers. The sailors, who admired his devotion, named the channel 'Heer Jan de Witt's Deep'.[9] However, these and other such expeditions were of great practical value for he showed that several inlets and channels, despite belief to the contrary, could be used by the largest ships of the line and so gave the navy greater flexibility in entering and leaving the roadstead. The news of Lowestoft had brought him at once to the Texel. He had boarded a half-sinking ship and remained there until she had been towed to safety. Thanks to his resolute administration after Lowestoft there was none of the collapse and disarray so confidently predicted by Downing, and the States continued to furnish men and resources at a level higher, in proportion to population, than England could provide. With de Ruyter returned, de Witt could now set aside Tromp as commander-in-chief. Tromp initially considered retiring, complaining that he 'did not propose to go to sea, now that, after he had got the fleet into good order, another man was put over his head'. De Witt allowed his naval obsessions to take him to sea with the fleet as a councillor pensionary, much to Tromp's irritation. At a reception on board the *Delffland*, Tromp guffawed when de Witt appeared in finery encrusted with gold and lace to dignify his new position, instead of the customary black. To counter his seasickness, de Witt had the great Dutch scientist Christiaan Huygens design him an ingenious hammock to alleviate it and was comfortable enough although he shared a single cabin with his two fellow deputies in 'a chaos like an ant's nest'.[10]

De Ruyter's first task was to sail north to shepherd the merchantmen home from Bergen and to intercept the English. Sandwich, determined to regain prestige lost at Bergen, sailed as soon as he could to prevent him. After a hasty survey of the fleet, he sent the least serviceable ships into harbour, employing their crews to help man the remaining ships, for 1,000 sailors had been invalided ashore. Then, with a bare fortnight's supply of provisions, he sortied on 28 August searching for de Ruyter off the Dogger bank. However, a northerly gale delayed his arrival until 3 September. The same gale had scattered the East Indies fleet and de Ruyter's escort but at mid-morning the English sighted seven or eight of their ships. The English frigates gave chase and by evening they had seized two large East Indiamen and four men-of-war, for the loss of the *Hector*, its captain and eighty men drowned. The *Hector* had been fighting with her lower gun-ports open, and Barlow on board the *Monck* saw how a sudden gust of wind 'pressed her down so much and the water came in at the ports so fast that she was presently full and sank immediately'.[11] News of more sightings came in each day, but no further spoils until the 9th, when they chased and took four men-of-war and two West Indiamen. Late in the day as they stood to westward they sighted thirty ships under Vice-Admiral van Nes, but were unable to weather them. They were now close in, at night, and in danger of being drawn upon a lee shore in 'misly and thick weather' so Sandwich called off the pursuit. Later his prudence would be condemned as covetousness.

The captured East Indiamen were golden eggs indeed. Pepys took horse to view them: 'Pepper scattered through every chink, you trod upon it; and in cloves and nutmegs I walked above the knees, whole rooms full. And silks in bales, and boxes of copperplate, one of which I saw opened.'[12] The ordinary seamen by custom could share any merchandise which lay between decks of ships taken as prizes. The two ships reportedly floated 5 feet higher after this ransacking. The flag officers could expect a share of the bulk of the cargo that lay in the holds, but were supposed to wait for their prize money until merchants had sold the goods and transmitted the proceeds to the Treasury. Sandwich let his flag officers and some of his commanders rifle the booty and reserved a large share himself. Only then did he apply to the king for a warrant for the procedure. This was foolish for it caused resentment among commanders who had been left out. Monck, Myngs and Ayscue loudly condemned it, eager to use the dispute to Sandwich's disadvantage. The treasure came ashore in wagonloads before gaping crowds. It was hoped that the booty would help towards paying the naval debts and provide for the setting out of the fleet next spring, but it proved less than anticipated. The expectation that the war would pay its way through the seizing of treasure was once more disappointed. Sandwich's irregular handling of the prize goods only encouraged the rumours that if Sandwich had not been so anxious to bring his prizes safely to port he might have trounced the entire Dutch fleet.

Both the king and James agreed that Sandwich had been sensible to withdraw but the duke of York still took umbrage. He should have been the conduit through which such rewards flowed, not Sandwich. The earl, he believed, either through greed or ambition to increase his popularity with the fleet, had robbed the duke of his right of patronage. No man had been less guilty of either fault, said Clarendon, 'Yet upon this blast the winds rose from all quarters, reproaches of all sorts were cast upon him.'[13]

Amid this furore the Dutch, who were supposed to be reeling after Lowestoft, reappeared along the Suffolk coast. De Witt had insisted that his admirals take the offensive as quickly as possible and hold the sea into autumn to rebuild their fighting spirit, rather than lie up in port or merely escort the merchant fleet as they had done after Scheveningen in 1653. For three weeks they blocked the approaches to the Thames, choking off the seaborne commerce of England, and only an outbreak of the plague in their ships and the late October storms drove them off. There was little Sandwich could do. England as yet had no mechanism for long-term borrowing or spreading the expenses of a major war. Besides Pepys reckoned that half the war taxation at least was not reaching the navy. Unpaid contractors refused to continue supplying on credit, dockyards had no provisions to repair the ships, the sailors and their families starved in the streets. Nor was there money to feed prisoners or their own seamen. John Evelyn, a Commissioner for Sick and Wounded Prisoners, despaired that he already had 2,500 sick and wounded prisoners perishing for want of food and shelter, and 'this barbarous exposure must needs redound to the king's great dishonour'.[14] The Navy Board had received no money to pay off the crews, and issued tickets, tokens which could be redeemed later for money, but the money was long in coming and the sailors were forced to sell their tickets at a heavy discount to obtain ready money.

The fleet itself had been rushed to sea in July, poorly provisioned and undermanned. Now in late September the council of war found only four ships of the line were in a fit state to sail. The jealous, the spiteful, the ambitious, among them Monck who wanted to return to sea, Coventry and the Duke of York, all worked to kindle resentment against Sandwich's management. The king feared that when parliament met it would move to impeach him and so appointed him ambassador to Spain to remove him from danger. Sandwich was happy to go, telling Clarendon that the common men were weary of the war and that too many in the fleet were preferred ahead of the best officers. He meant that Monck had been pressing hard for the removal of all the old tarpaulins. With Sandwich gone and Penn sidelined for his share in the disgrace, the king decided again for a joint command. Rupert abandoned his opposition and Monck accepted on condition that he had time to prepare his wife or 'she would break out into such passions as would be very uneasy to him'. Alas for his hope. Clarendon describes her fury, not out of concern for her husband's safety but because she thought it was a ruse to remove her husband from the influence and rewards of the court.[15]

The former Cromwellian, Andrew Marvell, mocked,

> United Gen'rals! sure the only spell
> Wherewith United Provinces to quell.
> Alas, e'en they, though shell'd in treble oak,
> Will prove an addled egg with double yoke.[16]

His sourness reflects the mood of the closing months of 1665 during which a worse enemy than de Ruyter had besieged London. The plague, which had been thinning the Dutch seamen for much of the year, now flared in London, and Pepys had seen the first red crosses daubed on house doors in Drury Lane in June. By early September he could hear little noise in the City but the tolling of bells.[17] The king, parliament and the law courts had moved to Oxford and the Navy Board to Greenwich. The comet which Sandwich had tracked with his telescope across the night skies of December 1664 and the early months of 1665 many now recalled as a harbinger of ill-omen.[18]

Councils of war immediately after Lowestoft had focused on repairing and revictualling but later they had turned to discussing battle tactics, and in particular how to prevent disorderly mêlées. Sandwich urged his captains to hold

Rupert, Prince Palatine of the Rhine and Duke of Cumberland, by Sir Peter Lely (National Maritime Museum, Greenwich, London)

their place in the line according to the order of battle, and if any accident prevented this they must 'put themselves in a line anywhere, to have their broadsides to the enemy'. Ships must not leave the line to seize a merchant prize till after victory was certain. Two additions to the *Fighting Instructions* specifically address blunders at Lowestoft: fouling one another by careless tacking, and firing at the enemy through their own ships if the line became bunched. Meanwhile parliament in October had agreed to supply £1.25 million to set out the fleet for 1666. The great ships were laid up for repair and orders for new ships were drawn up. Unluckier ships, including Edward Barlow's, stayed out to convoy the merchant ships coming down the North Sea, 'the mist freezing into ice, making the smallest rope in the ship as big as one's arm . . .', the flukes of their anchors 'worn as bright as silver with ploughing through the ground as we rid'.[19]

After Lowestoft de Witt also turned to the problems of fleet formation, recognising that the large number of squadrons had caused confusion. Three of the seven squadron commanders had paid no mind to overall attack, preferring to engage their swift ships in individual duels while leaving the slower sailers without direction, drifting downwind into trouble. Yet though disorderly fighting was condemned, the official commission which reported at the end of June, like the instructions to Obdam, still urged the fleet to grapple and board: 'it is to the greatest advantage of this nation that an enemy should be laid aboard and entered . . .' Nevertheless during the summer the flag officers must have been arguing for a battle order which more closely resembled that of the English, with only three squadrons, and fighting in line ahead, for the *Fighting Instructions* issued in August give their positions in the line, with Tromp in the centre, the second squadron ahead of him, the third astern. However, the formation was to provide some protection for the flag officers by adopting a snaking rather than a straight line, the first and last squadron closer to the enemy than the commander-in-chief's middle squadron, and within each squadron the first and last divisions closer to the enemy than the middle. De Witt admitted that only experience would reveal whether the planned formation could be achieved in differing conditions of wind and weather and other circumstances and the snake formation itself was probably never strictly observed. Nevertheless the Dutch navy had now accepted the line-ahead battle formation.[20]

In January 1666 Louis XIV at last fulfilled his treaty obligations to the Dutch by declaring war on England. Dutch collapse would cause the fall of de Witt and if the Orange Party came to power the country might become an 'English protectorate'. (Louis failed to foresee an even worse nightmare: England becoming a 'Dutch kingdom' two decades later.) However, he had no wish to risk his new and inexperienced fleet in battle, preferring to let Dutch and English wear each other out. De Ruyter took no account of French ships in his plans for the season's campaign, presciently thinking it 'too uncertain to judge', but the English alarm that French and Dutch might combine in a super fleet coloured their decisions.[21] They knew a French squadron of thirty warships under the Duc de Beaufort had left Toulon to join another at La Rochelle. They expected this combined fleet to then head up-Channel to join with the Dutch. The Dutch fleet had been gathering at the Texel since April and by 5 June it numbered eighty

The Zeven Provincien *at a Council of War in the Dutch Fleet by William van de Velde the Elder (Rijksmuseum, Amsterdam)*

fighting ships, 21,000 officers and men and 4,500 guns, and as de Witt happily observed more than 30 of the warships were 'more capital and of greater strength than the most capital ships of last year'. Tromp's dictum that unless they built ships to equal the English great ships they would be beaten as often as they fought them had at last been taken to heart. Ten of the new ships carried 80 guns, another twelve had 70, and the guns themselves were heavier. For the first time some 36-pounders were installed.[22] They had learned the lesson of Lowestoft. De Ruyter himself sailed in the brand new two-decker *Zeven Provincien*, 80, with her crew of 500, her stern ornamented with carved and gilded figures. A symptom of the republic's remarkable devotion to art was the presence in the fleet of William van de Velde the elder, for de Ruyter had instructed the skipper of a galliot to take him 'before, behind and in the fleet or in whatever way he will deem expedient for the drawings he is going to make . . .'[23]

Across the Channel Marvell's double-yolk had already split. The fleet had shifted from the Buoy of the Nore to the Downs and from there Rupert had sailed with twenty of the best ships to seek the French. We cannot know who made the decision to split the fleet, for at the later inquiry all concerned tried to blame others. Rupert claimed that the decision had been taken upon intelligence received that some French warships were at Belle Isle, with others expected shortly out of Brest, and that the Dutch were not expected to sortie for some weeks.[24] It seemed an opportune time to intercept the French fleet before it could join the Dutch. Pepys later repeated the gossip that Sir Edward Spragge persuaded the prince to it so that 'they might be doing something alone', implying that the glory would also be theirs alone. Monck claimed to have been much surprised by the proposition, for it would leave him too short of ships. He heard nothing more for a fortnight, during which time he agitated for the ships revictualling in the Thames and the Medway to join him, begged pay for the sailors and warned that if victuals did not arrive promptly he could sail nowhere. However, he failed to ensure his scout ships kept station along the Dutch coast. On 25 May he learned that Rupert had had orders on the 23rd to sail with his nineteen men-of-war to meet the French.[25] Next came the information that far from being unready the Dutch 'would very suddenly be out'. Reviewing the size of the remaining fleet Monck asked what he should do if the Dutch arrived before reinforcements came, for he needed seventy ships to match the Dutch for it 'went against his stomach' to retreat. He was uncharacteristically anxious to be backed up by official orders. Faction fighting (especially his own) had exiled Sandwich to Madrid. Now he was himself at risk from the faction who wanted all the old Cromwellian commanders outed. Yet he did not suggest that Rupert stay and Rupert sailed on 29 May. The next day, Monck had confirmation that de Ruyter had already left the Texel sailing westward. Urgent messages to recall Rupert were dispatched at once, while Monck decided that next day he would shift his fleet from the Downs to the Swin, an anchorage between the Gunfleet and the Middle Ground. There he could shelter more safely while awaiting the ships expected hourly from upriver and if necessary retreat further to the Buoy of the Nore. However, early on 1 June, the *Bristol*'s topmast lookout reported enemy in sight and her captain fired off three warning guns. De Ruyter with his three squadrons had come looking for prey, and was now at anchor off the North Foreland riding out the night and a strong south-west wind.

What should Monck have done, in the face of a far larger fleet, eighty-five warships against his fifty-four? He had the wind, and it was at his choice to fight or to sail to the Swin as he had planned. He could compel them to fight but they could not compel him. Yet with lookouts swaying from the rigging and counting enemy sail, the council of flag officers and captains found themselves agreeing to fight a fleet almost a third more than their size. Monck argued that with too many of his ships heavy sailers he could not have reached safety without a fight. Yet the wind in his favour gave him a head start and the Swin was only 25 miles away. However, if he had not stayed to fight de Ruyter might have conjoined with the French for all still believed the French to be approaching and the Dutch and French combined would have overwhelmed Rupert. (In fact the French were still as far away as the Tagus.) Moreover if he had fled to the Swin the morale of the men would flee also, with their fleet besieged in the Thames while the Dutch patrolled outside. The English attack also would have the element of surprise

The Four-Day Fight, 1–4 June 1666, by Abraham Storck (National Maritime Museum, Greenwich, London)

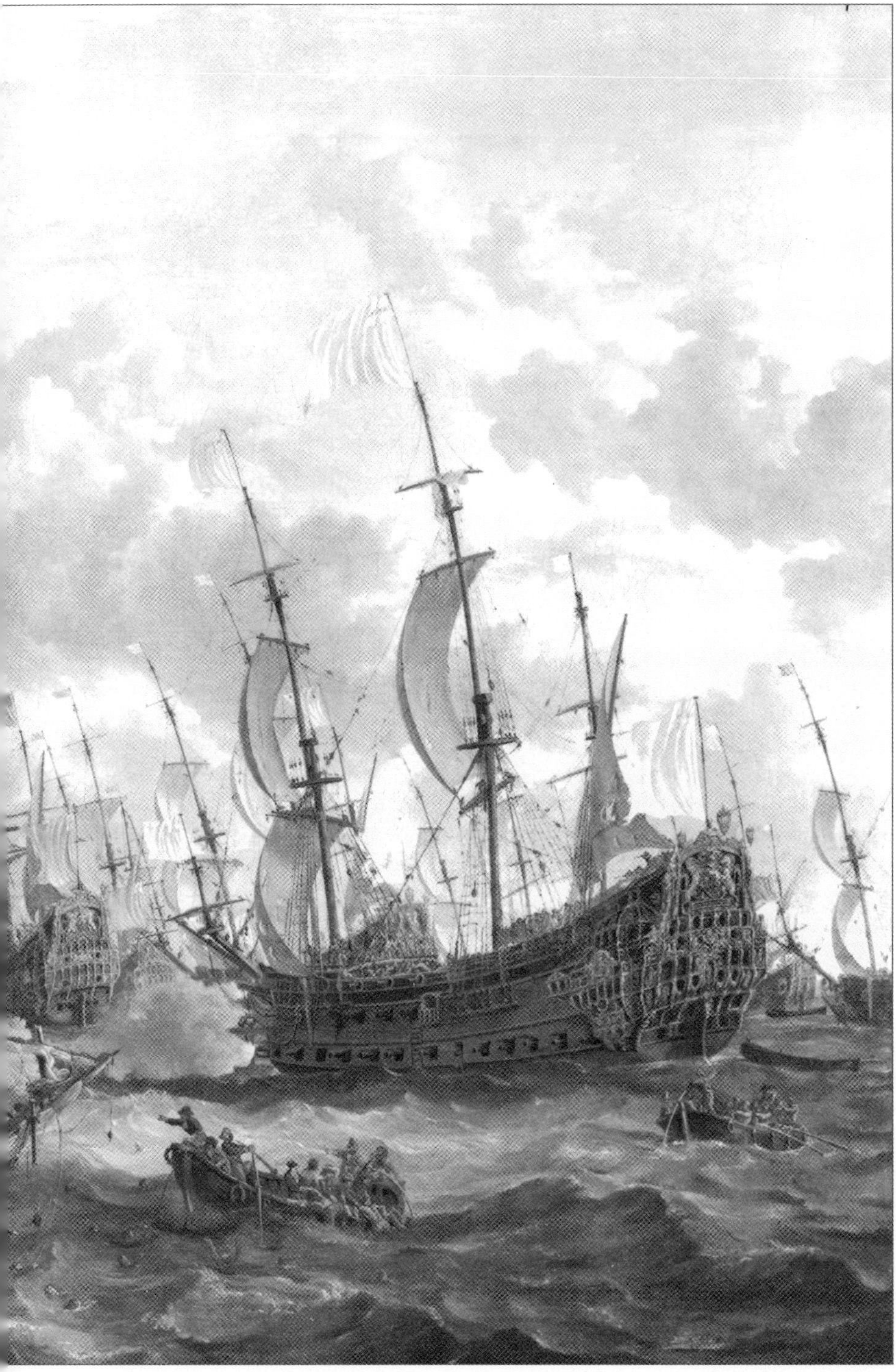

because the Dutch would not expect it. Penn's memory of the decision carried conviction: many of the captains thought it 'wholly against their judgement to fight that day with the disproportion of force', but agreed rather than be called cowards.[26] Monck, who had condemned Sandwich for caution, could not risk his own accusation. Perhaps most important of all, Monck had learned naval warfare under Blake who always expected to beat the Dutch at odds and only once failed to do so. Blake would have attacked and Monck would do no less.[27]

The fleet bore down upon the Dutch as they lay at anchor. De Ruyter flew his flag in the *Zeven Provincien* beside Aert van Nes in the new *Eendracht* in the centre; Cornelis Evertsen the elder commanded the van to the north-east; while the third squadron under Tromp with Meppel and van der Hulst was at the windward end, to the south-west. With their ships heeled over in the strong wind, the English could not run out the lower tiers of their guns, for the seas would have flooded in through the gun-ports. This had been the overriding reason not to fight, in Sir John Harman's view, but Monck must have discounted it in spite of his own belief earlier that morning that with the wind so high 'I think we shall not engage this day.' The Dutch also had problems in the heavy seas, struggling to cut their anchor cables and forced to fight on the leeward. Yet even so after this first pass, four or five English ships quit the fight and made back to port; 'and if the King do not cause some of the captains to be hanged, he will never be well served', wrote Clifford. In initiating this engagement Monck had remembered the ships he had defeated at the Gabbard and at Scheveningen in 1653. He would find the ships he now faced much more formidable. Tromp's squadron at the south-west took the brunt of the first impact, but the English by engaging head first, rather than in a passing line gave the Dutch centre and rear the opportunity to tack to the south-west and gain the weather gauge. Already in this pass, the *Swiftsure* and six or seven other ships in the English van were too far to windward to be effective. Monck in the *Royal Charles* had outrun the slower sailers in the rear, so the initial thrust had been blunted from the start with perhaps as few as thirty-four ships keeping up with him.

The second pass brought both fleets closer together. The Dutch gunners concentrated on the rigging and masts as in the past and soon had shredded the sails of the *Royal Charles*. The opposing crews traded shout for shout, the Dutch as Monck's flag was shot down, the English hallooing still louder as a new one ran up in its place. This pass had brought Monck a little ahead of the Dutch, so the *Royal Charles* and Sir Robert Holmes in the *Defiance* had a breathing space to anchor and fetch up new sail and mend the tattered rigging, shredded not only by the Dutch but by their own ships who had tacked away to the windward of Monck's ships and had then tried to fire through and over Monck's flagship.

Tromp's squadron again bore the brunt of this attack and with his flagship, the 80-gun *Hollandia*, dismasted after a collision he was forced to shift his flag. De Ruyter and Evertsen, who had so far seen little action, worked up into the wind and when both Monck and the Whites tacked back in a north-westerly direction to avoid the shoals, for they were now close to the Netherlands coast, he had the Dutch centre and van with their fresh ships closing up on either side. With de Ruyter to the windward and Tromp to the leeward, Monck's ships were

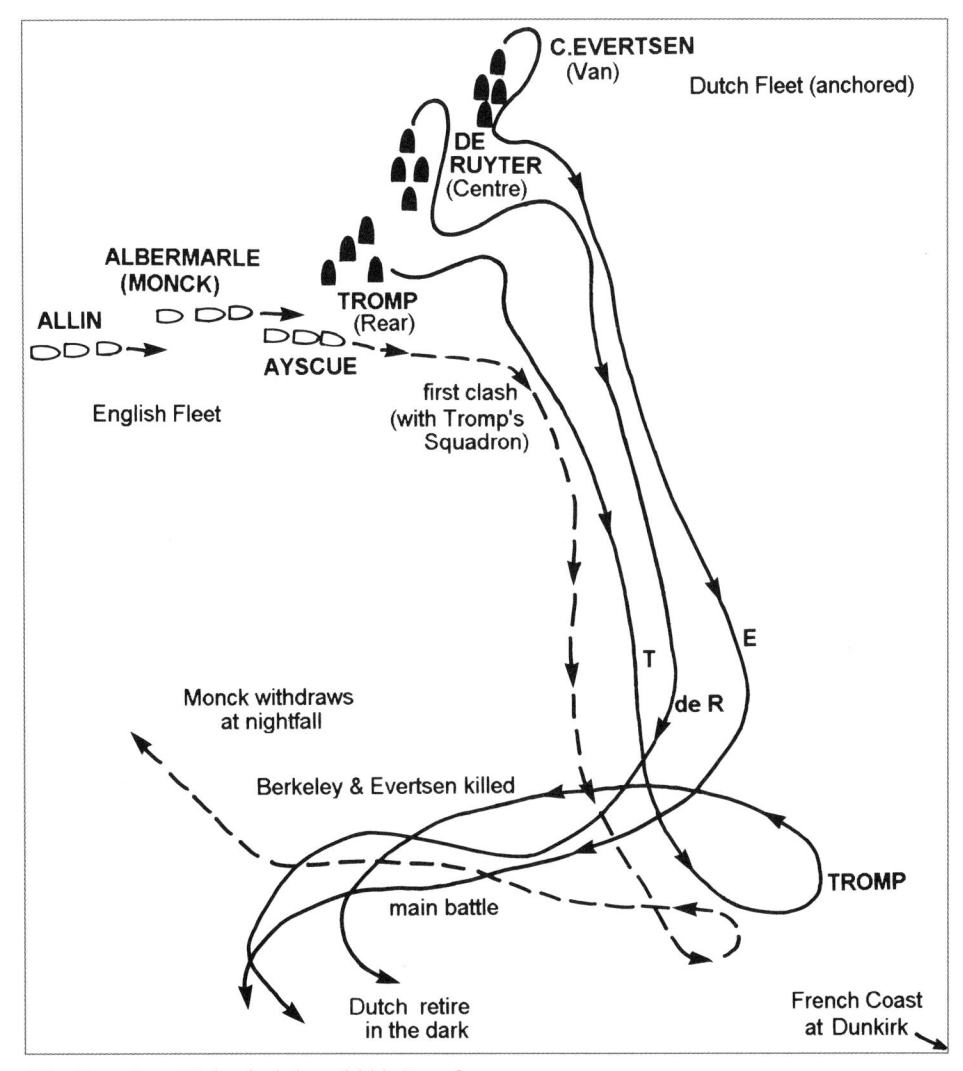

The Four-Day Fight, 1–4 June 1666. Day One

in the centre of the firing. In the mêlée which followed, Sir William Berkeley's *Swiftsure*, and two fourth-rates with her, the *Seven Oaks* and the *Loyal George*, were lost to the Dutch; although Berkeley fought like a man possessed to expunge the accusations of cowardice after Lowestoft. A Danish seaman fighting with the *Swiftsure*'s assailants describes Berkeley roaring his challenge to Andriansen the captain, 'You dogs! You rogues! Have you the heart then to press on board?' and firing broadside for broadside, until Andriansen let drop his foresail, grappled his victim, and led his men over the waist to cut the rigging to immobilise the ship.

The English, sheltering fore and aft, raked the waist with grapeshot but the Dutch overcame them. The living flung off their clothes as a signal of submission, the dead were piled up in heaps. Berkeley, shot through the throat, was unrecognisable for blood.[28] A more fortunate hero was Rear-Admiral John Harman in the *Henry*. He had managed to force his way clear of the mêlée but was badly mauled. One fireship after another had assailed him. Shaking off one fireship, another grappled and set the *Henry* alight, many of her crew leaping overboard, but Harman quelled the panic with brandished sword. As the fires were beaten out, her lower-deck guns sank a third fireship. Pinned to the deck by a fallen topsail yard Harman roared at Cornelis Evertsen who was offering him quarter, 'It's not come to that yet' and his gunners fired a broadside that killed Evertsen himself. Harman retired to Harwich, refitted during the night and rejoined the battle the following day. After his limping departure the fleets fought until they could no longer distinguish friend from enemy.

After a night of frenzied repair, they resumed battle, though Rupert still had not returned. Monck now had less than forty-five ships against the Dutch eighty, but he had the wind, pressed this advantage, and never let de Ruyter weather him. According to the Comte de Guiche, a gentleman volunteer on the Dutch side, 'the English fleet came back in admirable order; it advanced in line like an army, and when it approached, deployed and turned to bring its broadsides to bear'. At midday a frustrated Tromp in the rear broke ranks, abandoning the line, and tacked to get to windward to force direct combat. The van under Jan van Nes in the *Delft* stood further north, turning away from the English. Tromp was cut off and de Ruyter, to relieve him, signalled for his whole fleet to engage, then forced his way through the English line in a magnificent rescue. Tromp's ship was again so battered he came aboard the *Zeven Provincien*. Though the sailors cheered, de Ruyter roundly swore at his foolhardiness. Both commanders managed to rejoin their van and in some semblance of order again turned to the English though the *Zeven Provincien* had lost a mast, and Tromp shifted his flag once again, to the *Gouda*. (The English are said to have demanded 'Are there five or six Tromps with this fleet?')[29]

The third day still brought no sight of Rupert, though the anxious listeners in London believed the gunfire's resumption meant that he had at last arrived with his fresh ships. In fact, though Coventry had taken the Duke of York's orders to Arlington, to have them dispatched immediately by special messenger, his servants refused to wake him so the message went by ordinary post, and by the time it arrived the wind was fitful and Rupert could make little headway until the next day. With but thirty-four fighting ships left, the council of war resolved on withdrawal so Monck marshalled fifteen of his least damaged ships into line abreast at the rear as a bulwark to shelter the lamed ships home. The Dutch pursued but were unable to close in the light winds. An account otherwise critical of Monck's command here praises his personal bravery with everyone on deck issued with small arms 'to send a thousand deaths among those that should be bold enough to board him'.[30]

At 4 p.m. loud cheers resounded from ship to ship as Rupert's squadron at last appeared to the east. Monck ordered the fleet to close with Rupert, but the pilots,

The surrender of the Royal Prince *on the third day of the Four-Day Fight, by William van de Velde the Elder (Christies, London/Bridgeman Art Library, London)*

confused by all the changes of course during the fighting, ran three of the ships aground on the Galloper shoal. *The Royal Charles* and *Royal Katherine* came quickly off but the heavier *Royal Prince* was hard aground. Tromp bore down upon her with fireships, and though smaller English frigates closed up to defend her she struck her flag: so swiftly that Clifford expostulated, 'she yielded when she had not herself either shot ten guns in her defence or received ten shot from the enemy . . .' Van de Velde in his galliot sketched her as her ensign was lowered, a man at her main topgallant masthead hauling down Ayscue's flag as admiral of the White, boats ferrying her men prisoner to the *Gouda*. The Dutch next sent out twenty ships as bait to lure Rupert and his ships across the lurking shoal to engage them, hoping to ensnare the great ships but Monck, perceiving the tactic, sent a swift ketch to warn him off.

The Dutch now shifted clear of the shoals to gain more room, standing out in a north-easterly direction, but unable to refloat the *Prince* they left her burning. It was a far cry from that May day in 1660 when the king and his brother had dined in her great state cabin in the harbour at Scheveningen, the room wainscoted and gilded, furnished with linen fringed with gold, the silver plates piled high with roast beef, Obdam as their honoured guest. 'She was like a castle in the sea, and I believe the best ship that ever was built in the world to endure battering, but she is gone . . .' wrote Clifford. Sir George Ayscue and most of her 600 crew were taken prisoner, a lieutenant with sixteen men escaping in the longboat. When Rupert and his twenty-five ships arrived the two sides were at least evenly matched for all the Dutch ships had been battered over the previous three days whereas Rupert's were unscathed. The council of war decided to engage again on the following day. When day broke the Dutch could now only be seen from the topmast-head for they had sailed closer to their own coast. Once close to home, they took in sail and waited for the English to come up, the south-westerly wind giving them the weather gauge. The battle resumed about 8 a.m., the final day of the Four-Day Fight, and reading the accounts of the participants stresses the complexities of manoeuvring huge fleets across a large tract of sea choked by clouds of smoke as the fleets engaged in a deadly pavane.

Rupert's own account is brief, almost perfunctory. ('This is the plain matter of fact without descending to any particulars.') However, he emphasises the good order of his and Monck's squadrons as they tried to weather the Dutch during the five passes of the day. The Dutch for the most part, matching tactic for tactic, managed to keep most of their fleet to windward, until after the fourth pass, when several Dutch ships bore up to relieve others that had been caught to leeward. Rupert, with eight to ten frigates tacked a fifth time and at last got to windward of most of the Dutch fleet. With Monck in good order to their leeward, the Dutch were caught in the middle. Here their tactic of aiming at the rigging rather than the hulls reaped dividends, for even as Rupert's *Royal James* surged forward through the Dutch, most of her masts and rigging collapsed completely. Tromp would have shifted his flag and pressed his advantage but Rupert steered away, his squadron following suit. Monck's two accounts are little more detailed, reporting a day-long battle of pass, tack and pass again. In the first pass they were too far to the leeward to fire their guns, but in subsequent passes, 'we tacked and sailed towards the Dutch fleet and they towards us, in that tack we divided them into three or four parts and afterward we tacked and encountered again till seven or eight o'clock at night'. Yet in describing the battle as he does, Monck clearly demonstrates the development of manoeuvring a squadron as a whole. The squadron and the line of battle have become the tactical units, not the individual ships. As an earlier naval historian remarks: 'in it, for the first time, are we able to trace definite and effective tactical manoeuvring of squadrons. . . . Unavoidably did the lines become confused in the heat of battle, but they always proved capable of reforming.'[31]

Sir Thomas Clifford, on board the *Royal Charles*, praised the skill of the Dutch, able after each pass to form the line again 'with great art and dexterity'. He describes the turmoil of the last pass at about 5 p.m. Though the English succeeded then in dividing the Dutch fleet and were now chasing those to leeward, 'picking up some of their lame geese', de Ruyter leading those Dutch still to the windward immediately tacked and bore down on the English in turn and divided them, pouring the weight of their broadsides into Monck's ships before tacking again and falling upon the frigates to the rear of the squadron. Here, the *Essex* had tangled with the *Black Bull* which had just seized a Dutch

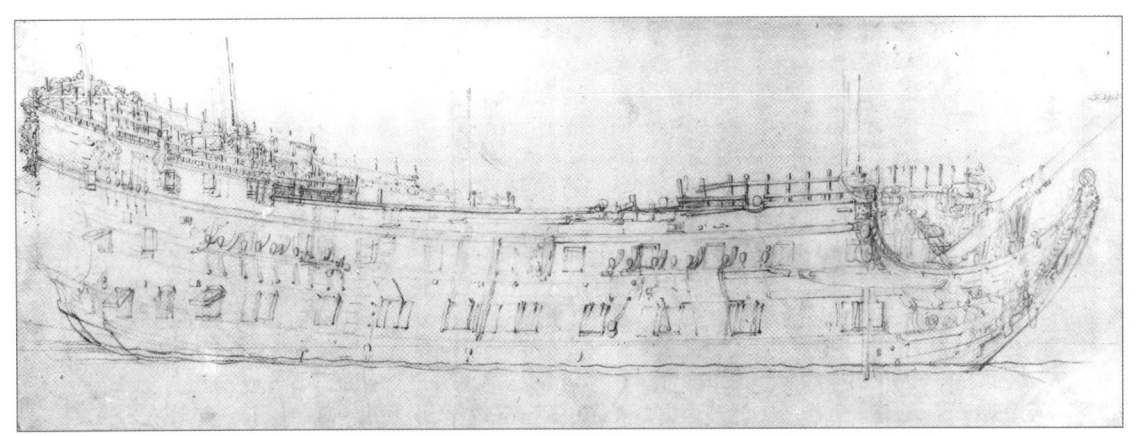

The damaged Swiftsure, *by William van de Velde the Elder (National Maritime Museum, Greenwich, London)*

ship, so tightly entangled they could not free themselves. The Dutch now took all three. Monck watched helplessly from the poop of the *Royal Charles*, unable to tack to their rescue because his main topmast was shot, his rigging shredded and the gunroom holed. He dared not tack until the holes were blocked, or the sea flooding in would have drowned his magazine, nor would his damaged foremast withstand the stress of the tack. The *Royal James* and Rupert's squadron having eased off to the north-west Monck bore after them and was able to take the *Royal James* in tow before de Ruyter could close on a new victim. By nightfall, with powder and shot almost spent and fog closing in, both sides stood for home and Barlow saw with relief that 'the Holens fleet made no great haste to follow us, being willing to leave off, having their bellies full as we'. When de Guiche went on board the flagship to congratulate de Ruyter, he found that austere republican sweeping out his cabin and feeding his chickens.[32]

John Daniel, a lieutenant wounded in the *Royal Charles* and sent ashore earlier that day, arrived on Pepys's doorstep with a fellow seaman. He was 'black as the chimney and covered with dirt, pitch and tar, and powder, and muffled with dirty clouts and his right eye stopped with oakum'. The two that evening told their version of the battle so far to the king himself. At least they had lived to tell the tale, and were given twenty gold pieces for it.[33] Monck put on a brave face, 'Never were men more willing than ours to engage again, nor enemy in a worse condition to receive us. They left us in the night and went homewards, having a much greater loss than ours.' No matter the boasts and bonfires most saw that this was not so. The English had lost two admirals killed and a third captured and four ships sunk or burned and six captured, including three third-rates against a Dutch loss of four ships. However, Monck had fought at heavy odds for three days and therefore should have been beaten or at the least, forced to retreat before Rupert could appear. One lesson Monck learned. The new Dutch great ships meant that the English could no longer count on winning at odds as in the past.

Hendrick van Minderhout and the van de Veldes repaired to their studios and began to paint the billowing sails, streaming pennants, carved and gilded sterns gleaming in the sun, men's heads bobbing like melons in the water. The *Swiftsure*, painted by van de Velde the elder and captioned 'the damaged *Swiftsure*', was refitted as the *Oudshoorn*, ready to fight against her former owners. The revellers celebrated with so many bonfires that Amsterdam seemed to be one entire fire. In some places effigies of the king, Monck and the Duke of York were set alight in tar barrels, that of the king made like a dog with a crown on his head. 'The lion's skin is sold. The Dutch must have England, the Danes Scotland and the French Ireland.'[34] The English told tales of Sir George Ayscue adorned with a tail and paraded for mockery through the streets of the Hague, and the body of Sir John Berkeley stuffed in a sugar chest. In fact Ayscue was escorted with much civility to Loevestein Castle and the Dutch embalmed the body of Sir John, laid it in honour in the Grote Kerk in the Hague, and then, saluting his bravery, sent it home to England.

CHAPTER 11
From Success to Humiliation

Battle at sea was quickly followed by quarrels on land. Monck claimed that he had never fought with worse officers in his life, that not above twenty of them had behaved as they should. His own conduct was heavily criticised, not least by the prejudiced Pepys: '. . . in his fighting at all – in his manner of fighting, running among them – in his retreat, and running the ships on ground – so as nothing can be worse spoken of'.[1] Most criticism centred around the decision to divide the fleet and the delay in recalling Rupert. Coventry made light of his decision to use the ordinary post, claiming that a special messenger would have lost so much time in fitting himself out that he would have arrived no sooner.[2] Clarendon scoffed at the excuse that Arlington's servants did not care to waken him. That would have been, he said, 'a tenderness not accustomed to be in the family of a secretary'. Edward Barlow, though he was reflecting years later and with hindsight, more ominously blamed the division on 'English papists and traitors . . . striving what they could to bring in a papist power'.[3] Pepys listened to the shifts of alliance as Monck singled out the protégés of Coventry and the Duke of York for blame and dismissal, in particular Jean-Baptiste du Teil, of the *Jersey*, who could speak so little English that he could scarcely give intelligible orders and was accused of firing more shots into English ships than Dutch. Coventry commended a captain whom Monck had put out and found fault with another whom Monck had kept on. One flag officer, Penn told Pepys, did not know which tack lost the wind or which kept it.[4] Rupert, remembering that fifth and final pass of the last battle, belatedly added to the *Fighting Instructions* that when a flagship was disabled the flag officer should shift his flag to another, 'that . . . his bearing away might not disorder his squadron'.[5] Though initially criticised, Teddiman was promoted admiral of the White. Holmes was confirmed as rear-admiral of the Red, but two of his rivals also gained promotion; Sir Jeremy Smith as admiral of the Blue and Sir Edward Spragge as his vice-admiral. The dead Sir Christopher Myngs could no longer fight for honours, but the sailors who had served him mobbed Coventry's coach at the funeral, imploring him to give them a fireship in the next battle with which to avenge his death.[6] Monck and Rupert remained as joint commanders; Allin in the White with Teddiman and Utber as vice- and rear-admirals; Jordan and Holmes vice- and rear-admirals of the Red; Sir Jeremy Smith commanded the Blue with Spragge and Kempthorne as vice- and rear-admirals.

The English fleet of eighty-nine ships included the newly-launched *Cambridge*,

Greenwich and *Warspite*, along with the *Loyal London*, at sea at last after much delay because all twenty-two of her 'cannon-of-seven' (the 42-pounders) burst at their proof trials. Clifford, looking at the fleet under sail and reckoning its length at 9 or 10 miles, confessed 'I was never more pleased with any sight in my life and there is a new air and vigour in every man's countenance . . . common men and all cry if we do not beat them now we shall never do it.'[7] The Dutch had eighty-eight ships, besides fireships and small craft. De Ruyter remained as commander-in-chief, while old Jan Evertsen, out of retirement and reinstated after Lowestoft, led the Zeeland squadron in the van. They had been at sea since 28 June, while the English ships were still being repaired at various points along the Thames, at Sheerness, Chatham and Harwich. One of the most startling aspects of these battles is the relative speed at which these ships could be repaired. The hulls themselves were very difficult to sink, and even severely damaged ships could be taken under tow back to port where the cannon-holes were soon plugged and new masts stepped. It is little wonder that men became emotionally involved with these ships which took so much punishment and yet struggled home and kept their crews alive. Barlow sailing once more in the *Monck*, sang the praises of his ship '. . . which deserves to be set in a ring of gold for the good services she has done, being a ship where I escaped many great dangers, and she shall have my good word so long as she is a ship'.[8] By 13 July the English fleet were ready to sail, but with the Dutch already off the Gunfleet, the fleet needed to emerge from the Thames estuary in a body or the Dutch would destroy it piecemeal. They anchored at the Middle Ground until a favourable tide and a westerly wind wafted them through the dangerous shoals into the Gunfleet on 22 July. The next day the fleet stood out to sea, drums beating, as the spectators on the shore watched them laying close to the wind, the more distant Dutch ships plying away in a southerly direction, till both fleets were out of sight. A storm struck on the night of 23 July and lightning which clove the *Jersey*'s mainmast from top to bottom. All next day the two fleets shadowed each other through a haze of dusky weather and rain, the wind in the north-east, both clapping on sail in an effort to draw ahead. The *Rainbow* and *Happy Return* were damaged in the tacking to gain advantage. Still the Dutch kept the wind and Arlington thought only their fear of fighting too close to the English coast saved the English from worse that day. 'The Dutch might have been upon us, if they had had metal in an hour, and at this time I assure your lordship our affairs looked with a scurvy face.'[9]

Both fleets anchored at night roughly 12 miles apart about 35 miles south-east of Orfordness. They weighed anchor at dawn, St James's Day, sails bellying out in a fine northerly, Allin in the *Royal James* leading the White squadron in the van, the Red squadron in the centre with Rupert and Monck on board the *Royal Charles* while Sir Jeremy Smith commanded the Blue in the rear. The Dutch fleet presented a crescent formation. Jan Evertsen in the van lay well ahead and to the windward of the centre and de Ruyter, while the rear under Cornelis Tromp lay astern, lagging well behind. James Pierce, the Surgeon General of the fleet, thought the resulting half moon was designed by them to avoid fireships, or to allow their van or rear by tacking to weather the English fleet. De Ruyter considered it simply poor management, especially by Tromp who sat too far

'The emblem of the King's ship called the Monk that was in the year 1666', a drawing by Edward Barlow (National Maritime Museum, Greenwich, London)

astern with his sails reefed and allowed the English to burst through the middle of the line.[10] The battle almost at once separated out into three, several encounters with the vans engaging at about 10 a.m. and the two centres an hour later, the rear squadrons not until noon. Svendsen, the Danish sailor on board the *Blaue Reiger*, remembered 'the wind quite dropped, so that both fleets clued up their sails and started firing against each other like it had been two castles. Thus it did not look like a naval fight, but more like murderous slaughter, because they scuttled each other . . .'[11] When the Dutch van opened fire the English responded with the flag of defiance, though some of Allin's squadron were still out of line when the battle began and fired through their own ships. The Dutch tactic of aiming high forced the *Royal Katherine*, the *Royal George*, the *Rupert* and then Robert Holmes in the *Henry* to lay by and send up fresh sails, but the superior fire-power of the English in a broadside duel told heavily too. Jan Evertsen was dead by early afternoon, his ship with command lost colliding and tangling with five others. Then with their two vice-admirals out of action, de Vries severely wounded and Coenders dead, the remainder of the van dropped their foresails and ran, in spite of de Ruyter furiously signalling them to stay. Allin pushed up so hard upon their rear, they could fire only their stern guns. That night the *Royal James* took two of their new ships; the *Snake*, 66, on her first voyage, with her yards and sails shot to pieces, and then Banckert's flagship, the *Tholen*, 60, badly shot and taking water. Banckert left her, her captain yielded. Her crew were taken off and she was fired. In the centre, the leviathans fought at musket-shot range. The *Royal Charles* was forced out for almost an hour to make and mend her shattered rigging, her place in the line taken by the *Royal Sovereign*. When the *Royal Charles* came back to the fray, she bore in so strongly that de Ruyter was forced to bear off, but she was soon so bereft of running rigging she had to be towed clear with longboats. By four, with the Dutch van already fled, their centre too began to give way and with these ships deserting the fight de Ruyter had to break off the action. There was no help from his rear, for though Tromp was to windward he held aloof. With his ships refusing to stand, de Ruyter signalled for van Nes to come on board who reproached his commander's anger and despair: 'I wish I were dead too, but one doesn't die just at the moment one wishes.' Then a cannon ball tore through the place where they had just been standing.[12] Yet though retreating, de Ruyter tacked back frequently to shepherd his maimed ships. One captain at least, despite his ship being badly disabled, could still demonstrate his skill in using the wind and tide to evade the pursuers. 'Like a very knowing seaman' he suddenly furled his sails and anchored. The English, caught unawares, swept past him.[13] Next day, 26 July, the Red and White squadrons kept chasing the main body of the Dutch, driving them like geese across the flats and banks until the great ships were compelled by the closeness of the shore to cry off the pursuit. Although the lighter frigates kept it up the Dutch sailed better in the light wind and slipped through the Durloo channel to anchor in safety in the Scheldt. The *Zeven Provincien* was by now dismasted and under tow. The battle had not been without its lighter moments: when the wind briefly dropped, the little sloop, *Fan Fan*, rowed up to de Ruyter's ship like a mouse against an elephant, firing broadsides with her two small guns, 'which was so pleasant a sight when no ship of either side could come near – there was so little wind – that all ours fell into a laughter, and I believe the Dutch into indignation to see their Admiral so chased'. Only when de Ruyter landed two or three shots 'between wind and water' did the *Fan Fan* prudently retire.[14]

The White and Red, baulked of their prey, stood out to sea again, and in mid-

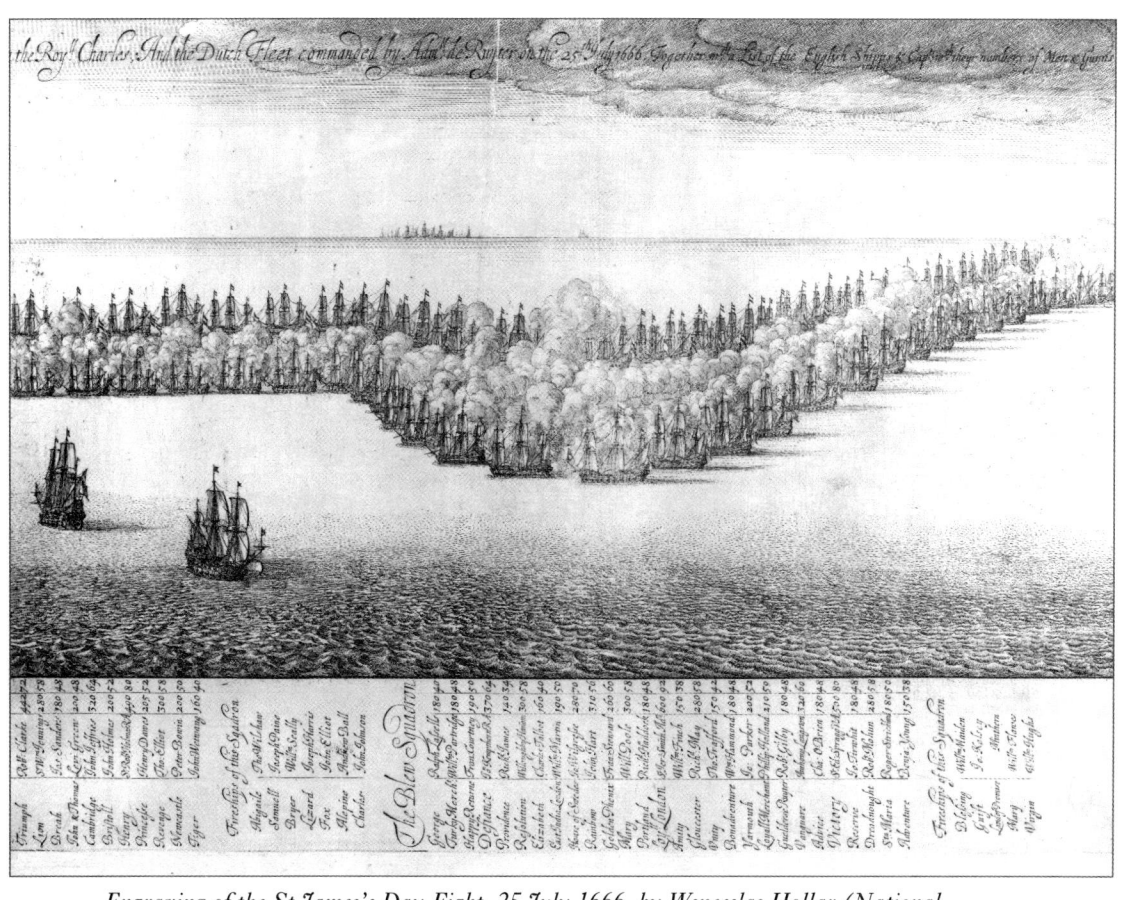

Engraving of the St James's Day Fight, 25 July 1666, by Wenceslas Hollar (National Maritime Museum, Greenwich, London)

afternoon sighted Tromp and the rump of the Dutch with the Blue to the windward chasing hard. Almost from the beginning of the fight the two rear squadrons had been fighting a separate battle well to the west. A number of heavy sailers in the Blue meant their swifter ships had a very hot time. A volunteer on board the *Royal Charles* recalled seeing them 'very far to the leeward and the Flag with many of his division all in a smoke intermixed with the Dutch colours, which confused fighting could not well please . . .'[15] Tromp was able to snatch the weather gauge and used it to send in a fireship to grapple the crippled *Resolution*. She shook free, but the fire itself had taken such a hold that her captain and his crew tumbled into boats sent by nearby ships. Kempthorne, leading the Blue, tried to save her by tacking about, with Jeremy Smith in the *Loyal London* and eight to ten ships following suit, but Smith could only get clear by having his ship towed round on the starboard tack. Both rear squadrons kept fighting to the westwards, and at an increasing distance from the rest of the fleet. When the wind shifted again into the south-west, the English snatched the advantage and Tromp retreated home. It was now that the Red and White squadrons sighted him. The generals gave order to tack and stand back toward the shore, to cut Tromp off, and about midnight Monck and Rupert anchored the *Royal Charles* to avoid being swept ashore by the tide. Clifford said they believed the same tide would bring the Dutch to them but the rest of the squadron, not hearing the warning signal, moved away. By 3 a.m. the tide had brought the Dutch to within cannon shot, but with few ships in support the *Royal Charles* dared not attack, and indeed might have been at the mercy of Tromp if he had closed. Nor was there sign of Smith and the Blue squadron. Warned by a pilot that they were too close in for safety he had stood off again. The next day, with the wind veering east to favour the Dutch, Tromp managed to slip past the English into the safety of the shoals. The Dutch had been 'beaten into their harbours' crowed an English report, and, forgetting the false bonfires in England in June, mocked their bells, bonfires, and boasts of victory. The Dutch, wrote another, 'must have thought that every oak in England was grown into a ship since the last battle'.[16]

Deciding to press their advantage, Rupert and Monck shifted to the *Royal James*, sent in the worst-damaged ships and held a council of war which debated how to take the war to the enemy beyond his defences of shoals and sandbars. A Dutch ship's captain who had quarrelled with de Ruyter treacherously betrayed his knowledge of the shoals and anchorages, the whereabouts of Dutch storehouses, and in particular the ill-guarded islands of Vlieland and Terschelling. Robert Holmes would lead a squadron of fifth- and sixth-rates and fireships and several companies of soldiers to raid, sink or burn any ships harbouring there, loot the storehouses, seize 'the better sort' of inhabitants for ransom and re-embark before the victorious sailors drank themselves silly or began killing the civilians. Holmes sailed with his detachment and anchored just 5 miles off-shore. The next morning, 9 August, a southerly carried them into the channel of the Vlie and there before him stretched a forest of ships and masts that would blaze more brightly than any forest fire once his fireships reached them. With the instincts of a true professional, Holmes recast the plans for what had been intended as a glancing coastal raid into the destruction of a large part of the Dutch merchant fleet, guarded only by two men-of-war. By the evening the merchantmen lay smouldering down to the waterline. The victors left on the flood tide, the tall towers of smoke and flame signalling their success to the waiting fleet. The next morning, unable to land on Vlieland because of the worsening weather, Holmes took eleven companies of men in longboats to Terschelling and marched into the town of Westerschelling 'very clean and sweetly kept' with gardens of vines and apple trees, and by now utterly deserted, so ripe for plunder that Holmes beat the drums for assembly in vain. He was compelled to fire the town to smoke them back to the waiting ships. The victorious Holmes could afford to relate his success with telling brevity: 'Our own loss was not very considerable, having not above twelve men killed and wounded. The number of the ships burnt I suppose to be between 150 and 160 sail.'[17] The Dutch estimated their losses at £1.25 million.

The English fleet could do no more. The crews had been on short rations since

2 August. They needed to return to Sole Bay to reprovision. By sunset of the 14th, Dunwich steeple lifted into sight, and the fleet came safe to anchor only to resume their customary quarrelling. Uncharitable eyes observed Charles Talbot 'walking the deck in his silk morning gown and powdered hair' on a ship which had lost no masts or sails.[18] Robert Holmes accused Sir Jeremy Smith, who had been promoted for his bravery at Lowestoft, of cowardice. Holmes claimed that Smith could have pursued Tromp more tenaciously and caught him before he reached the shoals. Monck defended his protégé, 'he had more men killed and hurt in his ship than in any of the fleet and his ship as it appears at present has received more shot'.[19] Smith laid a counter-charge and only intervention by the king prevented a duel. A later inquiry by the House of Commons cleared Holmes but although agreeing that Smith had yielded too easily to his pilot, his reputation survived and he was appointed vice-admiral under Sir Thomas Allin.[20] Though many of the accusations still reflected Civil War allegiances, the flag officers clearly lacked the sense of common purpose which nurtures group loyalty. Former Cromwellians had led the denunciations against Sandwich, Monck savaged his former colleague and protégé Penn. The contrast with the First Dutch War is glaring. 'The bitter feuding inevitably damaged the fleet's performance. It was hard for commanders to make sensible decisions when they knew colleagues and subordinates were waiting to denounce almost any course of action as either cowardly or rash.'[21]

The Dutch engaged in quarrels of their own. The Orangist Zeeland and Friesland squadrons had suffered most damage and their provincial deputies blamed de Ruyter. De Ruyter, the staunch republican, accused Tromp of gross irresponsibility, but when Tromp was banished to his country estate many attributed his disgrace to his allegiance to the Orangist cause. Van Ghent was appointed in his place and at least accepted by the men without the rioting and mutiny de Witt anticipated. Banckert replaced Jan Evertsen, with Cornelis Evertsen the younger as his vice-admiral. The French, according to the Venetian ambassador, were not displeased at the overall outcome, 'and that victory should alternate between the two parties is considered a piece of good fortune for this crown. That the Dutch do not always conquer will serve to keep them humble, and will prevent them from being the arbiters of the ocean, and that is what is wanted.'[22] De Ruyter was back at sea by 26 August, heading towards the Strait of Dover with a fleet of eighty ships to try to rendezvous with the elusive French, now at least as close as the Bay of Biscay. Monck and Rupert followed and soon after midday on the 31st sighted the Dutch just off Longsands Head. The English made towards them, assured by the pilots of a good depth of water, but almost at once the *Royal Charles* struck the Galloper sands and it took hours to refloat her.

The chase kept up throughout the night, in a hard gale, running past the coast near Calais to just south of Cap Gris Nez where de Ruyter tacked north, the English following. The next day, de Ruyter once again demonstrated his seamanship by using the shelter of the coast to bring his fleet into smoother water, while the English further out in the force of the gale had sails blowing to pieces and ships unable to answer the helm. Allin, unable to record in his journal ships taken or burned, gave battle honours to the wind. 'The *York* lost his mainmast about 5 o'clock and bore away, the *West Friesland* after him. The *Plymouth*'s two topsails flew away together and Sir Thomas Teddiman's fore topsail. Two their foresail and several others their topsails, all in half an hour. I never saw the like. We split two fore topsails that day, part of our main topsail, our mizzen.'[23] Holmes tried tacking, but de Ruyter tacked too, and Monck and Rupert abandoned the fight, the Red flag was lowered, and the fleet retired to St Helens Road. The gale now swooped on a large victim. In London in the first hours of 2 September, in a criss-cross of narrow alleys and cramped timber houses, a baker's house at the end of Thames Street near the Tower caught alight, and the wind which at sea had stopped two fleets from grappling cast the flames from Pudding Lane to the Leadenhall, then west to the Guildhall and St Paul's. Pepys watched the fire grow, the drops and flakes of fire raining down 'and as it grew darker, appeared more and more, and in corners and upon steeples and between churches and houses, as far as we could see up the hill of the City, in a most horrid malicious bloody flame'.[24] Charles rushed Monck from the fleet to direct the fire-fighting and keep order in the devastated city. For three days it raged, destroying 13,000 buildings and 87 parish churches, over 100,000 were homeless and the cost of rebuilding was reckoned at over £10 million. The Dutch, remembering Holmes's bonfire, called it a retribution from God.

The fleet with Rupert in sole command, patched and mended as best it could be, received news that the Duc de Beaufort with about forty ships had arrived in Dieppe and was starting out to meet the Dutch off Zeeland, so set out to intercept them. The French backed off at once, though six stragglers strayed into the path of Allin and the White squadron, who had anchored apart from the rest of the fleet to ride out a storm. One of them, the *Rubis*, mistook Allin's White flag for the colours of Beaufort and came in close. The English ships could not run out their lower guns but by tacking and firing what broadsides they could they soon compelled her to yield. The next day, Allin made for St Helens to rejoin the fleet. On 23 September fever compelled de Ruyter to go ashore to recuperate, handing over command to van Nes. At the next encounter, off Dover on 25 September, Rupert at once put out the flag for the fleet to draw into line, but in yet another rising gale went about to the westward and anchored; 'the violence of the weather was more dreadful than the appearance of the Dutch'.[25] The Dutch themselves disappeared to the south-east.

All that winter the bulk of the fleet lay at Chatham, the river freezing over two or three times. Barlow iced up with them grumbling more at the victuals, 'a little brown bread made of the worst of their wheat, and drinking a little small beer, which is as bad as water bewitched, or as the old saying is amongst us seamen – "Take a peck of malt and heave it overboard at London Bridge and let it wash or swim down the river of Thames as low as Gravesend, and then take it up."'[26] By now the disillusion with the war was complete. Less than a quarter of the seamen who returned with Rupert were paid and they rioted regularly between October and January. The warships lay at anchor unrepaired and unsupplied. Victuallers and contractors refused to supply except for ready money which was non-existent and unpaid dockyard workers refused to work. The chronic shortage of money led to unending cannibalism, for '... we have not credit left us for procuring lead for covering of a furnace, but have been forced to melt our very weights to answer that occasion with: For want of broom we are reduced at this day to the emptying our tar-cask for the getting their staves for firing and in want of resin for graving of ships are put to the paying them with pitch ...'[27] Parliament had become increasingly reluctant to supply the huge sums needed without accountability. 'They say that the king hath towards this war expressly thus much ... £5,590,000. The whole charge of the Navy, as we state it for two years and a month, hath been but £3,200,000. So what is become of all this sum [of] £2,390,000?' The king detested the scrutiny parliament demanded, not surprisingly, as Pepys heard a rumour in December that Charles had diverted £400,000 of this money to his personal use. The French navy may have been keeping well clear, but the locust horde of French privateers were relentlessly pillaging the merchant fleet so customs receipts fell even below the level of the previous year. With their trade languishing the merchants who had welcomed war now clamoured for peace. The excesses and corruption of the court sickened even royalists, 'A sad, vicious, negligent Court and all sober men there fearful of the ruin of the whole Kingdom this next year ...' wrote Pepys in his last entry for 1666.[28]

The Dutch, in spite of the devastation at the Vlie, kept on finding the money to fit out their fleet: Charles could not. Clarendon had often warned the king that 'the Dutch could endure being beaten longer than he could endure to beat them'.[29] By May, Charles had resolved to lay up the big ships and rely instead on frigates riding off the coasts to harass Dutch merchantmen and give early warning of the Dutch fleet. The first- and second-rates were to be towed well up the Medway, the naval bases fortified and the river below the main dockyard at Chatham guarded by shore batteries with a giant chain slung across the water, a naval Cerberus. The Dutch coming out, finding no fleet to attack and the coast itself too strongly fortified, would eat up all their supplies and go home empty-handed. That at least was the reasoning, though Coventry forecast 'we shall soon have enough of fighting in this new way'.[30]

Charles had decided to seek peace at Breda, relying on Louis to make his allies amenable and believing the Dutch would not prejudice the negotiations by further attacks. Far from being contained by the French, de Witt was preparing the Dutch fleet for sea. It would be, he said, 'the best plenipotentiary for peace', a strike which would force major concessions and secure an honourable treaty.[31] To achieve this and avenge the humiliation of Holmes's fireships, he planned a counter-raid. In 1664 he had sent a scout to inspect the approaches to Chatham and in October 1665 while his fleet blockaded the Thames, had repeated his earlier surveying exploits by going in a galliot to sound and chart the channels at the river mouth. Now that the English had laid up their great ships along the Medway was the time to pluck the fruit. He scoured the prisons for English seamen who would act as pilots or sailors. The colonel in charge of his newly formed marines was also English. The republican Thomas Dolman had served with the Dutch since the 1650s, had been a friend of both Monck and Cromwell, and helped negotiate the peace of 1654.[32] De Witt could not absent himself from

The Dutch raid on the Medway, by Romeyn de Hc (National Maritime Museum, Greenwich, London)

hester, op den 22 en 23 Junij A.º 1667

Breda so when the fleet sailed for the Essex coast on 7 June his older brother Cornelis sailed as plenipotentiary to press the assault in the face of the more reluctant admirals. For even de Ruyter flinched at the hazards of the proposal: the narrow winding Medway before them, the English squadrons out at sea who could return at any time and shut the gate behind them. Cornelis de Witt resolved his doubts with an alternative plan. The main fleet under de Ruyter in the *Zeven Provincien* would anchor at the river mouth, sending a smaller party to scout in Dover Strait to warn of any English return. Meanwhile a raiding party of seventeen smaller ships with four fireships and a number of yachts and galliots under van Ghent and a thousand soldiers under Colonel Dolman would strike along the River Thames at the West India merchantmen sheltering just below Gravesend. The English had not even removed the marker buoys. Though this initial foray was frustrated by a turning tide and falling wind, and the uncertainty over the preparedness of the defence, the Dutch had come determined to make more of a mark than a few barns burned on Canvey Island, or some sheep taken for provisions. Indeed de Ruyter had issued strict commands that landing parties were not to plunder private property and civilians despite the English behaviour at Terschelling. Jan de Witt had urged his brother to capture warships. Cornelis now persuaded van Ghent to attack the richest target of all: the ships anchored in the Medway and at Chatham Dockyard itself. Sheerness Fort, which guarded the approaches, was still only partly built, poorly garrisoned, and its sixteen guns so badly mounted as to be almost unserviceable. It was protected by a single frigate which fired only one broadside before retreating upriver in the face of a blazing fireship. When Dutch troops landed nearby, the gunners at the fort fled and the invaders hoisted their flag. Not until this day, 10 June, with Sheerness taken by the raiders the Dutch fleet itself pushing up the Thames towards Hope Reach, did the English admirals or the Navy Board begin to take action beyond sending and receiving letters and reports. News of the Dutch fleet's preparations to sail in late May had been dismissed as but a 'bravado'. A newsletter of 30 May had assured its readers that wherever the Dutch fleet landed 'we need not question but authority has an eye to their motion'.[33]

Monck at Gravesend further up the Thames found pitiful defences, as the fort on the Kent side had few guns ready mounted. Next morning (Tuesday 11 June) when he crossed to Chatham on the Medway, little better greeted him. Of the 800 men supposedly in the king's pay only a handful remained, and those too frightened to be manageable. The thirty boats he thought were there had been grabbed by panicky men to ferry away themselves and their goods. The resident commissioner, Peter Pett, had remained but he too had commandeered boats to rescue his ship models.[34] A chain had been stretched across the Medway at Gillingham, but it sagged so badly that most of it was well below water – or shallow Dutch keels. Three ships guarded it, but these apart, there were no defences and no resolute men. Monck had come attended 'with a great many idle lords and gentlemen, with their pistols and fooleries', thought Pepys; and their superfluity of orders and counter-orders soon did worse than their presence. Though Monck directed his soldiers to set up two shore batteries to cover the chain, they had no tools until they broke into the storehouses. He saw the weakness of the chain itself and ordered fireships sunk before it. Then when he checked the work on the batteries, he found instead of thick oaken planks to absorb the guns' recoil, only flimsy deals. The *Royal Charles*, whose great guns might have assisted the defence, lay an empty shell. 'There was neither sponge, ladle, powder, nor shot in her.' Monck ordered her to be taken further upriver the next tide but now Pett was too busy sinking more ships at the chain. In the morning she lay there still and by that evening the Dutch had snatched her. Two ships had been sunk at the chain but the much larger *Sancta Maria* had been caught by the ebbing tide as they brought her down, and ran aground uselessly rather than blocking the channel. The next morning the Dutch raiders began their push upriver. The narrowing of the channel forced the ships in line ahead, exposing the leaders to concentrated firing from the shore batteries and guardships at the chain, besides the broadsides from the two frigates covering the approaches, and the assault might well have faltered at this point but for the determination of one man to salvage his own reputation. Captain Jan van Brakel, under arrest for letting his men plunder the Isle of Sheppey two days before, persuaded de Witt to restore him to his command, the *Vrede*, undertaking to sail up to the chain, taking the brunt of the English fire, while the fireships under cover of smoke and confusion attempted to breach it.

Van Brakel sailed straight at the foremost guardship, withholding his fire until the last moment. One broadside from the Dutch, then the two ships ground together, the Dutch pouring aboard, while her patched-up crew of Thames watermen tumbled overboard to escape capture; the longboat guarding her to prevent them doing just that, slipped away at the *Vrede*'s approach. One of the Dutch fireships crashed through the chain as if it had been rotten string; then both fireships ran their flames into the other guardships until they exploded and burned. Every shot fired from the shore battery drove the wheels through the deal board, rendering its firing ineffectual. The English ships lay all along the reaches of the Medway 'like molting fowl, a weak and easy prey'.[35] The Dutch frigates coming up close behind poured their bombardment into the shore batteries. The *Monmouth*, lying just above the chain, was towed hastily further up into Upnor Reach. There was no one left aboard the *Royal Charles* to check the Dutch tide. A trumpeter signalled their triumph, sounding out the mocking notes of 'Joan's placket is torn'. Monck, watching in anguish from the shore, and dissuaded from rushing aboard to defend her to his death, gathered up the few men he could muster and retreated to Upnor Castle further up the Medway to strengthen its defences. He still hoped to save the great ships further up.

The victorious Dutch, halted only by the ebbing tide, met on board the *Royal Charles* and it was from her great cabin in mid-afternoon that Cornelis de Witt composed his detailed account of the success to the States General. Beyond the great ship lay even more possible prizes: *Royal Oak*, *Loyal London*, *Royal James* and Chatham Dockyard itself. Monck ordered all three ships run aground and then holed. By that afternoon the main Dutch fleet had moved to the entrance of the Medway and de Ruyter joined de Witt and van Ghent. By the following midday (Thursday) a body of fireships from the fleet, guarded by four frigates and numerous smaller craft, moved towards the great ships stranded below

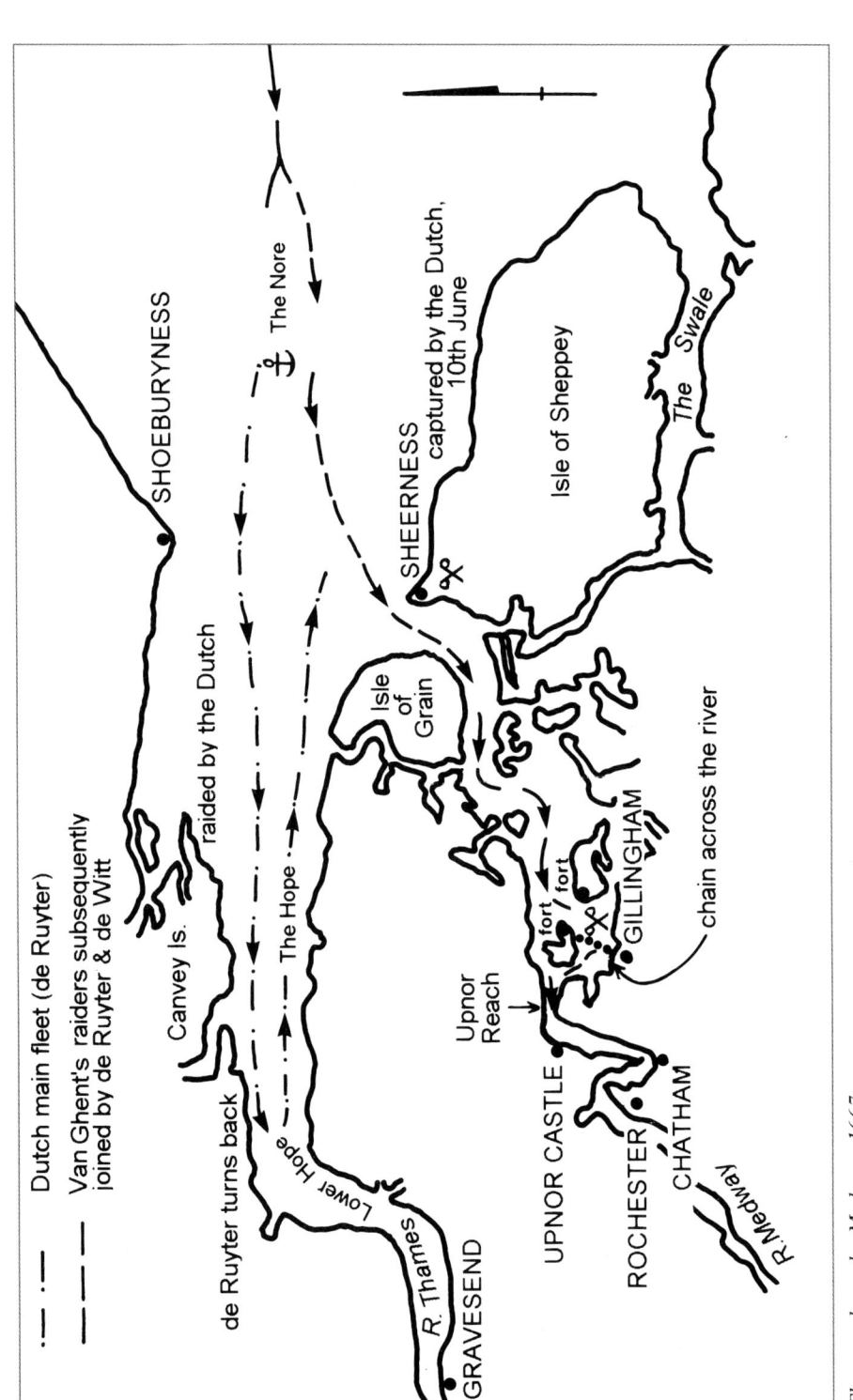

The assault on the Medway, 1667

Upnor Castle. The wind had died away, and with the leading ships now coming under fire from Upnor Castle and the batteries which Monk had managed to set up on the opposite bank, de Ruyter, de Witt and numbers of other commanding officers took to the river in longboats, to direct operations and exhort the men. The three great English ships had only been partially sunk, their demoralised crews having fled. Little wonder that de Ruyter is supposed to have told a fleeing English seaman who promised to guide the Dutch further up, 'If you are so brave a man as you have represented yourself to be, I will send you back again to your master the King, he has now occasion for such valiant men as you are.' One man alone remained on the *Royal Oak*, a Scottish captain, Archibald Douglas, who refused to desert the ship and died in her flames as she burned to the waterline. Monck with a handful of remnant volunteers did what they could to tow the remaining ships further up, others were deliberately beached along the reach to slow the progress of the Dutch as they passed into the range of the shore batteries guarding Chatham. But the Dutch went no further, and by late that afternoon, drew back down the Medway on the ebbing tide, those English sailors now fighting for the Dutch yelling out, 'We did heretofore fight for tickets; now we fight for dollars.'[36]

Edward Gregory, a clerk at Chatham, relayed the casualties to Pepys: 'I'll grapple with a fit of melancholy to answer your expectation. The *Royal Charles* with 32 brass guns in her, and the *Unity* were taken, the *Royal James*, *Loyal London*, *Royal Oak*, *Matthias*, *Charles V* and *Sancta Maria* were burnt, the *Marmaduke*, 5 fireships, 2 ketches, 1 flyboat and a dogger sunk . . . as to the enemies damage, he had 10 fireships burnt, one man-of-war . . . blown up by themselves, and one other great ship burnt also by themselves.'[37] As they withdrew they took the *Royal Charles*, handling her so skilfully that the dismayed watchers could only admire how she was heeled to one side to reduce her draught and slide her into deeper water, the Dutch firing her cannon in jubilation. Nor had they finished, for throughout all of July their ships raided at will up and down the estuary. De Ruyter sailed a squadron down the channel to alarm the merchant fleets and terrify the coastal towns, while van Nes kept the Thames closed. London swarmed like an ants' nest as a terrified people gathered their valuables and prepared to flee. John Evelyn, who went to Chatham to see for himself, wondered in dismay 'how triumphantly their whole fleet lay within the very mouth of the Thames, all from Northforeland, Margate, even to the Buoy of the Nore, a dreadful spectacle as ever any Englishmen saw and a dishonour never to be wiped off.' Sir William Batten cried, 'By God I think the Devil shits Dutchmen.'[38]

Charles ordered the peace negotiations concluded as quickly as possible and the treaty was signed on 31 July. The Dutch held Surinam and were allowed to import into England goods of their own, or from Germany and the South Netherlands. The English conceded the principle of 'Free Ship, Free Goods' save for weapons of war. The contentious matter of saluting the flag was rendered as 'in the British Seas, in the same manner as was used in former times'. The English retained New Amsterdam and New Netherland, both called New York, but these seemed far away and of little consequence. No bonfires burned and no

The Royal Charles *carried off by the Dutch, June 1667, by Ludolf Bakhuizen (National Maritime Museum, Greenwich, London)*

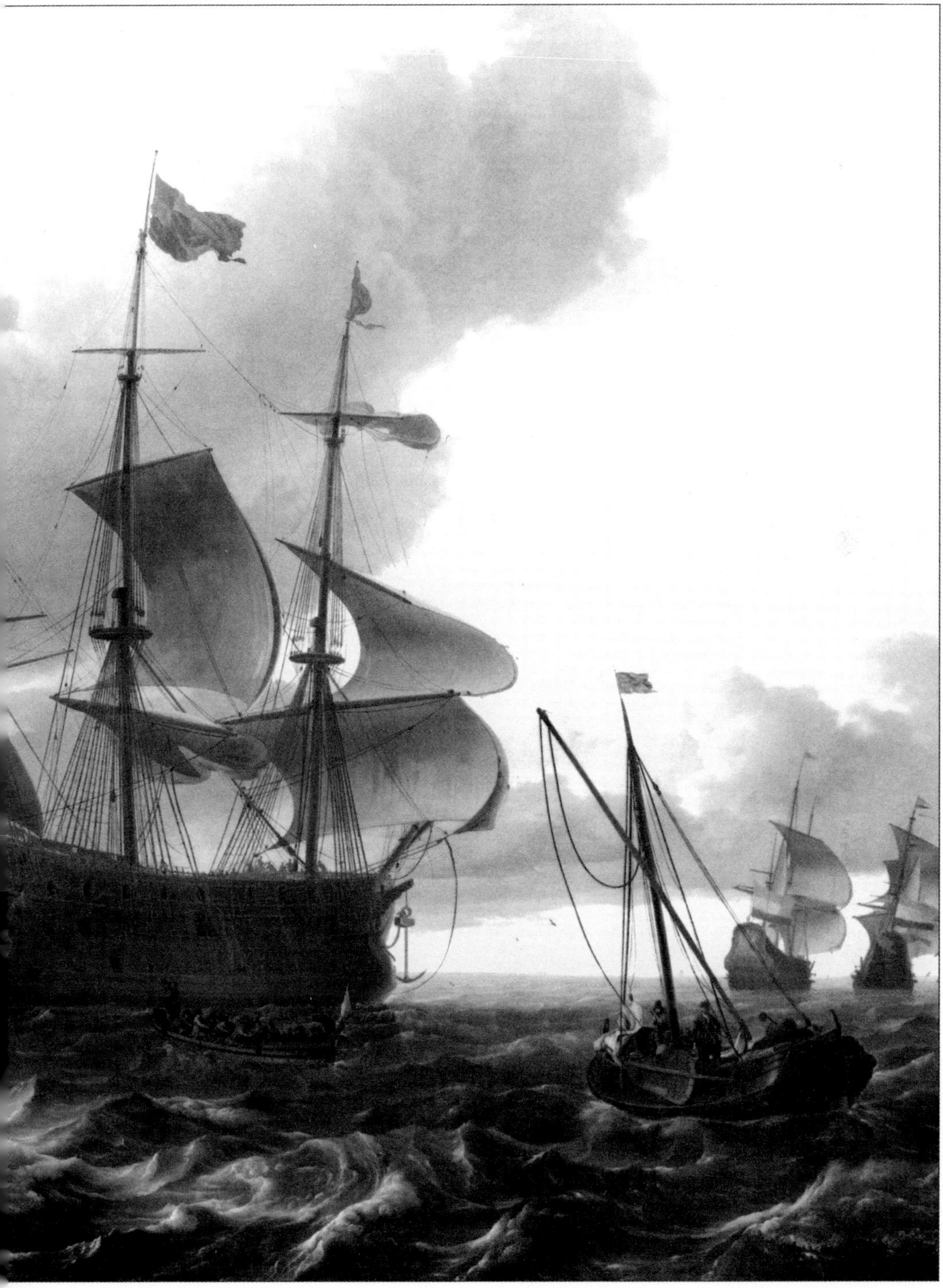

Cornelis de Witt as Victor of the Medway, by Jan de Baen (Rijksmuseum, Amsterdam)

one talked of the peace, 'but are silent in it, as of a thing they are ashamed of . . .'[39] The clamour and rage to blame and punish were permitted to fall on the king's chief minister, Clarendon, in the hope that such a spectacular scapegoat would absorb the wrath. He had never pushed for war, had so little notion of the sea that he did not know where Sheerness was, and his only idea when upon the river was to get back to shore as soon as possible. However, he had few friends, many enemies and was deeply unpopular, so Charles deserted him. Parliament impeached him on the grounds that he had blocked advice to his king and Clarendon had no choice but to flee abroad. His letter protesting his innocence was ordered to be burned by the hangman.[40] The *Royal Charles* lay in exile too, though the husband of the king's mistress argued that a ship built for Oliver Cromwell (as *Naseby*) was doomed to such a fate. No doubt many reflected in discreet silence that had Cromwell been alive England would have been spared this humiliation.

The navy itself became the subject of scrutiny by parliament in October, and a frenzied round of wound-tearing began. Sir Robert Holmes again aired his fury at both his old rival, Harman, and Henry Brouncker (the two closely linked to the Duke of York); Coventry denigrated Monck's conduct at Chatham, and savaged Sir Edward Spragge while Spragge blamed Coventry's administration for the shortage of sailors. Rupert blamed naval maladministration and the dockyards. Monck focused on the débâcle of Chatham. Rupert and Monck then turned on Penn and Sandwich and the earlier prize goods scandal. Sea officers and administrators alike settled old scores and advanced their own prospects; while across the channel, a painting of Cornelis de Witt, crowned with laurel as victor of the Medway, hung in Dordrecht Town Hall and de Ruyter was fêted and celebrated; the republic triumphant.[41]

CHAPTER 12
A Conspiracy of Princes

> Surely this was a quarrel slenderly grounded, and not becoming Christian neighbours, and of religion, and we are like to thrive accordingly.[1]
>
> John Evelyn

Outwardly the Peace seemed a success, especially as Jan de Witt was able to negotiate a further agreement with England six months later against a threat from his former ally Louis XIV. Since 1663 French territorial ambition had increasingly centred on the Low Countries as the crumbling Spanish empire withdrew its forces from the region. In April 1667, the French invaded the Spanish Netherlands, a move as threatening to England's interests as it was to the Dutch, given that the French army was now the most powerful in Europe. A third major Protestant power, Sweden, joined them in an armed coalition, the Triple Alliance signed in May 1668. Louis, forced to halt his armies, turned instead towards annihilating the interfering Dutch; to strip the sails of this alliance and isolate de Witt. The way lay through his cousin, Charles II.

The Dutch war's crippling effect on English maritime trade had severely eroded the crown's ordinary revenue and Charles had no hope of convincing parliament to grant the funds necessary to renew the fight. Louis bribed him with a large cash payment, sufficient to pay for a knock-out strike, to circumvent the necessity of summoning parliament. In return Charles agreed to assist in the French invasion of the Netherlands which they planned to carve up between them; two royal crowns and ancient kingdoms against an upstart republic of merchants. While Louis stormed overland from the south and east, a combined English and French battle fleet, having crushed the Dutch at sea, would land troops to link with Louis's army. This secret treaty was signed at Dover in May 1670; secret because parliament had already voted Charles money to spend on the Triple Alliance and secret because parliament was instinctively suspicious of Catholic France and their monarch's admiration of it, 'they saw popery and slavery lay at the bottom'.[2] This perception was acute. By two further, still more secret clauses (only known to his Catholic ministers) Charles agreed to suspending the penal laws against 'nonconformists' (which included Catholics) and to announce his own conversion at some unspecified future time. This was a secret within a secret. He was encouraged to take this dangerous road by Sir Thomas Clifford, now Treasurer of the Household, and the Duke of York, both intent on increasing the power of the crown and debilitating parliament

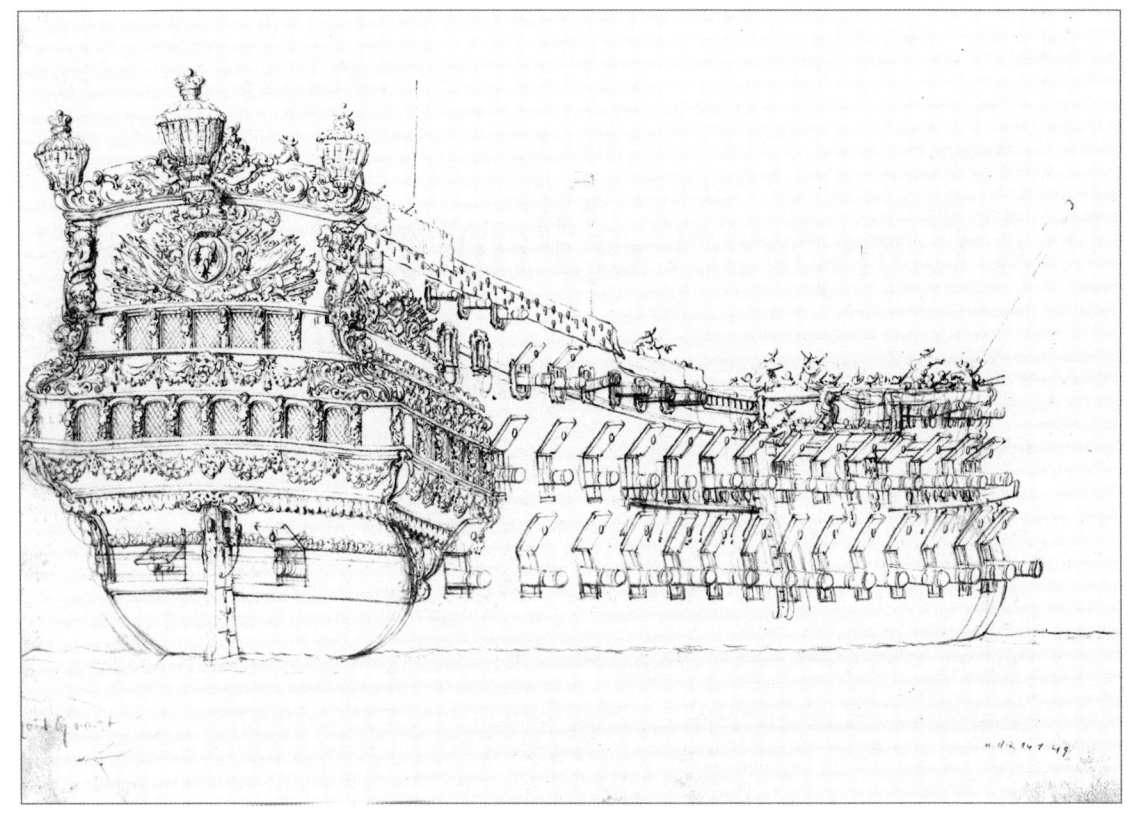

The French 70-gun Superbe *by Van de Velde (National Maritime Museum, Greenwich, London)*

while strengthening ties with the Bourbon monarchy they dreamed of emulating.[3] No powerful merchant groups lobbied for this war, Charles had few genuine pretexts and they were feeble. The public display of the captured *Royal Charles* at Helvoetsluys was offensive. He made what he could over the grumblings of East India planters. He took care to recall Sir William Temple, the envoy who had negotiated the peace, a champion of Dutch toleration and freedom. Next he claimed the Dutch fleet outraged his sovereignty of the seas. In August 1671 the royal yacht *Merlin*, taking Temple's wife back to England, passed by the Dutch fleet in the North Sea. De Ruyter took the gun shot from this cockleshell for a salute, and answered the courtesy. Van Ghent, who knew Lady Temple well, went on board to greet her, but also to enquire why shot and not merely powder had been fired. Her captain demanded the entire fleet strike their flags to his 6-gun vessel. He was in no position to enforce it although one source claims he had been instructed to seek out the Dutch, pick this quarrel and try to shoot down de Ruyter's flag. The king in a fury that both sides had robbed him of his excuse for war by parting with courtesies clapped him in the Tower and sent that Dutch-hater Sir George Downing to replace Temple. Small wonder that Dutch merchants in English harbours were said to keep watch 'with matches lighted and in a fighting posture'.[4]

What better way to begin a war than have Sir Robert Holmes attack the Smyrna convoy when it refused to strike flag? They met off the Isle of Wight on 13 March 1672, but the well-armed merchantmen fought back, and '. . . we received little save blows, and a worthy reproach', wrote Evelyn.[5] Nevertheless it served Charles's purpose. With Louis's subsidy he had as yet no need to summon parliament and by the end of the month both England and France had declared war on the United Provinces. The well-bribed Swedes remained neutral. Those who insisted on the link between popery and arbitrary government had their fears confirmed by two other closely linked events. First, Charles accepted Clifford's expedient to stave off bankruptcy by proclaiming the 'Stop of the Exchequer' on 2 January, whereby he suspended his payment of interest on bankers' loans for twelve months, a move which outraged the financiers and merchants. Then two days before war was declared Charles bypassed parliamentary statute, and by his own Declaration of Indulgence granted toleration of worship to nonconformists. 'Many persons have said that the King, having undertaken the war without notifying Parliament, and decided arbitrarily concerning religion', observed the Venetian secretary, 'it was evident that he intended to destroy the authority of that assembly.'[6]

The French under the supervision of Louis's chief minister, Jean-Baptiste Colbert, had amassed a formidable navy. By 1666 their then allies the Dutch had built them six new men-of-war of about 74 guns apiece ('which they would do for any other prince for money, making shipping a trade rather than a secret', said Pepys.) Then in 1668 the French began building six massive three-deckers at Toulon and Brest using Dutch and Venetian shipwrights. By the early 1670s twenty more ships of 60 to 80 guns had joined the fleet. The Dutch had launched no new great ship since 1667. In England, the destruction in the Medway and the determination to match the rapid French naval expansion saw three new 100-gun ships launched between 1670 and 1673; the *Prince*, the *Royal James* and the *Royal Charles*. Four slightly smaller three-deckers of 90 to 96 guns were also completed by 1670; the *St Michael*, the *St Andrew* and the *Charles*. The combined English and French fleets numbered seventy-four ships of 40 guns or more, the Dutch sixty-two, giving the former a seven to six superiority in ships and six to five in guns.[7] At the end of 1665, Louis had reckoned that any Dutch defeat or major threat to their territory would bring about the collapse of de Witt's republican government and usher in the House of Orange. His prediction began to come true early in 1672. Prince William III, now close to his legal majority had become an alternative focus of power and the States General voted him captain and admiral-general for life; though de Ruyter and Cornelis de Witt as States General plenipotentiary retained daily charge of the fleet. In spite of knowing themselves heavily outmatched these experienced men decided they must attack before the English and French fleets combined. Once again the pilots swore there was not enough draught in the Slenk to get the ships through, once again Jan de Witt sat in a boat at the Spaniard's Gate and plumbed the depth to prove them wrong, though the rough weather held the ships in until the very end of April. Then the Zeeland authorities, fearing an attack by an invasion fleet, refused to let their division sail from Flushing before they heard that de Ruyter had left the Texel, and he was obliged to sail down to meet it. The Dutch arrived too late off the North Foreland. The English had left the Nore for the Isle of Wight, meeting the French on 7 May at St Helens.

The Duke of York was again in command for Monck had died in 1670 and the French were readier to accept overall command from the heir to the throne rather than the Protestant Rupert. The Comte d'Estrées acted as second in command, his thirty ships to be the White squadron. Within the fleet all the factional jealousies had been reignited by the poor showing of Holmes over the Smyrna convoy. His detractors blamed it on his jealousy of Sir Edward Spragge; for Spragge had been close by on 10 March, returning from Algiers, and could have been summoned to help – but as senior officer he would then have assumed command. Holmes loathed him and, his accusers said, wanted the glory and all the prize money for himself and his squadron. Had the two squadrons combined the convoy could hardly have escaped. Sandwich had returned as rear-admiral though he was opposed to the war and knew that his caution in the 1665 campaign had damaged his standing. 'I must do I know not what to save my reputation', he told Evelyn who had come to farewell him. Somebody recalled the gouty and now unwieldy admiral, leaning on two young men for support, and foretelling their death and his own.[8] While the combined fleet laboured back up the Channel against adverse winds, Jan de Witt urged a pre-emptive raid against a small squadron still in the Thames. Van Ghent obliged as far as Sheerness but finding the fort more strongly fortified since 1667 backed off and the Dutch withdrew. On 19 May, a hazy Sunday morning, the scouts fired signal guns and let fly their top-gallant sails as they raced in with sightings of the Dutch. Hampered by the raw and unpractised French squadron it was late afternoon before the allies came within range. Conditions could not have been better, they were to windward, the water smooth enough to run out the lowest guns. De Ruyter had also counted the odds and by 7 p.m., with darkness gathering in, brought into play the shoals and banks off Nieuport and Ostend. If he had to fight downwind he would do so along his own coast and on his own terms. Throughout the night the English shadowed them, close enough in the faint light of a young moon for John Narborough, second captain on the *Prince*, to see their hulls 'and hear the shot sing as they flew past our ships', the Dutch appearing and disappearing in brief clearings of fog with muffled musket fire, ringing bells and beating drums. The haze lifted during the following morning and the Dutch shimmered back, but de Ruyter tacked away toward the coast, refusing to engage with the wind against him and determined to draw closer to the shoals. With the wind now blowing hard and the seas too rough to run out the lower guns, the duke signalled to turn northward and anchor for the night.[9] The following day, 21 May, with not a Dutch sail in sight, the fleet returned to Sole Bay to take on provisions and fresh water. The duke insisted they ride unmoored 'to be the sooner ready in case we should be alarmed by the enemy'. For all the *qui vive*,

Dockyard model of the St Michael *(National Maritime Museum, Greenwich, London)*

they were caught napping, though Narborough in his journal records the comings and goings of the scouts, writing on 26 May, 'keeping a good watch, for I expect the enemy will be with us in a morning, if the wind hang easterly'. An east wind was a Dutch wind. Yet if Narborough was alert, the fleet was ill-disposed. The three squadrons were strung out along the coast, the French who were to be the van to the south, between Dunwich and Aldeburgh, the rear under Sandwich to the north. With the wind in the east it was also a lee shore. With extraordinary insouciance Captain Cox ordered that his *Prince* be careened and at first light the men set to work shifting the ballast to tilt her. Other ships were still provisioning, many of their crews ashore in the ale houses. De Ruyter, meanwhile, was prowling closer. Having seized a collier he knew more about his enemy than they did of him and had conceived a plan to offset their superior numbers. He took six ships and six fireships from each of the three squadrons, and formed these into a spearhead commanded by the fiery van Brakel. A French scout spotted them as they moved in from the north-east. It was as well for the English that the wind began to die away, giving them some time to right the *Prince* and beat the drum for the shore parties.

Sandwich, at the north of the fleet, was closest to the Dutch. With the wind east by south and his ships' heads lying northwards in the flood tide, he sortied on a starboard tack for had he paid off on the port tack he risked running foul of the centre squadron. The duke followed as soon as the *Prince* could be got under way. Given the situation James had decided to reverse the normal order of the fleet: but without signalling his intentions. Lacking fresh orders d'Estrées to the south led his squadron off in a south-easterly direction to get into a position from which they could lead the fleet. When he had sent for commands the duke replied only 'that he desired he would keep his wind as much as he could'. The Zeeland squadron under Banckert, their southernmost squadron, peeled away to follow d'Estrées and by pressing the French away from the main action successfully reduced the odds against de Ruyter.

Sandwich had come out in considerable disorder. The smaller ships – the fourth-rates and fireships – almost becalmed closer to the shore could not get out so quickly and his larger ships were slow in getting into line, so the *Royal James* was to the windward of the rest of Sandwich's squadron and soon deep among the enemy. The Dutch had caught them ill-prepared and could use the wind to fight in the way they liked best, by mêlée and surrounding the trophy flagships. It was now 7 a.m. Van Brakel, one of the advance squadron, then van Ghent and his seconds followed by two fireships cornered the *Royal James*. Sandwich sent out urgently for help, a light pinnace to the ships astern; a barge ahead to Sir Joseph Jordan; but the pinnace never returned, and though Jordan tacked and got to windward of the Dutch he kept moving south and, said Richard Haddock, 'passes by us to windward very unkindly' and took no notice of them. Jordan later claimed he had his hands full. He had weathered the Dutch only to find himself contending with van Ghent's squadron, who were striving to recover the wind; and 'in this smoke and hurry we could not well discern what was done to leeward; but sometimes saw the enemy battering at our fleet, and ours at them'. Nor was there help for Sandwich from his own rear-admiral. Sir John Kempthorne, in the *St Andrew*, passed to leeward with the Dutch division assailing him.

The burning of the Royal James *at the battle of Sole Bay, May 1672, by William van de Velde the Younger (National Maritime Museum, Greenwich, London)*

It was as perfect a summer day as could be, the sea 'smooth as a bowl of milk', wrote Narborough, then again, as if to emphasise the contrast with the horror, 'the sea was all day as smooth as a fish-pond, and the day very hot and fair sunshine, the fairest day we have seen all this summer before'. In the light wind the dense pall of smoke clung about the ships so that each one seemed to be islanded, isolated, remote from their fellows, and when the murk shifted briefly they found it impossible to distinguish friend or foe. When Kempthorne caught a glimpse of the *Royal James*, he saw a ship by her boards but thought it was one of their own; and for most of the day he fought 'not seeing any flag beside our own, in regard of the constant firing and great smoke standing still to the northwards . . .' When Sandwich farewelled Evelyn he had said, 'they will not have me live'. Now to his flag captain he said 'we must do our best to defend ourselves alone'.[10] They could not do it. Though they had beaten off the fireships, the ship had been eaten out with shot by van Brakel, and after by van Ghent and his ships. Then van Brakel rammed the 60-gun *Groot Hollandia* aboard under her bowsprit, using the

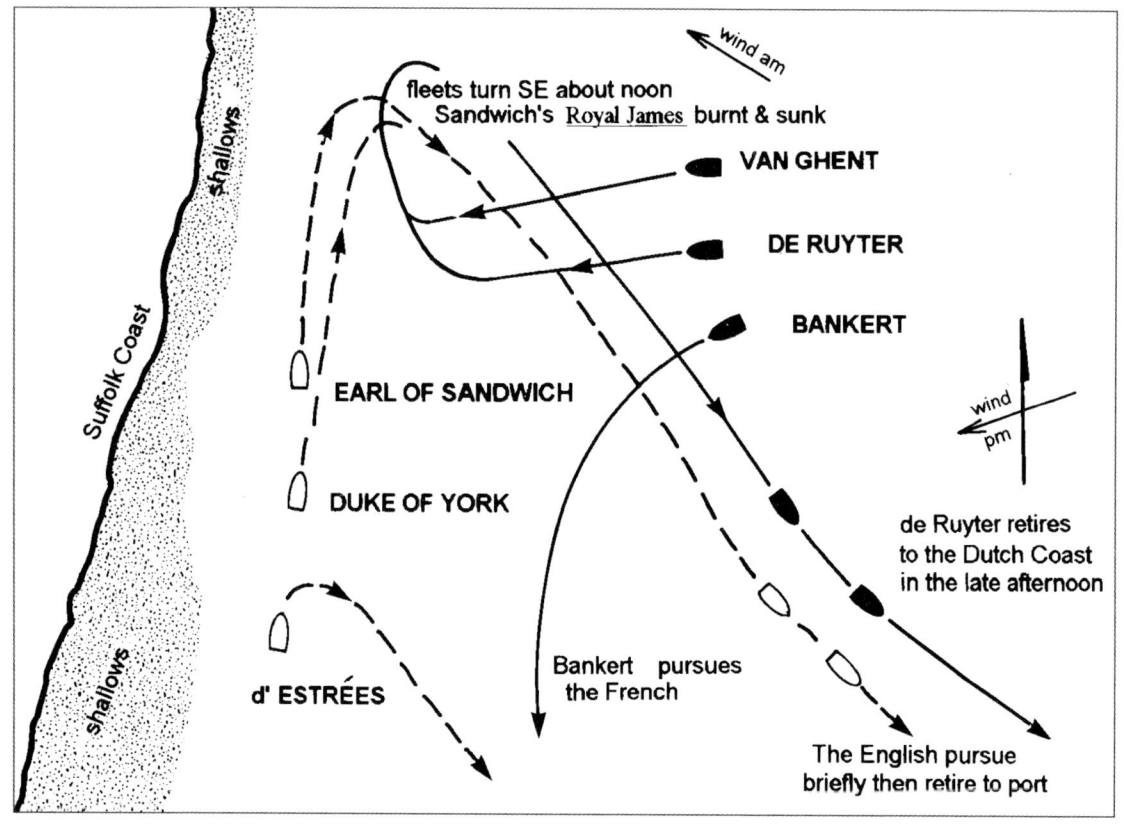

The battle of Sole Bay, 28 May 1672

force of the flood tide to lock her close, out of reach of any broadside. With 300 men already killed or wounded, the guns on the upper deck silent with dead crews beside them, they were too few to board and still have enough to repel boarders in return. The rain of musket shot, said one witness, made the sea boil as though filled with whales. Van Ghent loomed up to reinforce van Brakel but the wind would not bring the *Dolfijn* under the English stern and caught in the fire of the lower guns van Ghent himself was killed. Haddock, shot in the foot and on his way below saw with relief that the flood tide was done: now if they anchored by the stern, the ebb would bear the *Hollandia* away. A wrecker's yard of fallen rigging still bound the two ships so at his order a raiding party swarmed briefly aboard the Dutch ship to hack it loose. Haddock, even while the surgeon attended him, next sent orders to cut the cable and allow the ship to bear up. However, Sweers in the *Olifant* came up with a fireship which grappled and set the *Royal James* alight. The glare of her burning leaps at us still from van de Velde's painting.[11] Remarkably, among the few of the *Royal James*'s crew who managed to escape was her injured but indomitable captain.

In the centre the *Prince* too had been fighting for most of the morning in her own pool of smoke and death against at least seven Dutch ships, thought John Narborough, with de Ruyter in the *Zeven Provincien* on their quarter and van Nes in the *Eendracht* a musket shot off their bow. 'We being all alone made it the warmer with us; none of our squadron could get up with us for their lives, they being so becalmed.' Nevertheless the heavy guns of the *Prince* kept firing, the duke urging his quartermaster to luff her still closer to the enemy. By midday Cox, her captain, had been killed, and the main topmast had crashed down, the ship so entangled with broken wood and rigging that they could not keep her to the wind, nor use the guns on the upper deck, nor send men aloft into the hail of shot. Through the smoke and chaos they saw two fireships being towed towards them. Their own fireships lay useless astern, one burning, the other sinking but Narborough, *Prince*'s new captain, got two boats launched to tow her northward towards the rest of their squadron and greater safety. However, the *Prince* could fight no more so the duke shifted his flag aboard Robert Holmes's *St Michael*. Though it scarcely flapped in the still air to signal the change, the Dutch dropped on him like a swarm of bees. A flag lieutenant from the *Royal James*, plucked from the sea by the *Zeven Provincien*, begged de Ruyter to let him stay on deck and marvelled at the tactics: 'Sir, is this fighting? It is not yet noon and there is more done already than in all the Four Days in 1666.'[12] By midday, with the tide pushing them ahead and wind backing east-north-east, the northern squadrons of both fleets were forced onto the port tack to avoid the Red Sand shoals off Lowestoft, and as they went about van Nes bore down on the 82-gun *Royal Katherine*, capturing her and removing her officers. Here a weakness of the mêlée tactics worked in her favour. A badly disabled ship cannot readily be worked up to windward to join the fleet which has captured her. When her crew herded below decks began to shout 'The ship sinks!' the Dutch released the crew to help save her which indeed they did by overmastering their captors.[13] Both fleets were now fighting back along the coast in a southerly direction. In mid-afternoon the *Prince*, rigged with makeshift sails, came upon the smouldering hull of the *Royal James*, her survivors clinging to a litter of scorched yards and booms which spread like driftwood around her. The Earl of Sandwich was not among them. Both fleets were now fighting in a series of ragged parallels. The *St Michael*, pounded between two lines of Dutch ships, began to ship so much water that the duke again shifted to Spragge's *London*. The number of crippled ships grew; the *Resolution*, the *Cambridge*, the *Royal Katherine*, the *Henry* with her captain dead and 'scarce a rope in her', and the *Phoenix* with no cartridges left nor paper to make any. Only the weight of Sir Joseph Jordan's division bearing on de Ruyter's saved them from worse. Late in the afternoon William van de Velde the elder labelled part of his drawing 'My galliot trying to luff to be out of the way of the work.'[14] About sunset, seeing the Zeeland squadron coming up from their fight with the French, de Ruyter signalled his ships to join them. So ended the battle of Sole Bay, for though the council of war on board the *Prince* decided to stay at sea with those ships still seaworthy dense fog succeeded by a rising gale compelled both sides to abandon the fight. The Dutch had lost the *Stavoren*, 48 and *Josua*, 54 but they had destroyed the 100-gun *Royal James* and sent a superior fleet back to their ports so battered they would lose a month of the campaigning season refitting it. Ten days after the battle the crew of a ketch casting around for lost anchors found the body of Sandwich. There had been, the men said, many porpoises about him.[15]

What were the reasons for such a humiliating reversal? Full honours go to the tactics of de Ruyter who had practised manoeuvres in the North Sea in the summer of 1671 with most of his flag officers. In the English fleet, there had been a marked break in the continuity of senior officers. With James at sea, Rupert controlled admiralty business ashore, Sir Thomas Allin and Sir Jeremy Smith had been appointed to the Navy Board, and Sir George Ayscue had just died. While ten of the fourteen Dutch flag officers had been in the same squadrons in 1666, only four of the nine English flag officers had served in that rank on St James's Day. James preferred gentleman officers even though inexperienced. The Earl of Ossory, for example, was given command of a third-rate early in 1672 after only a few months' experience as a volunteer. Samuel Pepys thought that their opponents 'cannot be offered a greater advantage than that of our meeting them with landmen in the head of our fleets'.[16] Their growing numbers rankled among the tarpaulins, contemptuous to see 'so many green fellows' who had scarce seen salt water preferred as lieutenants. Most criticism, however, was levelled at the seasoned Sir Joseph Jordan and his apparent failure to help Sandwich. His appointment as vice-admiral of James's own squadron shortly after did not quieten those who saw the earl's death as 'a sacrifice to faction'. Richard Haddock had his own small revenge. He commissioned a painting from William van de Velde of the *Royal James* with the union jack at the foremast forever signalling for the van of the squadron to tack as a reminder of Jordan's unkindness. One ghost at least had vanished in this war. Factional strife remained bitter but it no longer sprang from Interregnum rivalries. Nobody questioned the loyalty of former Interregnum officers.[17] The French claimed that Banckert's squadron, despite being to windward, had refused to engage closely. Only the French *Superbe* was badly damaged but their engagement had been fiercer than a mere skirmish, 450 casualties as against 340 for the Dutch squadron. Official accounts said nothing against the French, but public opinion certainly did, and a correspondent reporting to Holland noted '. . . the daily graving jealousy against the French, which the king must dissemble against his will', least he be reproached for having too hastily engaged himself. The Danish envoy said succinctly, 'this union is not destined to last long'.[18]

In the Netherlands all was turmoil. During early June Louis's army of over 100,000 had overrun four out of the seven provinces and Holland and Zeeland were only saved by cutting the dykes and letting the overwhelming waters spread out before the invaders. De Ruyter, his ships stripped of sailors and marines, guns dragged off to bolster the land defences, and a third of the fleet decommissioned by the end of June, could do no more than prepare to defend against seaborne invasion. In the hysteria wild accusations of treachery against the de Witts raged across the country, particularly in the strongly Orangist provinces such as Zeeland but spreading also into the States of Holland. A young hothead attempted to kill Jan de Witt. The grand painting of Cornelis in the Town Hall of

Dordrecht was slashed into pieces and the fragment depicting Cornelis was pasted to a gibbet. As rioting and pandemonium spread to most towns first the Dutch assembly then the States General voted William of Orange into the office of stadtholder. De Witt resigned his office as Pensionary of Holland shortly after, and Cornelis was arrested on a fabricated charge of plotting to murder William. The torture which followed failed to produce the expected confession but Cornelis was sentenced to banishment from the province of Holland. After Jan arrived at the prison in the Hague to carry his brother home, the frenzied mob yelled, 'We've got the two traitors inside', broke in and tore them to pieces. Parts of their bodies were sold in the streets. A finger joint sold for six stivers; the market price for a Dutchman's ear was more than twenty.[19]

The English loathed the war although without taking to the streets. Unlike the Dutch they were not under threat. However, conflicting opinions on how the campaign should proceed were reflected in the results. While James urged attacking de Ruyter again Charles insisted he concentrate on the East Indiamen, clinging to the illusion that booty could pay for the war because England could not fight on unless it did. The French subsidy was insufficient to pay the huge naval costs, still less compensate for customs revenue lost by the severe curtailment of trade. James's eighty ships sailed at the end of June into two months of dismal failure: the fleet expensively battered by unseasonable storms; the victualling fleet unable to rendezvous for the weather; sailors on short rations sickening of scurvy and booty-filled Indiamen escaping into the Ems. With no English scouting frigates on watch de Ruyter was even able to bring them unscathed to the Texel. The French departed to winter in Brest on 22 September. Spragge's small squadron patrolled the North Sea for a few weeks longer, seeking the Dutch fishing fleet but the twenty-five fishing buses he captured did nothing to swell the Treasury. Blake would have sent them home. The merchants' opposition grew bitter, their trade obliterated by growing numbers of Dutch privateers which seemed to raid as they pleased, and what convoys were assembled never seemed to be effective.

The Danish envoy in London had noted at the very beginning of the war, 'Time will show what the parliament will say if the king is obliged to come to his subjects for money.'[20] The king, compelled to call parliament for the first time since the war began, found out in the stormy session of February–March 1673. Most of the MPs seemed to agree that the war must continue but dissatisfaction over its conduct merged with other longer-standing causes of disquiet: the fear of arbitrary government, concern over the number of Catholics at court and suspicion that the Duke of York might himself be one. Salacious stories of debauchery at court and the sway held by Charles's Catholic mistresses circulated widely in coffee houses and through broadsides and news-sheets.[21] Determined to avoid becoming a pawn of France, parliament made supply conditional on Charles overturning his Declaration of Indulgence and assenting instead to a Test Act which would force all office holders to swear an oath against Catholicism. Did Charles believe that his brother would acquiesce? He had again decided that James should not risk his life at sea but now James refused the oath and resigned as Lord High Admiral. Charles put the office in commission with Pepys as secretary and Rupert was given command. Though his notorious dislike of the French was unlikely to promote allied cooperation the king needed Rupert's Protestant zeal to mollify parliament. James, however, did not resign his interest in the fleet, and he was not prepared to let Rupert have a free hand, particularly in the appointment of officers. Spragge's appointment as admiral of the Blue angered Rupert's supporters, who considered him too closely linked to the Duke of York's faction. Rupert complained that he had no real authority and had too few of what he described as 'undertaking officers', especially as Narborough, on an expedition to Tangier, might not be back for the next campaign and Sir John Harman was incapacitated by gout. Rupert repeatedly asked for Sir Robert Holmes but Rupert's faction believed that the duke's party were deliberately undermining the coming campaign by blocking Holmes's appointment.[22]

De Ruyter had worked well with the de Witts and expressed what dismay he dared at their death. He was not punished because he was the essential Dutch hero of 1673. His tactical skill and bravery would match that of the greatest admirals. He planned to begin with a pre-emptive strike by sinking a number of his own ships in the main channel of the Thames estuary to imprison the ships berthed there and in the Medway, then sail down the Channel to engage the French and the few English ships which had wintered at Portsmouth. Though he lost the race, again through the unreadiness of the Zeeland squadron, the sight of him off-shore reminded English spectators that their coast was as familiar to him as his own backyard. De Ruyter now turned to defensive tactics to bait, then thwart the allies by lying in the Schooneveld channel off Walcheren; his 'narrow hole', as the English dubbed it. This useful channel led out to Flushing in the north and towards the mouth of the Maas at the south. A series of banks, some always covered by shallow water, others such as the Oyster bank drying out, lie along its outer edge. Rupert, with his combined fleet of larger ships, would find it a narrow hole indeed, but if de Ruyter would not be drawn into the open sea, he either had to go back to port or tackle the Dutch on their own ground. He arrived off the Schooneveld on 22 May, the Dutch in full view, but the rough weather kept both fleets at anchor for some days. Spragge, seeing how poorly the English charts matched what was in front of them, remembered how the Dutch escaped obliteration in the previous war: 'no entire victory is ever to be had of the enemy except we are well acquainted with their ports, so as to be able to pursue them into them . . .'[23] At a council of war before the fleet sailed, Rupert had decided to mimic de Ruyter's tactic of an advance squadron, selecting thirty-five men-of-war, thirteen fireships and twenty-four tenders. He also decided to put his own Red squadron as the van, appointing the French (the White squadron) to the centre in an effort to force them into the main action. However, having the admiral of the fleet so far ahead was a poor tactic. (Later Spragge would be sharply critical, at least in his journal. In a long line of battle he could not see any signal the admiral made, and he feared the innovation 'may prove of ill consequence to us . . . I know not any reason he has for it except being singular and positive'.)

De Ruyter had one other addition to his numbers. William of Orange had restored Cornelis Tromp as Lieutenant Admiral of Amsterdam. The gale finally moderated on the 27th and the English flag officers resolved to attack at ten the following morning after the flood tide had done. At their advance the Dutch formed into line; Tromp in the *Golden Leeuw* leading the van north-easterly along the channel, de Ruyter in the *Zeven Provincien* in the centre and a little to the leeward, Banckert in the rear, leeward again. The south-westerly wind of early morning had begun to veer west-north-west. The numbers of the two fleets were roughly three to two – de Ruyter having fifty-two ships with 3,171 guns against the allies' seventy-six ships with 4,812 guns.[24] Though Rupert had copied de Ruyter's line of battle, he did not employ the tactics best suited to it: that of the mêlée, of boarding or destroying with fireships. The fleet's best weapon was its broadsides delivered from ships in line ahead. The smaller ships chosen as the spearhead lacked the fire-power to knock out Dutch ships and simply got in the way of the heavily armed bigger ships. However, according to one report the Dutch attacked too quickly for all the advance squadron to get organised. Nor did the concentration of spearhead and Red squadron drive Tromp from the field. The *Royal Charles* and then one of the French spearhead ships, the 56-gun *Conquerent*, were able to cripple the *Goulden Leeuw* so that Tromp had to shift flag; and the 50-gun *Jupiter*, another of the Dutch van, was so badly damaged that the boarding crew Legge sent from the *Royal Katherine* also abandoned her. Tromp eased away into shallower water but he was not driven out of the line completely. By 3 p.m. the English van, in danger of running aground in the Banjard sands, put their ships about to continue the fight first in a south-westerly direction, then north, then south again, a switchback of fighting which lasted until dark. De Ruyter described the allied formation as a half moon, for the French in the centre under d'Estrées lagged until after Spragge at the rear had engaged. Though the ships at the rear of the French division fought tenaciously, they took on the leading ships of Banckert's squadron in the rear instead of engaging with their Dutch counterparts. This left d'Estrées with far fewer ships in his section: ten to twelve against eighteen Dutch and in the fighting against them the *Zeven Provincien* and Aert van Nes's *Eendracht* together lost only three men killed. When Banckert's flagship the *Walcheren* was disabled, de Ruyter and his squadron were able to tack and push their way through d'Estrées's ships, cutting the allied fleet in two, a feat which gained him the wind and forced Spragge to bear away to westward.

At 5 p.m., de Ruyter and Banckert turned north to pick up with Tromp, then their combined fleet again turned south. This brought Tromp abreast of Spragge, who, seconded by the *Cambridge*, bore in to attack. Spragge had boasted to the king that he would bring Tromp back, dead or alive but he only forced him to shift flag as first the *Prins te Paard* and then the *Amsterdam* were dismasted; in return the *Cambridge* had to be towed to safety by the boats of the *Glorieux*. At dark the Dutch retired to 'their lurking holes' and the English to sea before anchoring early next morning almost at where they had begun the previous day. Rupert had nothing to show for the day's work. Only fireships had been lost by either side and both had equal numbers of disabled ships. 'It proved a very ill fighting place for so great a number of ships. And in truth as ill fought of our side as ever yet I saw' was Spragge's summary. Their great ships had been hampered

The first battle of Schooneveld, 28 May 1673, by William van de Velde the Elder (National Maritime Museum, Greenwich, London)

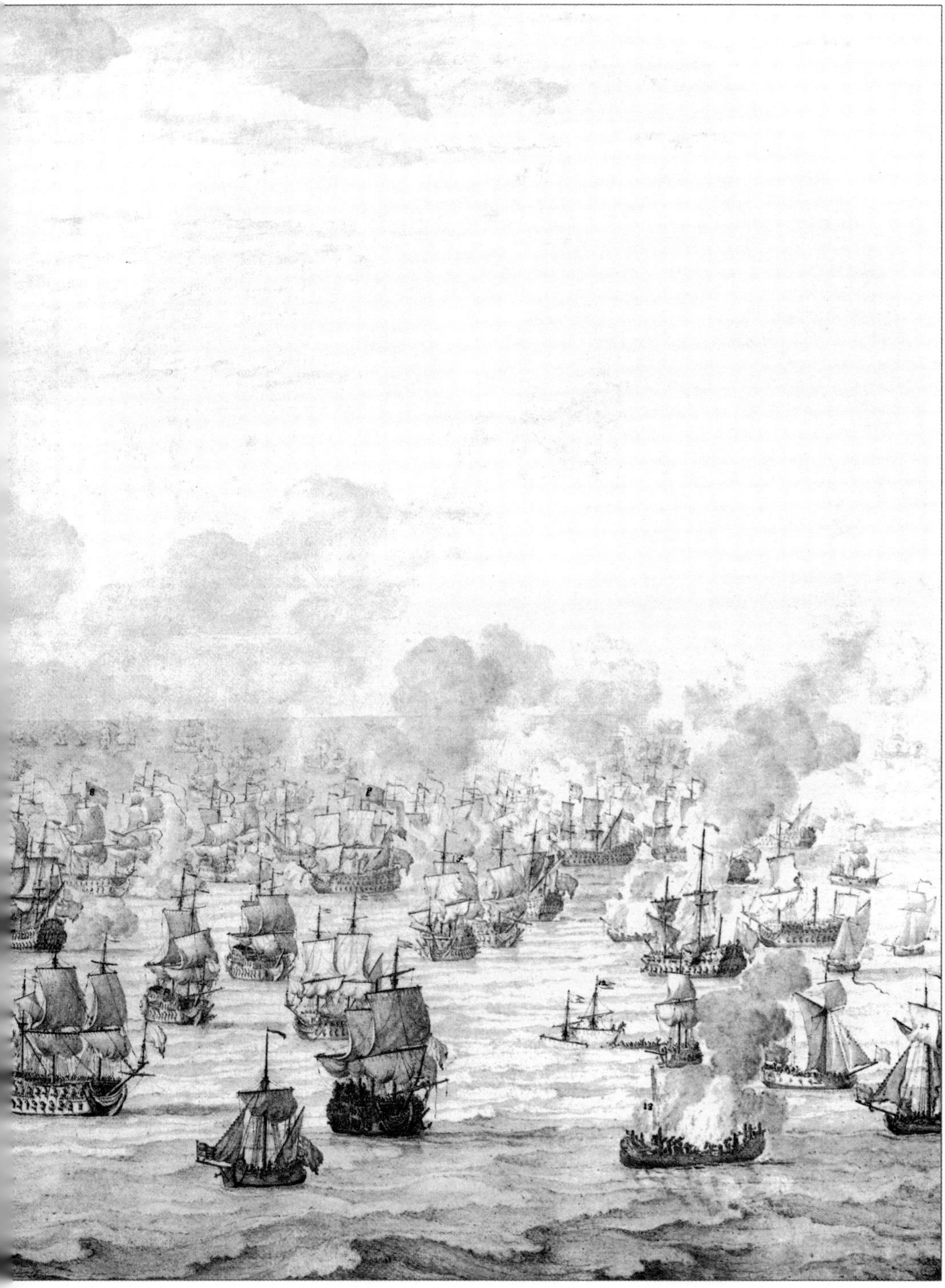

Sir Edward Spragge (National Maritime Museum, Greenwich, London)

by fighting near the shoals, and George Legge thought that most captains had been more frightened of losing their ships by running aground than to enemy fire. Tromp had not lost his ability to fight and wrote to his sister the day after battle, 'I have entered into the dance and thank God I am still in good health. I have enjoyed myself like kings.'[25] The new *Royal Charles* had heeled so badly and let so much water in by her lower gun-ports even in fair weather as to be almost useless.

The French (apart from those with Spragge) simply refused to engage closely and had let de Ruyter rescue his far weaker rear squadron.

Rupert shifted his flag to the *Royal Sovereign*, redirected the fleet's anchorage with an eye to getting into line smoothly, and cobbled up the damaged masts and rigging as best he could during a week of rough weather. De Ruyter, knowing he could repair and recruit more thoroughly from shore, waited for the weather to moderate and then bore down to attack on 4 June. Again, he caught them unready. Spragge had set out to visit Rupert, a distance he judged as 10 miles, and though he saw the *Sovereign*'s fore-topsail loose and could see the Dutch moving into line, persisted in continuing. Rupert dismissed him back to his own ship but, losing patience, decided to lead out himself. The ships in his wake moved out north-north-westerly in a jumbled formation. Spragge at first tried to regain the lead and draw the ships astern into a good order after the chaotic beginning he helped cause, but then backed his topsails in response to a challenge from Tromp: 'you would have thought by his (Tromp's) vapouring and fierceness we were to be eaten alive'. In fact Tromp played him like a fish, keeping carefully well to windward, firing long shots and refusing to close in; a strategy echoed all along their line as it continued northwards. De Ruyter, too, fenced defensively at a distance until midnight, then steered away for the coast; Tromp followed him at daylight. To launch a seaborne invasion the allies needed to defeat the Dutch comprehensively but the Dutch did not have to defeat the English, merely keep their squadrons intact. As de Ruyter remarked: 'They will fight with me when I please, but I won't when they please.'[26]

One naval historian asserts that 'the conclusion from both the Schooneveld battles must surely be that the English high command had fallen from the standards set by the Commonwealth generals-at-sea'.[27] However, given that de Ruyter could win simply by avoiding battle, it is difficult to see how Rupert could flush out a fox determined to stay in his hole. De Ruyter would come when it suited him, as was demonstrated infuriatingly when the Dutch returned to the mouth of the Thames on 26 June while the allied fleet still refitted. Though sickness forced the Dutch off, it was further demonstration that de Ruyter could keep to the seas more easily than the allies. Rupert returned to the Dutch coast, this time with strict instructions not to fight in the 'narrow hole', but to show himself and then sail north towards the Texel in the hope of drawing de Ruyter out. The strategy appeared to work, but a bad wind-shift just as the allies tacked isolated Spragge to windward and forced them to retire. The allies then moved up the coast toward the Texel, beacons flaring, 'and . . . jangling their bells and drums beating all night to call the country in'.[28] De Ruyter preferred to hang back off the mouth of the Maas from which he hoped to protect the coast from the Texel to Walcheren from the still-expected invasion. The stand-off ended on 2 August when William visited the fleet. The English, he was certain, had only one battle left in them. The council of war responded by heading at once for the Texel, although stormy weather kept both fleets struggling simply to stay in position. During the night a Dutch East Indiaman blundered among the allies and the French *Bourbon* dismasted the stray while still at anchor, 'a kind of little miracle', Spragge called it, perhaps hoping for a bigger one. As the weather moderated both fleets weighed anchor and by mid-morning, 10 August, the lookouts had sighted the Dutch. De Ruyter accepted battle, though again the allied fleet was numerically superior; eighty-six ships of more than 40 guns against his sixty, and the allies had the weather gauge.

He outmanoeuvred them almost at once, for as both fleets ran towards the coast on a southerly course that day and into the night, the Dutch pressed on as much sail as they could. The allies, uncertain of the shoals so close in, shortened to topsails so, as Narborough recorded, the Dutch 'shot ahead of us at a great pace'. Once well ahead they would be able to tack. Narborough dryly commented that it was clear to all seamen in the fleet that the Dutch would gain the weather gauge before morning. With water sounding at 12 fathoms the allies tacked north about one in the morning, but de Ruyter had tacked an hour ahead of them, and as day broke they saw his sails well ahead and indeed to the windward. An anonymous 'Relation', by a person eager to exculpate Rupert, blamed the French van who against specific orders twice slackened sails during the night.[29] Rupert's own relation says nothing of this for it begins at daybreak, 11 August with both fleets sailing northwards, the wind at east-south-east and fair. As the Dutch attacked, Rupert calculated the various concentrations: the rear division only of the Zeeland squadron with just seven men-of-war against the whole French squadron; Tromp with twenty-six against Spragge's Blue squadron; and de Ruyter and Banckert with the rest of the Dutch closing on the centre. It was an example of de Ruyter's tactics for fighting a bigger force at its clearest: concentrating most force on the enemy's main body, not spreading too thinly along the whole line. Firing began at eight amid fog and rain which a south-west wind cleared several hours later. This, said Rupert, allowed d'Estrées to tack and cut through his opponents and, by gaining the wind, could now attack effectively. However, d'Estrées did nothing with his advantage, hanging off at least 6 miles away. By this time the battle had split into three separate engagements. In the Red squadron, both the leading division and the centre were heavily engaged by the combined weight of de Ruyter and Banckert. Sweers in the *Olifant* had pushed the Red's rear division hard, forcing John Chicheley away to leeward. By noon, Rupert's division was under fire from two sides, with 'de Ruyter and his squadron on my lee quarter, an admiral with two flags more on my weather quarter, and the Zeeland squadron [Banckert's] upon my broadside to the windward'. The *Royal Katherine* under Legge lay astern to second him, enabling Rupert to edge his way towards an embattled Chicheley – a rescue in Rupert's eyes, a retreat in de Ruyter's – and then make towards the Blue well to the leeward to try and re-form the fleet. At this, de Ruyter also bore away to assist Tromp.

From the very beginning, Spragge in the rear aboard the *Royal Prince* anticipated a battle of his own, laying his foretop sail to the mast as he had done in June at Schooneveld, waiting for Tromp and the *Golden Leeuw*. Tromp came in close for this encounter, 'within fair gun shot' by 8 o'clock, the English saluting him with trumpets sounding, the crews yelling three cheers. But Narborough reckoned the Dutch shooting was recognisably faster and more accurate. It was three hours before a man aboard the *Golden Leeuw* was killed while the *Prince* was savaged. By midday the shrouds and rigging of the *St Michael* were being cut by

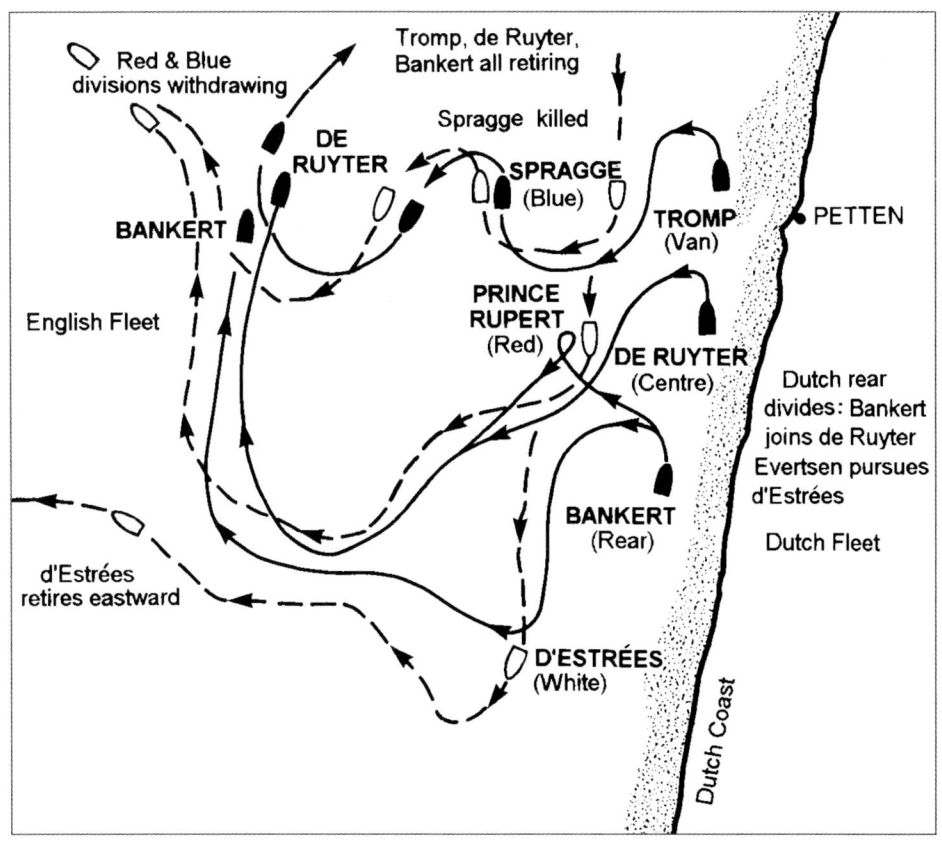

The battle of the Texel, 11 August 1673

Dutch shot faster than her seamen could get them up again until a wind change to the south-west put Tromp to leeward, and both stood apart for an hour to make repairs. The *Prince* tried to work back into action in the early afternoon, but as she took the wind her mainmast crashed to the deck knocking most of the mizzen mast into the sea as it went. In a flurry of exchanges, Spragge shifted flag to the 70-gun *St George*, and put a fireship by the *Prince* to repel boarders. The *St George* in her turn had her fore topmast shot, and Spragge took to a boat to shift flag again. A well-placed shot caught him on the water, shattering the boat. The night before, Spragge had noted in his journal Tromp's position. 'He will, I hope, fall to my share in the Blue squadron tomorrow . . .' It had proved his final entry. 'We ever looking when the Blue flag would be put up', remembered Narborough. When they took up Spragge's body, his head and shoulders were above water but his hands had gripped the sides of the boat so tightly they could hardly disengage them.

Ossory in the *St Michael* had stuck close to the stricken *Prince*, shepherding

The battle of the Texel, by William van de Velde the Younger (National Maritime Museum, Greenwich, London)

her as she went ahead. It was now hard to tell which ship had the most damage – the *St Michael*'s topsails cut asunder like rags, the bolt rope of the fore topsail broke and the sail collapsed into the sea, the only working sail left was a badly rent foresail. However, the *Prince* continued firing and the *Golden Leeuw* at last fell astern, sails and masts shot out, and at 3 p.m. Tromp moved his flag to the 70-gun *Komeetster*. An hour later, Narborough spotted a great fleet of ships to windward, the watching men anxiously trying to identify their flags and colours. The crowded sails were both English and Dutch: de Ruyter and Rupert bearing down in parallel lines. Tromp had sent two fireships against the *Prince*. The bulwarks of her upper decks had been flattened but her gun-crews kept firing and the fireships burned uselessly astern. Two frigates took the stricken ship in tow. Rupert then flew the great Blue flag from his mizzen peak and fired off his guns, a signal to call those ships to windward to bear up in his wake and form into line to renew battle. Most of the Blue were now repaired enough to get them under way, and Narborough on the *St Michael* was ready for more: 'We had now much the advantage of the Dutch in having more ships, and not much the worse for the day's fight, and the weather gauge of them.' Tromp at de Ruyter's approach tacked and stood to westward to join him, but the fighting was almost done. Rupert claims further fighting 'very sharp and close' but Narborough thought the enemy were too distant. The Dutch fell astern until their lights could no longer be seen. The French stayed resolutely aloof, still at least 6 miles distant, but there was no doubt that they had seen the huge flag flying from the mizzen peak. Now that battle was certainly over a query arrived from d'Estrées asking its meaning. Narborough may have guessed he was writing the war's epitaph as he concluded this day's entry: 'Thus the enemy and our fleet parted; we having the weather gauge of the enemy, stood away from them, a sight unpleasant to the English seamen. I hope never to see nor not hear of the like again. I had rather fall in battle than ever to see the like more, that so mighty a fleet of ships as ours is to stand away, as now we do, from so mean a fleet as the Dutch fleet is to ours, without the loss of one ship or any other damage considerable to us.'[30]

Charles, desperately trying to keep the alliance alive, tried to choke off the howl of criticism against the French which poured out from officers and seamen alike as letters or the men themselves came ashore, as printed pamphlets appeared, as the talk raged in the taverns and coffee houses: that the French had behaved as traitors or at the very least, cowards. Charles ordered Rupert to try to limit the damage. Rupert did not denounce the French in general but his opinion of d'Estrées's behaviour was unequivocal '. . . his squadron was to windward of the enemy drawn up in very good order and never bore within cannon shot of the enemy . . . my witnesses shall be his own officers and mariners and the rest of both fleets friends and foes . . .'[31] In fact, anger at the French muffled criticism of his own tactics. The truth in any case was now immaterial. The English had come to believe that from the first 'we were engaged by the French that they might have the pleasure to see the Dutch and us destroy one another, while they knew our seas and ports, and learned all our methods, but took care to preserve themselves'.[32] Those who they now believed were not in fact the true enemy, the Dutch, corroborated this even before battle began. By sending a derisory number of ships against the French de Ruyter had already passed judgement.

Meanwhile, the Dutch had found another Medway in the west. Commanded by a member of one of the great Dutch naval families, Cornelis Evertsen the youngest, a small contingent of four Zeeland ships had sailed from Flushing in late December 1672 to raid the American colonies of England and France. By the time he arrived off Staten Island, he had been joined by Jacob Benckes and a squadron of six Amsterdam men-of-war. Between them, they would subdue three English colonies, depopulate a fourth and seize over twenty-two vessels. For months, New York had been hearing rumours of a possible invasion fleet and though its governor Francis Lovelace had made noises about it being 'high time to buckle on our armour' nothing was done about defences or planning. As the frequent alarms and wild rumours failed to turn into actual ships, he allowed himself to think there was no danger at all. By mid-1673 he was so unconcerned that he left the colony in July to visit the neighbouring governor of Connecticut, John Winthrop. No sooner had he gone than the Dutch flotilla appeared off Sandy Hook. Captain John Manning, a former smuggler and now acting governor, was caught as empty-handed as Monck had been in 1667. Most of the heavy guns at Fort James were pointing landwards, not out to sea, and 'the platforms and carriages were also bad, either the carriages broke or they could not bring them to pass again'. In effect, he had little more than half a dozen guns to command. The troops in the city were summoned to the fort, sailors ordered back to their ships, and provisions to withstand a siege were hauled in. And just as Monck had few men to work with, so Manning laboured to prepare for the confrontation in a city with a large Dutch population and in a countryside where many of the English settlers were disgruntled with the Lovelace administration. The ships came through the Narrows, to ride at anchor under the island to wait for the flood tide to bear them within firing range of the fort. As they waited, Evertsen sent for a formal surrender, while Manning, playing desperately for time in the hope that Lovelace would return, or reinforcements would arrive, prevaricated by demanding to see Evertsen's commission. Manning would find it, he replied, 'stuck in the muzzle of a cannon'. The hundred or so defenders of the forts locked their gates as a forlorn hope against the 600 marines ready to swarm off the ships. The fighting lasted perhaps as long as an hour, before Manning flew a flag of truce. New York had fallen as swiftly as it had once been taken.[33]

In England, the Dutch propaganda which now seemed to wash in with every tide supported what the nation at large had already come to believe, that a continuing alliance with France would betray their law, liberties and religion. The mood of the nation compelled Charles to accept the peace proposals offered by the Dutch and the Treaty of Westminster was signed in February 1674. The Dutch agreed to strike the flag in the Narrow Seas, offer reasonable terms for the settlers in Surinam, return New York and pay a modest indemnity (which was almost at once returned to them as payment of debts owed by the House of Stuart to the House of Orange). Charles had gained nothing by the war which he could not have had in peace, while he had allowed an unexploded mine to be put under the throne: the secret treaty of Dover, the terms of which might be betrayed at any time. Henceforth Charles, willingly or unwillingly, was under the unshakeable influence of the King of France.

Epilogue

There was little gain for either English or Dutch in the Anglo-Dutch Wars of the seventeenth century. Grand Pensionary Pauw was even more right than he knew when he declared in 1652 that the Dutch would be attacking a mountain of iron if it engaged in war with the England of the Commonwealth. The problem for the English of the Dutch preponderance in international trade would be solved by other means and over a long space of time but in the end very much in England's favour. England had a long struggle against rivals in the East and West Indies and in North America, which lasted for much of the eighteenth century, but it would not be a struggle against the Dutch. The rivals would be the French and the Spanish, particularly the former, and the Dutch would be perceived as almost as irrelevant to the remarkably swift emergence of Britain as an imperial power in the East Indies as they were in North America or the West Indies. None of these developments could be foretold when the last Dutch war rumbled away into history.

Yet there were certain possibilities in the situation of England and the United Provinces which pointed to the future. The politically influential in England were inveterately hostile to Catholicism and the heir to the throne stood revealed as a Catholic. Even Charles II – perhaps especially Charles II since he knew his brother better than anyone – was not optimistic about the long-term prospects of James's reign although he did what he could to ensure that James would inherit the throne peacefully and with the government stable. The overwhelmingly Anglican majority among the ruling class were opposed to all nonconformity in religion because they associated it with the nonconformity in politics which had brought, as they saw it, the deprivations of life and property of the era of the Civil Wars and the republic. Nevertheless they were opposed to Catholicism even more strongly during the 1670s because of the danger from Catholic France. The ogre of Louis XIV damned all hope of reconciliation between Catholic and Protestant in England then and after, just as the ogre of Phillip II of Spain had done during the reign of Elizabeth I. However, any danger to England from Louis's enormous war machine was modest compared to the danger to the United Provinces. The Dutch survived after much bitter struggle and terrible cost in lives and treasure and flooded lands during the war with France and England. The Dutch under their new stadtholder, William of Orange, had no doubt that this was only the first round in a long struggle. With the old loathing and fear of Spain now transferred to France in both England and the United Provinces a close association was both natural, necessary and in the long run as certain as anything in history could be. It could not happen with a Catholic friend and ally of Louis on the English throne but by 1688, only three years after his accession, James had so alienated the Protestant landed classes among his subjects that a Dutch fleet carrying a Dutch army led by William of Orange was able to land in England and march on London largely unopposed as James's army either melted away or joined the prince. James fled into exile. William and his English wife were proclaimed joint rulers and the Dutch and the English had now achieved that unity which men like Cromwell had spoken so enthusiastically about as early as 1649 and which Strickland and St John had sought in vain in 1651, although in circumstances which would have horrified the old republicans.

Now the war against France could be fought to a finish. Unfortunately it took nearly a quarter of a century and during it some of the evil consequences of too close an association with England which had been foreseen by the Dutch republicans of 1651 were fulfilled – not politically but economically. If by 1714 the French monarchy was almost bankrupt, the Dutch state was also exhausted, its commerce declining, its vast merchant fleet shrunk, its people impoverished by the demands of war. In the maritime states of the United Provinces the situation after apparently endless campaigns in fulfilment of treaty obligations with England, was sad indeed. Even that remarkable infrastructure – shipyards, dry docks, sail-lofts, roperies, foundries – which had sustained its shipping industry were falling into ruin and decay. Nothing could symbolise this decline more poignantly than that during the eighteenth century the surviving ship-building yards often sought Englishmen to manage them and English artificers to bring to them skills which were already becoming rare in a region which had been so richly endowed with them.[1] In England, by contrast, the wealth of the land seemed inexhaustible and the remarkable financial experiments which produced the Bank of England and the funding of the national debt had made the state better able to withstand the financial excesses of war. England steered into the eighteenth century with a strong navy and huge commercial, agricultural and manufacturing wealth which would sustain the gradual if unplanned expansion of its overseas empire.

During England's wars with France the role of the navy had been and continued to be crucial. Its victories in the end confined France's territorial aspirations to continental Europe even under Napoleon and largely deprived her of her pre-nineteenth-century overseas empire. In the history of the development of that navy as a significant instrument of power the Anglo-Dutch wars had played a significant role and if only for that reason those wars should not be forgotten. It was then that the 'big ship, big gun' policy, which not all English admirals had favoured in the past, was revealed to be the correct path to victory. Its permanent adoption brought two further developments of crucial significance. The first was the gradual elimination of armed merchantmen as a serious naval resource and with that the emergence of a permanent, professional navy in which professionally skilled men might seek a career both in war and peace. Secondly, there was the development of the line of battle as a formation in which large numbers of warships could engage the enemy to greatest effect. In time skilled and talented commanders could devise and execute successful tactics for their fleet because they could control and manoeuvre that fleet through increasingly elaborate signals. Ironically the line-of-battle formation's success doomed the very ships which first employed it, Monck's second- and third-rates and smaller frigates. Although larger and better armed than their adversaries of the First Dutch War they were too small for the line of battle of the future. That would be composed of ships bearing from 74 to 100 guns, and although there would be far fewer of them in any fleet entering a battle, their fire-power was much heavier than that which Blake and Monck in 1652–3, or York and Rupert, Sandwich and de Ruyter in the later wars, had brought to bear on their enemy. Nevertheless the commanders of the Dutch Wars were pioneers in a new and terrible trade, and the Anglo-Dutch Wars of the seventeenth century, however unnatural such conflicts appear today, are a very important chapter in the history of naval warfare.

Notes

1. First Blood

1. An anonymous spectator in a letter from Dover, 20 May 1652, S.R. Gardiner and C.T. Atkinson (eds), *Letters and Papers Relating to the First Dutch War, 1652–1654* (London, 1898–1930) (hereafter *FDW*), i, 192.
2. *Calendar of State Papers, Domestic Series* (hereafter CSPD), *Commonwealth*, vol. 4, 243.
3. Although the leading ex-soldier naval commanders were called then 'generals-at-sea', other military men sent to sea were called rear-admiral, vice-admiral and captain (naval) where appropriate. In the interests of consistency the more usual title is given in these pages.
4. They were the *Andrew*, *Triumph*, *Fairfax*, *Entrance*, *Centurion*, *Adventure*, *Assurance*, *Greyhound* and *Seven Brothers*. Rear-Admiral Bourne's 'Relation', 29 May 1652, *FDW*, i, 251. Although Blake tends in dispatches to refer to his subordinate as 'Major Bourne' the latter had been a captain in the navy since the reorganisation of 1649. He was appointed a rear-admiral on 19 May. *CSPD*, *Commonwealth*, vol. 4, 185.
5. The Fairlight was a headland below Fairlight Down, a few miles north-east-by-east of Hastings.
6. *FDW*, i, 418–21.
7. For the action off Dover, *FDW*, i, part iii, *passim*.

2. The Rival Republics

For the political, social and economic development of the Dutch republic during the previous seventy years and English commercial rivalries with it, see Jonathan Israel's magisterial *The Dutch Republic: Its Rise, Greatness and Fall 1477–1806* (Oxford, 1995) and Israel's 'Competing Cousins: Anglo-Dutch Trade Rivalry', *History Today* (July 1988), 17–22; J.R. Jones, *The Anglo-Dutch Wars of the Seventeenth Century* (1996) which is particularly illuminating on the political background of the wars; and Charles Wilson, *Profit and Power: a Study of England and the Dutch Wars* (1956) which stresses the commercial background at the expense of the political, an emphasis which has more recently come under question.

1. Bernard Capp, *Cromwell's Navy* (Oxford, 1989), 73.
2. This fatherless infant had an improbable destiny. Forty years later he would rule over Great Britain as King William III. That he was the third of his name for both the Dutch and the British is a coincidence.
3. Israel, *Dutch Republic*, 179.
4. For a detailed analysis of the English ideological enemies of the Dutch, see Steven C.A. Pincus, *Protestantism and Patriotism* (Cambridge, 1977).
5. J.E. Farnell. 'The Navigation Act of 1651, the First Dutch War and the London Merchant Community', *Economic History Review* (1963), 2nd series, vol. xvi, 439–54.
6. Wilson, *Profit and Power*, 53.
7. Christopher Clay, *Economic and Social Change: England 1500–1700*, ii: *Industry, Trade and Government* (Cambridge, 1984), 188–9.
8. J.R. Bruijn, *The Dutch Navy of the Seventeenth and Eighteenth Centuries* (Columbia, SC, 1993).
9. Bruijn, *Dutch Navy*, 5 ff.
10. Bruijn, *Dutch Navy*, 74.
11. Quoted in Brian Tunstall, *Naval Warfare in the Age of Sail: the Evolution of Fighting Tactics 1650–1815* (1990), 1.

12. This was James I's giant flagship of 1610 totally reconstructed in 1641. Brian Lavery, *The Ship of the Line* (1984), 158. The *Sovereign of the Seas* was named *Sovereign* under the Commonwealth, and *Royal Sovereign* after 1660.
13. The additions in chronological order 1642–7 were *Assurance*, 34 guns, *Adventure*, 32, *Nonsuch*, 32, *Dragon*, *Elizabeth*, *Phoenix* and *Tiger*, all 38; see the valuable analytical lists in Lavery, *Ship of the Line*, 158–61.
14. Bruijn states forty-five additions, of which twenty were new-built; *Dutch Navy*, 69.
15. Partly based on the list in M. Oppenheim, *A History of the Administration of the Royal Navy from 1509 to 1660* (London, 1896), 332, but even more on Lavery.
16. *Dutch Navy*, 70. 'Even smaller English ships were considered to have greater fighting power than Tromp's flagship.'
17. Oppenheim, 341.
18. For much interesting data on naval gunnery see Peter Padfield, *Guns at Sea* (London, 1974), passim.

3. First Campaigns: From the Shetlands to the Casquets

1. *FDW*, i, 363.
2. Council of State to Blake, 10 June 1652, *FDW*, i, 301.
3. Council of State to Thompson, 11 June 1652, *FDW*, i, 309.
4. *FDW*, i, 311.
5. *FDW*, i, 325.
6. *FDW*, i, 327.
7. Council of State to Admiral Blake, 14 June 1652, *FDW*, i, 313
8. My emphasis.
9. Ayscue to the Earl of Pembroke, President of the Council, *FDW*, i, 342–3. On 4 July he ordered the Admiralty Committee to supply Ayscue with two ketches 'for intelligence'.
10. *Loc. cit.*
11. See his letter to Penn, 1 July 1652, J.R. Powell (ed.), *The Letters of Robert Blake together with Supplementary Documents* (1937), 168.
12. 'Information from Yarmouth', 22 July 1652, *FDW*, i, 384–5.
13. *FDW*, i, 404.
14. A letter to the Council dated 22 August, author unidentified, reported that Ayscue had only thirty-eight ships not counting four fireships and four small scouts, *FDW*, ii, 121.
15. Referring to Ayscue's gallant charge a letter from Plymouth of 20 August remarks 'Had some of the merchants' ships in the fleet done the like he had banged the Dutch fleet to the purpose', while a letter from Exeter observes that some captains '. . . were cowards and did not their parts'. *FDW*, ii, 116 and note.
16. *FDW*, ii, 121.
17. *FDW*, ii, 148.
18. A staff with a fork to hold a lighted match or fuse at one end.
19. *FDW*, ii, 122.
20. See chapter 13.

4. From Triumph to Defeat

1. Blake to the Council of State, 26 August, *FDW*, ii 134–5.
2. S.R. Gardiner, *History of the Commonwealth and Protectorate* (3 vols, 1897–1901), ii, 103.
3. During his long wait for the Plate fleet of Cadiz a few years later he was nearly to drive his treasure-obsessed crews to distraction by his cautious refusal to move prematurely but by then he was much more campaign-hardened and also physically depleted by illness and long sea-time. See D.R. Hainsworth, *The Swordsmen in Power. War and Politics under the English Republic, 1649–1660* (Stroud, 1997), 214.
4. The waters in which the Dutch War battles were fought were shallow enough for ships to anchor. Few areas are as deep as 120 feet, most no more than 80. Jones, *Anglo-Dutch Wars*, 19.
5. Penn to George Bishop, 2 October 1652, *FDW*, ii, 276.
6. 'Captain Mildmay's Relation', 1 October 1652, *FDW*, ii, 269.
7. Badiley's ship, probably an armed merchantman, is not named in contemporary reports. Badiley should not be confused with Richard Badiley who currently commanded Commonwealth naval forces in the Mediterranean. They may have been brothers.
8. Penn to George Bishop, 9 October, *FDW*, ii, 277.
9. Account of the battle of Kentish Knock in a 'Letter from Blake's Fleet', *FDW*, ii. 283.

10. *Ibid.*
11. 'Captain John Mildmay's Relation', 1 October 1652, *FDW*, ii, 269–70.
12. See above, 12.
13. An island and an anchorage north of the Scheldt.
14. J.S. Corbett, *England in the Mediterranean* (London, 1910), i, chapter xv.
15. Tromp to the Estates General, 28 October 1652, *FDW*, ii, 19–22.
16. *FDW*, ii, 20.
17. Tromp to the Estates General written from Boulogne, 4 December 1652, *FDW*, ii, 116.
18. Same to same, 7 December 1652, *FDW*, ii, 137.
19. Blake to Admiralty Commissioners, 1 December 1652, *FDW*, ii, 91.
20. Blake to the Council of State, 4 December 1652, *FDW*, ii, 114–15.

5. Portland

1. Gardiner, *Commonwealth and Protectorate*, ii, 154, 150 and note.
2. Capp, *Cromwell's Navy*, 219–20. Despite their heavy reliance on the death penalty the Interregnum navy was remarkably merciful. Capp can find evidence of only one sailor hanged for an offence committed on board ship between 1649 and 1660.
3. Capp, *Cromwell's Navy*, 80.
4. John Aubrey's story that 'the seamen would laugh that instead of crying "tack about" he would say "wheel to the right"' is probably as apocryphal as most of his biography of Monck. *Aubrey's Brief Lives*, (ed.) Oliver Lawson Dick (London, 1949).
5. John Bourne was the brother of Nehemiah Bourne who was left at Gravesend working to find more men for the fleet. See his letters in *FDW*, iv, *passim*.
6. Absent presumably because of the drain on men of ships mounting between 80 and 100 guns.
7. *FDW*, iv, part ix, *passim*.
8. M. Baumber, *General-at-Sea: Robert Blake and the Seventeenth-Century Revolution in Naval Warfare* (1989), 172 and Powell, *Blake*, 212, give differing accounts of the relative positions of the Dutch squadrons but it is all conjectural. The documentary evidence is inconclusive, *FDW*, iv, *passim*.
9. 'Extracts from the *Monnikendam*'s Journal', *FDW*, iv, 180–1.
10. Tromp to States General, 22 February, *FDW*, iv, 121–2.
11. 'Extracts from Evertsen's Journal', *FDW*, iv, 187.
12. Ships' hulls were at their widest close to the waterline with the sides sloping inward toward the bulwarks above. This slope was the 'tumble-home'.
13. Tromp to the States General, 22 February 1653, *FDW*, iv, 123.
14. Only seven survived from the sinking of the two ships according to one report.
15. 'Extracts from the *Monnikendam*'s journal', *FDW*, iv, 181.
16. For the *Struisvogel* and Munnick's ship see 'A Letter from aboard the *Waterhound* sent from the Dover Road on 21 February 1653', *FDW*, iv, 88. See also 'A Relation of the Late Engagement', *FDW*, iv, 81. De Ruyter's 'Journal' states, however, that Munnick's ship was taken and burned late on the previous day, *FDW*, 195. For de Wildt see Tromp's report to the States General, *FDW*, iv, 119.
17. *FDW*, iv, 120.
18. Tromp to the Estates General, 22 February 1653, *FDW*, iv, 120–1

6. The Last Battles

1. Monck to the Lord President of the Council, 31 July 1653, *FDW*, v, 347.
2. Jones, *Anglo-Dutch Wars*, 126 and note.
3. See 'The Pause in Operations', *FDW*, iv, part x.
4. A doctoral graduate of both Oxford and Leyden, the Linacre Reader in Medicine at Oxford, Whistler was successively Registrar and President of the Royal College of Physicians. *Dictionary of National Biography*.
5. *FDW*, iv, 232. See also Monck and Deane's letter, 234; Penn's letter of 3 April ('we have many sick in the fleet and more daily falling down'), 229 and Whistler's detailed recommendations for the future treatment of naval casualties of 21 March, 241.
6. After one of its more colourful members, a London leather-seller called Praise-God Barbon. For the crisis and its causes see Hainsworth, *Swordsmen in Power*, chapter 8, *passim*.
7. *FDW*, iv, 263. (My emphasis.)
8. *FDW*, v, 68.
9. *FDW*, v, 100, 109. Thurloe had been made

secretary to the Council of State the previous year and would be Cromwell's Secretary of State and highly efficient master of intelligence under the coming Protectorate.
10. Monck, once more a general, would in the winter and spring of 1659–60 skilfully engineer the recall of the Long Parliament and then the holding of a general election which he knew would accomplish the Restoration of Charles II. Hainsworth, *Swordsmen*, chapters 14 and 15, *passim*.
11. *FDW*, v, 100.
12. Tromp to the States General, *FDW*, v, 69–70.
13. Richard Lyons, from the *Resolution*, to the Council of State, 4 June, *FDW*, v, 84.
14. Prisoners taken by the English numbered about 1,350; *FDW*, v, 87.
15. *FDW*, v, 87.
16. Tromp to the States General, 8 August 1653, *FDW*, v, 341.
17. *FDW*, v, 367.
18. *FDW*, v, 369.

7. The Peacemakers

1. For de With's northern voyage, in which he was accompanied by de Ruyter and Floriszoon, and the disaster off the Texel see the large number of documents in *FDW*, vi.
2. For a thorough discussion of the peace process see Jones, *Anglo-Dutch Wars*, 136–44; and the detailed account in Gardiner, *Commonwealth and Protectorate*, ii, chapter xxii, *passim*.
3. Time mercifully concealed from the Protector and his advisers that the infant William III would not only one day hold these offices but use the Dutch navy to invade England and then take the English throne. Hainsworth, *Swordsmen in Power*, 192.
4. John Thurloe, *A Collection of the State Papers of John Thurloe*, ed. John Birch (1742) ii, 257.

8. The Uneasy Peace

1. For a detailed examination of de Witt's impact on the navy, see Bruijn, *The Dutch Navy*, 'Jan de Witt's New Navy', 75–82.
2. Israel, *Dutch Republic*, chapter 30, *passim*.

3. Clay, *Economic and Social Change*, ii, 189–90. Clay points out that the long wars between the Dutch and the English and the French between 1665 and 1714 also contributed to this decline.
4. Edward Hyde, *The Life of Edward, Earl of Clarendon* (two volumes, 1827), ii, 49. Colbert: 'Le plus grand quereller des diplomates de son temps'. *Dictionary of National Biography*.

9. A New War: Lowestoft

1. The Marquis of Newcastle, quoted in Steven Pincus, 'Popery, Trade and Universal Monarchy: The Ideological Context of the Outbreak of the Second Anglo-Dutch War', *English Historical Review*, January 1992, 27. See also Pincus, *Protestantism and Patriotism. Ideologies and the Making of English Foreign Policy, 1650–1668* (Cambridge, 1996).
2. Charles himself undertook to subscribe £6,000 but never actually paid the money; P.G. Rogers, *The Dutch in the Medway* (1970), 19.
3. Quoted in Richard Ollard, *Man-of-War: Sir Robert Holmes and the Restoration Navy* (1969), 86.
4. D.G. Shomette and R.D. Haslach, *Raid on America: The Dutch Naval Campaign of 1672–1674* (Columbia SC, 1988), 17–18.
5. East India Company memorandum to Earl of Southampton, 25 May 1664, in Pincus, *Protestantism and Patriotism*, 244.
6. Clarendon, *Life*, ii, 9; R.C. Latham and W. Matthews (eds), *The Diary of Samuel Pepys*, 11 vols (1970–83), v, 137.
7. Pepys, *Diary*, ix, 402.
8. Rowen, *John de Witt*, 461.
9. Pepys, *Diary*, v, 352.
10. *Calendar of State Papers Venetian*, 1664–6, 11. Some 200 Dutch ships were seized before war was officially declared.
11. R.C. Anderson (ed.), *The Journals of Sir Thomas Allin* (1939), 193. A Navy Board discussion of leaky ships in early 1667 blamed 'the over-gunning of ships [which] make ships old too soon', and ships running into each other, which the captains 'do in vanity because one or t'other will not bear up'. *Samuel Pepys and the Second Dutch War*, ed. R.C. Latham (1995), 132. The captains blamed the use of 'green' or unseasoned timber. *CSPD*, 1667, 429.

12. Frank Fox, *Great Ships. The Battlefleet of King Charles II* (Greenwich, 1980), 174.
13. Pepys, *Diary*, ii, 69.
14. The costs of naval warfare were prodigious. Paying debts and obligations in the month of March 1665 alone gobbled up £500,000 and it was reckoned that three-fifths of the parliamentary grant would be spent by November of that year. Frank Fox, 'The English Naval Shipbuilding Programme of 1664', *Mariner's Mirror*, 78 (1992), 277–92.
15. J.R. Tanner (ed.), *Samuel Pepys's Naval Minutes* (1926), 250.
16. *CSPD*, 1664, 75.
17. J.D. Davies, *Gentlemen and Tarpaulins: the Officers and Men of the Restoration Navy* (1991); Bernard Capp, *Cromwell's Navy* (1989).
18. Pepys, *Diary*, iii, 122; Tanner, *Pepys's Naval Minutes*, 26.
19. Granville Penn, *Memorials of the Professional Life and Times of Sir William Penn* (1833), ii, 293 and 301; Clarendon, *Life*, ii, 82 and 85.
20. For the development of the *Fighting Instructions*, see Brian Tunstall, *Naval Warfare in the Age of Sail: the Evolution of Fighting Tactics 1650–1815* (1990), 22 ff.
21. The accounts of the following battles are based on R.C. Anderson (ed.), *The Journals of Sir Thomas Allin* (1939); ——, *The Journal of Edward Mountagu, First Earl of Sandwich* (1929) and B. Lubbock (ed.), *Barlow's Journal of his Life at Sea in King's Ships, East and West Indiamen, and other Merchantmen from 1659 to 1703*, 2 vols (1934).
22. *CSPD*, 1665, 275.
23. A.H. Taylor, 'Galleon into Ship of the Line. II', in *Mariner's Mirror*, 45, 2 (1959), 15; Rowen, *John de Witt*, 578, gives the figure as 103 great ships, almost 500 guns and 21,000 crew.
24. Peter Padfield, *Tide of Empires: Decisive Naval Campaigns in the Rise of the West* (1982), ii, 32.
25. *CSP Ven.* 1664–6, 51. Downing reported to Arlington that all the new ships were to have brass guns. H.T. Colenbrander, *Bescheiden uit Vreemde Archieven omtrent de Groote Nederlandsche Zeeorlogen*, (1919), i, 172. The new 80-gun *Hollandia* had a gun deck length of 177 feet which was large even by English standards.
26. Downing to Bennet, Colenbrander, *Bescheiden*, i, 142.
27. Downing to Arlington, in Colenbrander, *Bescheiden*, i, 184.
28. W. Voorbeytel Cannenburg, 'The Van De Veldes', *Mariner's Mirror*, 36, 3 (1950), 191. See also Michael Robinson, *The Paintings of the Willem Van De Veldes* (1990).
29. Rowen, *John de Witt*, 578.
30. *A Second Narrative of the Signal Victory . . . Licensed by Roger L'Estrange* (1665), 6.
31. John Dryden, *Of Dramatic Poesie*, ed. George Watson, 2 vols (1962), i, 18–19.
32. Downing to Arlington, Colenbrander, *Bescheiden*, i, 198. Downing stayed in Holland until September, when he returned to London.
33. Pepys *Diary*, vi, 122; Clarendon, *Life*, ii, 137. But see his moving tribute to Sir John Lawson, ii, 133–6.
34. Downing to Arlington, Colenbrander, *Bescheiden*, i, 238.
35. *CSP Ven.* 1664–6, 144–7, 150, 152.
36. *CSP Ven.* 1664–6, 109.
37. Pepys, *Diary*, vi, 129.
38. Pepys, *Diary*, vi, 129.
39. Pepys, *Diary*, vi, 135, 148; E.S. de Beer (ed.), *The Diaries of John Evelyn*, 6 vols (Oxford, 1955), iii, 618.
40. *Essay Upon the late Victory obtained by His Royal Highness the Duke of York*, by the Author of Iter Boreale (1665).

10. The Four-Day Fight

1. Sandwich, *Journal*, 248.
2. 'Lord Sandwich's Narrative', Colenbrander, *Bescheiden*, i, 257.
3. Rochester to his mother, C. Hartmann, *Clifford of the Cabal* (1937), 50.
4. Hartmann, *Clifford*, 46–81. The governor told Clifford the treasure 'cannot be less worth than six million pounds of sterling'.
5. C.R. Boxer, review of J.C.M. Warnsinck, *De Retourvloot van Pieter de Bitter (1664–1665)*, *Mariner's Mirror*, 15 (1929), 324.
6. Teddiman's report, Sandwich, *Journal*, 263.
7. '. . . which indigent and disunited condition of the fleet . . . being the root whereunto in all probability may be assigned the missing de Ruyter in his return, and surprising the Dutch East India ships in the open sea . . .' 'Lord

Sandwich's Narrative', Colenbrander, *Bescheiden*, i, 251.
8. Bruijn, *The Dutch Navy*, 82.
9. Rowen, *John de Witt*, 581–2. Gilbert Burnet credits him with inventing chain shot. Osmond Airey, *Burnet's History of my Own Time* (1897–1900), i, 409.
10. Rowen, *John de Witt*, 582.
11. 'Lord Sandwich's Narrative', Colenbrander, *Bescheiden*, i, 261; *Barlow's Journal*, 110.
12. Pepys, *Diary*, vi, 300.
13. Clarendon, *Life*, ii, 196.
14. Pepys, *Diary*, vi, 211; *CSPD*, 1665, 577.
15. Clarendon, *Life*, ii, 212; Pepys, *Diary*, vii, 11.
16. Andrew Marvell, 'Third Advice to a Painter', *Poems on Affairs of State*, ed. G. de F. Lord (Newhaven, 1963), 69.
17. By the end of the year, the death toll from the plague was over 100,000, perhaps a quarter of London's total population.
18. 17 December 1664: 'I saw the Blazing Star again in the main topsail of the Argo Navis . . . the tail of him streamed in the fashion of a birchen besom . . .', Sandwich, *Journal*, 158.
19. Sandwich, *Journal*, 270; *Barlow's Journal*, i, 113.
20. R.E.J. Weber, 'The Introduction of the Single Line Ahead as a Battle Formation by the Dutch 1665–1666', *Mariner's Mirror*, 73 (1987), 5–19.
21. P.J. Blok, *The Life of Admiral de Ruyter* (1933), 225.
22. Blok, *de Ruyter*, 70; Tromp quoted in Clarendon, *Life*, ii, 131; Jones, *Anglo-Dutch Wars*, 52.
23. *The Second Dutch War 1665–1667, De Tweede Engelse Orlog* (1967), 42.
24. 'Rupert's Narrative to the House of Commons, 31 October 1667', in J.R. Powell and E.K. Timings (eds), *The Rupert and Monck Letter Book, 1666* (1969), 286.
25. Pepys, *Diary*, vii, 180; 'The Duke of Albemarle's narrative of miscarriages, in the message sent to the House of Commons, 31 October 1667', in *Rupert and Monck Letter Book*, 283.
26. Sir John Harman told Pepys that to begin the fight then was against his reason, and 'the reasons of most sober men there . . .' Pepys, *Diary*, vii, 161.
27. The account of the battle is based on accounts and letters in *Rupert and Monck Letter Book*.
28. W.R. Prior, 'The Naval War with the Dutch, 1665–7. The Diary of a Danish Sailor', *The United Services Magazine*, 43 (1911), 357.
29. Blok, *Life of Admiral de Ruyter*, 238.
30. 'Notes upon the June Fight; 1666', *Rupert and Monk Letter Book*, 210.
31. A.W. Tedder, *The Navy of the Restoration* (1916), 165.
32. *Barlow's Journal*, i, 121; C.R. Boxer, 'M.A. de Ruyter, 1607–1676', *Mariner's Mirror*, 44 (1958), 10.
33. Pepys, *Diary*, vii, 146.
34. Newsletter from Amsterdam, Colenbrander, *Bescheiden*, i, 396.

11. From Success to Humiliation

1. Pepys, *Diary*, vii, 158.
2. Pepys, *Diary*, vii, 179.
3. Clarendon, *Life*, ii, 271; *Barlow's Journal*, i, 116 and 119.
4. Pepys, *Diary*, vii, 163, 172, 174, 195.
5. 'Notes upon the June Fight; 1666', *Rupert and Monck Letter Book*, 214.
6. Pepys, *Diary*, vii, 165.
7. *CSPD* 1665–6, 512.
8. *Barlow's Journal*, i, 123.
9. *Rupert and Monck Letter Book*, 276.
10. *Rupert and Monck Letter Book*, 268.
11. *Diary of a Danish Sailor*, 359.
12. Blok, *Life of Admiral de Ruyter*, 245.
13. 'London Gazette, 23 July', *Rupert and Monck Letter Book*, 272.
14. *Rupert and Monck Letter Book*, 277.
15. R.C. Anderson (ed.), 'Naval Operations in the Latter Part of the Year 1666', *Naval Miscellany iii* (1928), 12.
16. *Rupert and Monck Letter Book*, 268; 'A Short Account of what happened after the June fight 1666', Colenbrander, *Bescheiden*, i, 416.
17. Anderson, *Naval Operations*, 23; Ollard, *Man-of-War*, 157.
18. *CSPD* 1665–6, 591.
19. *Rupert and Monck Letter Book*, 271.
20. *Rupert and Monck Letter Book*, 285; *CSPD* 1665–66, 40.
21. Capp, *Cromwell's Navy*, 386.
22. *CSP Ven.*, 1666–68, 50.
23. *Rupert and Monck Letter Book*, 147; *Journals of Sir Thomas Allin*, 286–7.
24. Pepys, *Diary*, vii, 271.
25. Anderson, *Naval Operations*, 44.
26. *Barlow's Journal*, i, 127.

27. Navy Board to Duke of York, 31 March 1667, Pepys, *The Second Dutch War 1665–1667*, 35.
28. Pepys, *Diary*, vii, 317, 426.
29. Clarendon, *Life*, ii, 365.
30. Pepys, *Diary*, 1 April 1667.
31. P.G. Rogers, *The Dutch in the Medway* (1970), 63.
32. Jones, *Anglo-Dutch Wars*, 178.
33. Rogers, *Dutch in the Medway*, 75.
34. Though a later House of Commons committee, determined to make him a scapegoat, mocked him for this, he asserted with some truth that the models were in fact more valuable than the ships themselves. Rogers, *Medway*, 137.
35. Andrew Marvell, 'The Last Instructions to a Painter', *Poems on Affairs of State*, 125.
36. Pepys, *Diary*, viii, 267.
37. Edward Gregory to Pepys, Colenbrander, *Bescheiden*, i, 585.
38. Evelyn, *Diary*, iii, 486; Pepys, *Diary*, viii, 345.
39. Pepys, *Diary*, viii, 399.
40. Clarendon, *Life*, ii, 371.
41. Davies, *Gentlemen and Tarpaulins*, 149–58; Rogers, *Dutch in the Medway*.

12. A Conspiracy of Princes

1. Evelyn, *Diary*, iii, 606.
2. Burnet, *History*, ii, 6.
3. Jones, *Anglo-Dutch Wars*, 96–9. For a deliberation on the likelihood of Charles's conversion, see Ronald Hutton, 'The religion of Charles II', in R. Smuts (ed.), *The Stuart Court and Europe* (Cambridge, 1996), 228–46.
4. Crow was shortly released, but according to Pepys's list was put out of command. Jones, *Anglo-Dutch Wars*, 181, captures the cynical motives behind the incident with 'One suspects that it had been hoped that fire would be returned; a dead Lady Temple would have been an ideal *casus belli*.'
5. Holmes's account, *CSPD*, 1671–2, 204–8; Evelyn, *Diary*, iii. 605.
6. Girolamo Alberti to Doge and Senate, *CSP Ven.*, 1672, 225.
7. Tanner, *Pepys's Naval Minutes*, 242; R.C. Anderson (ed.), *Journals and Narratives of the Third Dutch Wars* (1946), 14.
8. Evelyn, *Diary*, iii, 616–7 and Harris, *The Life of Edward Montagu, First Earl of Sandwich*, ii, 249.
9. Contemporary accounts of the engagements in R.C. Anderson (ed.), *Journals and Narratives of the Third Dutch War* (1946).
10. Evelyn, *Diary*, iii, 617.
11. See van de Velde the younger's *The Burning of the Royal James*, p. 175.
12. Boxer, *M.A. de Ruyter, 1607–1676*, 13.
13. *CSPD*, 1672, 95. In a separate action the *Henry* who had also been boarded and captured, was retaken by men from the *Plymouth* and survivors of her own crew.
14. After this engagement both van de Veldes moved to England, and van de Velde the elder's drawings of the battles of Schooneveld invariably show his vessel on the English side. In 1674, Charles awarded each a yearly salary of £100.
15. We do not have accurate numbers of the killed and wounded for the battles of the Third Dutch Wars. Padfield, *Tides of Empire*, ii, 88, reckons 2,500 for each fleet for this battle. For the retrieval of Sandwich's body, *CSPD*, 1672, 191.
16. Bruijn, *Dutch Navy*, 88–9; Davies, *Gentlemen and Tarpaulins*, 160 ff; Pepys, *Samuel Pepys and the Second Dutch War*, ed. R.C. Latham (1995), 224. For his distrust of gentleman captains, see 221–6.
17. *CSPD*, 1672, 342; Capp, *Cromwell's Navy*, 391. The observation on the painting of the *Royal James* is by Frank Fox, in Richard Ollard, *Cromwell's Earl. The Life of Edward Mountagu 1st earl of Sandwich* (1994), 259.
18. *Journals and Narratives*, 16–17; Colenbrander, *Bescheiden*, ii, 125; Harold Hansen, 'Opening Phase of the Third Dutch War described by the Danish envoy in London, March–June 1672', *Journal of Modern History*, 21 (1949), 107.
19. Rowen, *John de Witt*, 861–82. William did not order their murder, but he protected and rewarded the ringleaders.
20. Hansen, 'Opening Phase of the Third Dutch War', 99. For changing attitudes to the war, see Pincus, 'From Butterboxes to Wooden Shoes: the Shift in English Popular Sentiment from anti-Dutch to anti-French in the 1670s', *Historical Journal*, 38 (1995).
21. 'Charles's scepter and his prick are of a length/Yet she who plays with one may sway the other/and make him little wiser

than his brother' – the Earl of Rochester had turned to satire since the battle of Bergen. 'A Satire on Charles II' in *The Complete Poems of John Wilmot, Earl of Rochester*, ed. David Vieth (New York, 1968).
22. Rupert to Arlington, *CSPD*, 1673, 232; 'An Exact Relation of the Several Engagements, Anno 1673', *Journals and Narratives*, 373. Rupert wrote later 'That how great soever my endeavours were to get Sir Robert Holmes into the fleet, I could not prevail'. Colenbrander, *Bescheiden*, ii, 310.
23. *Journals and Narratives*, 319.
24. *Journals and Narratives* (introduction) 29.
25. Tromp's letter, Bruijn, *Dutch Navy*, 122.
26. E. Chappell (ed.), *Tangier Papers of Samuel Pepys* (1935), 247.
27. Padfield, *Tides of Empire*, ii, 101.
28. Newsletter from Rotterdam, Colenbrander, *Bescheiden*, ii, 293.
29. 'An Exact Relation of the Several Engagements Anno 1673', *Journals and Narratives*, 380.
30. *Journals and Narratives*, 361.
31. *CSPD*, 1673, 509.
32. Burnet, *History of My Own Time*, ii,18.
33. *Raid on America*, chapter 13.

Epilogue

1. J.J.A. Wijn, 'Shipbuilding and strategy, an ever changing interaction: a history of the construction of men-of-war in the Netherlands', *Revue Internationale d'Histoire Militaire*, 58, 198.

Bibliography

Primary Sources

A Second Narrative of the Signal Victory . . . 1665 (1665).
Allin, Sir T., *The Journals of Sir Thomas Allin*, ed. R.C. Anderson (1939).
Anderson, R.C. (ed.), *Journals and Narratives of the Third Dutch War* (1946).
—— 'Naval Operations in the Latter Part of the Year 1666' in Navy Records Society, *The Naval Miscellany*, iii (1928).
Barlow, E., *Barlow's Journal of his Life at Sea in King's Ships, East and West Indiamen, and other Merchantmen from 1659 to 1703*, ed. B. Lubbock, 2 vols (1934).
Burnet, G., *Bishop Burnet's History of his Own Time*, ed. Osmond Airey, 2 vols (1897–1900).
Calendar of State Papers, Domestic Series (1886–1939, 1960–72).
Calendar of State Papers, Commonwealth.
Calendar of State Papers and Manuscripts, Relating to English Affairs, Existing in the Archives and Collections of Venice, and in other Libraries of Northern Italy (1932–1947).
Clarendon, Edward Hyde, Earl of, *The Life of Edward Hyde Earl of Clarendon . . . in which is included a Continuation of his History of the Great Rebellion*, 2 vols (Oxford, 1827).
Colenbrander, H.T. (ed.), *Bescheiden uit vreemde arcieven omtrent de groote Nederlandsche zeeorlogen 1562–76*, 2 vols (The Hague, 1919).
Corbett, J.S. (ed.), *Fighting Instructions 1530–1816* (1905).
Dryden, J., *Of Dramatic Poesy*, ed. George Watson, 2 vols (1962).
Essay Upon the late Victory obtained by His Royal Highness the Duke of York, by the Author of Iter Boreale (1665).
Evelyn, J., *The Diary of John Evelyn*, ed. E.S. de Beer, 6 vols (Oxford 1955).
—— *Navigation and Commerce, Their Original and Progress* (1674).
Gardiner, S.R. and C.T. Atkinson (eds), *Letters and Papers Relating to the First Dutch War, 1652–1654* (1898–1930).
James, Duke of York, *Memoirs of the English Affairs, Chiefly Naval, from the Year 1660 to 1673* (1729).
Journals of the House of Commons, 8–9.
Mulgrave, John Sheffield, Earl of, *The Works of John Sheffield, Earl of Mulgrave, Marquis of Normanby, and Duke of Buckingham* (1740).
Penn, G., *Memorials of the Professional Life and Times of Sir William Penn, Knt*, 2 vols (1833).
Pepys, S., *The Diary of Samuel Pepys*, ed. R.C. Latham and W. Matthews, 11 vols (1970–83).
—— *Samuel Pepys and the Second Dutch War. Pepys's Navy White Book and Brooke House Papers*, ed. R.C. Latham (1995).
—— *Samuel Pepys's Naval Minutes*, ed. J.R. Tanner (1926).
—— *The Tangier Papers of Samuel Pepys*, ed. E. Chappell (1935).
Poems on Affairs of State, ed. G. de F. Lord (New Haven, 1963)
Powell, J.R. (ed.), *The Letters of Robert Blake together with Supplementary Documents* (1937).
Powell, J.R., and Timings, E.K. (eds), *The Rupert and Monck Letter Book, 1666* (1969).
Sandwich, Edward Mountagu, Earl of, *The Journal of Edward Montagu, First Earl of Sandwich*, ed. R.C. Anderson (1985).
Temple, Sir W., *Observations upon the United Provinces of the Netherlands*, ed. Sir G. Clark (Oxford, 1972).
Thurloe, J., *A Collection of the State papers of John Thurloe*, ed. John Birch (1742).

SECONDARY SOURCES

Baumber, M., *General-at-Sea: Robert Blake and the Seventeenth-Century Revolution in Naval Warfare* (1989).
Blok, P.J., *The Life of Admiral De Ruyter* (1933).
Boxer, C.R. *The Anglo-Dutch Wars of the 17th Century* (1974).
—— 'Some Second Thoughts on the Third Anglo-Dutch War, 1672–4', *Transactions of the Royal Historical Society*, 5th series (1969).
—— review of J.C.M. Warnsinck, *De Retourvloot van Pieter de Bitter (1664–1665)*, *Mariner's Mirror*, 15 (1929).
—— 'M.A. de Ruyter, 1607–1676', *Mariner's Mirror*, 44 (1958).
Bruijn, J.R., *The Dutch Navy of the Seventeenth and Eighteenth Centuries* (Columbia, SC, 1993).
Capp, B., *Cromwell's Navy: The Fleet and the English Revolution 1648–60* (Oxford, 1989).
Cannenburg, W. Voorbeytel, 'The Van De Veldes', *Mariner's Mirror*, 36 (1950).
Clay, Christopher, *Economic and Social Change: England 1500–1700*, ii: *Industry, Trade and Government* (Cambridge, 1984).
Corbett, J.S., *England in the Mediterranean*, 2 vols (1904).
Davies, J.D., *Gentlemen and Tarpaulins: The Officers and Men of the Restoration Navy* (Oxford, 1991).
—— 'A Lover of the Sea and Skilful in Shipping. King Charles II and his Navy', *Royal Stuart Society Papers*, xii (1992).
Ekberg, C.J., *The Failure of Louis XIV's Dutch War* (Chapel Hill, NC, 1979).
Farnell, J.E., 'The Navigation Act of 1651, the First Dutch War and the London Merchant Community', *Economic History Review*, 2nd series, xvi (1963).
Fox, F., *Great Ships: The Battlefleet of King Charles II* (1980).
—— 'The English Naval Shipbuilding Programme of 1664', *Mariner's Mirror*, 78, 1992.
Gardiner, S.R., *History of the Commonwealth and Protectorate*, 3 vols (1897–1901).
Hainsworth, D.R., *The Swordsmen in Power. War and Politics under the English Republic 1649–1660* (Stroud, 1997).
Hansen, H., 'The Opening Phase of the Third Dutch War Described by the Danish Envoy in London, March–June 1672', *Journal of Modern History*, 21 (1949).
Harris, F.R., *The Life of Edward Mountagu, K.G., First Earl of Sandwich*, 2 vols (1912).
Hartmann, C.H., *Clifford of the Cabal* (Kingswood, 1937).
Hutton, R., *The Restoration: A Political and Religious History of England and Wales, 1660–7* (Oxford, 1985).
—— *Charles II: King of England, Scotland and Ireland* (Oxford, 1989).
—— 'The religion of Charles II', in R. Smuts (ed.), *The Stuart Court and Europe* (Cambridge, 1996).
Israel, J.I., *The Dutch Republic: Its Rise, Greatness and Fall 1477–1806* (Oxford, 1995).
Jones, J.R., *The Anglo-Dutch Wars of the Seventeenth Century* (1996).
Lavery, B., *The Ship of the Line*, 2 vols (1983, 1984).
—— *The Arming and Fitting of English Ships of War, 1600–1815* (1987).
Ollard, R., *Man-of-War: Sir Robert Holmes and the Restoration Navy* (1969).
—— *Cromwell's Earl. The Life of Edward Mountagu 1st Earl of Sandwich* (1994).
Oppenheim, M., *A History of the Administration of the Royal Navy from 1509 to 1660* (1896).
Padfield, P., *Guns at Sea* (1974).
—— *Tides of Empire: Decisive Naval Campaigns in the Rise of the West, 1481–1654*, vol. i (1979), vol. ii (1982).
Pincus, S., 'Popery, Trade and Universal Monarchy: The Ideological Context of the Outbreak of the Second Anglo-Dutch War', *English Historical Review* (January 1992).
—— *Protestantism and Patriotism. Ideologies and the Making of English Foreign Policy, 1650–1668* (Cambridge, 1996).
—— 'From Butterboxes to Wooden Shoes: the Shift in English Popular Sentiment from anti-Dutch to anti-French in the 1670s', *Historical Journal*, 38 (1995).
Powell, J.R., *Robert Blake General-at-Sea* (1972).

Prior, W.R., 'The Naval War with the Dutch, 1665–7. The Diary of a Danish Sailor', *The United Service Magazine*, 43 (1911).
Robinson, Michael, *The Paintings of the Willem Van De Veldes* (1990).
Rogers, P.G., *The Dutch in the Medway* (1970).
Rowen, H.H., *John de Witt: Grand Pensionary of Holland* (Princeton, NJ, 1978).
Seaward, P., 'The House of Commons Committee of Trade and the Origins of the Second Anglo-Dutch War, 1664', *Historical Journal*, 30 (1987).
The Second Dutch War 1665–1667, De Tweede Engelse Orlog (1967).
Shelley, R.J.A., 'The Division of the English Fleet in 1666', *Mariner's Mirror*, 25 (1939).
Shomette, D.G. and R.D. Haslach, *Raid on America: The Dutch Naval Campaign of 1672–1674* (Columbia, SC, 1988).
Taylor, A.H., 'Galleon into Ship of the Line. i, ii and iii', *Mariner's Mirror*, 45 (1958, 1959).
Tedder, A.W., *The Navy of the Restoration* (Cambridge, 1916).
Tunstall, B., *Naval Warfare in the Age of Sail: the Evolution of Fighting Tactics 1650–1815* (1990).
Weber, R.E.J., 'The Introduction of the Single Line Ahead as a Battle Formation by the Dutch 1665–1666', *Mariner's Mirror*, 73 (1987).

Index

Abelson, James, 125
Act of Exclusion, 93, 98, 99, 101
Admiralty Commissioners (formerly Admiralty Committee), 53, 59, 89
Admiralty of the North Quarter, 18
Africa, 103–4
Africa Company, 104, 108
Ahlefeldt, Claus von, 131
Albemarle, duke of, *see* Monck, George
Albemarle, duchess of, wife of above, 135
Algiers, 172
Allin, Sir Thomas, 110, 129, 133, 149, 150, 152, 155, 156, 178; attacks Smyrna convoy, 110
Amboyna, 'massacre' of, 12, 17, 93
Amsterdam, 11, 15, 71, 99, 133, 148
Amsterdam admiralty, 18
Anglo-Dutch relations, 7–22, *see also* union proposal, peace negotiations
Antwerp, 12
Appleton, Henry, 49–50
Arlington, Henry Bennet, earl of, 104, 149, 150
Aukes, Douwe, 33
Ayscue, Sir George, 3, 23–8, *27*, 31; at the Casquets, 32–3; retires, 34; 35, 39, 113, 134, 145, 146; taken prisoner to Holland, 148, 178

Badiley, Captain, at Kentish Knock, 43, 46, 196
Badiley, Richard, 36, 49, 73, 196
Ball, Andrew, killed at Portland, 64
Baltic Sea, 11, 13, 14, 15, 23, 48, 57, 58, 71, 74, 89, 93, 97, 99, 129, 131
Banckert, Adriaen, 152, 155, 174, 178, 181, 186
'Barebones' Parliament, *see* Parliament, Nominated
Barlow, Edward, 124, 134, 149, 150, 156
Batten, Robert, killed at Dungeness, 52
Batten, Sir William, 111, 163
Beaufort, duc de, 137, 156
Bennet, Henry, *see* Arlington
Bergen, 75, 129, 131, 133; raid on, 131
Berkeley, Charles, earl of Falmouth, 125
Berkeley, Sir William, 111, 127, 143, 144
Blake, Benjamin, 39, 58
Blake, Robert, 4–8, 17, 22; and the Northern Voyage, 23–31; first sorties against de Ruyter, 35; against the French expedition, 36; Vendome demands dismissal of, 37; second sortie against de Ruyter, 37–9; and the Kentish Knock, 41–7; defeated at Dungeness, 52–3, 56, 57, 58, 59; and battle of Portland, 60–70, *67*, 72, 73, 74; and the battle off the Gabbard, 75, 80; ill-health, 82, 90, 97, 98, 113, 142, 179, 197
Blake, Robert, the Younger, 80
blockade, *see* tactics
Boulogne anchorage, 56
Bourne, John, 61, 64, 73
Bourne, Nehemiah, 4–6, 39, 41–3, 73
Boyle, Roger, 125
Brakel, Jan van, 161, 174–6
Breda, 157, 160; Treaty of, 157, 163, 169
Brest, 139, 171, 179
Brouncker, Henry, 125, 127, 167
Buckingham, George Villiers, 1st duke of, 13
Buoy of the Nore, 127, 138, 139, 163, 172

Cardenas, Alonso de, Spanish ambassador, 36
Carew, John MP, 59
Carr, Sir Robert, 106
Carteret, Sir George, 111, 127
Casquets, the, 32
Channel Islands, 73
Charles I, King of England, 7–8, 13, 19
Charles II, King of England, 7, 76, 92, 97, 99, *100*, 101, 104, 108, 110, 113, 129, 134, 148, 156, 157, 163, 166, 169, 170, 171, 179, 189, 190, 191, 198, 201
Charles X, King of Sweden, 99
Chatham dockyards, 53, 56, 58, 111, 127, 150, 156–7, 160–1, 163, 167
Chicheley, Sir John, 186
Clarendon, Edward Hyde, earl of, 101; opposes war, 108; 113, 125, 134, 135, 149, 157; exiled, 166
Clifford, Sir Thomas, later baron, 107, 131, 142, 145, 146, 150, 154, 167, 171
Colbert, Jean Baptiste, 101, 171
Continental Congress of the United States, 10
Commons, House of, committee to investigate trade, 107–8
Commonwealth government, *see* Council of State
convoys, Dutch, 2–6, 13, 17, 26, 28, 29, 31, 32, 34, 35, 37–9, 53, 56, 61, 66–70, 71, 74–5, 76, 82, 89, 108, 115
convoys, English, 31, 49
convoys, Smyrna, 110, 116, 117, 171
Copenhagen, 99, 129

Coppin, John, 39
Cortenaer, vice-admiral, 117, 124–5, 127
Council of State, 4, 23–4, 36, 48, 57–9; *see also* Parliament, Purged
Coventry, Sir William, 104, 111, 127, 135, 144, 149, 157
Cromwell, Oliver, 7, 9, 13, 58, 61, 73; as Protector, 90–3, *91*, 97, 98, 101, 110, 157, 166, 192
Cromwell, Richard, 97
Cubitt, Captain, 85, 86

Daniel, John, 147
Danzig, 99
Day, John, 65
Deal Castle, 28
Deane, Major-General Richard, 20, 53, 59, 72, 73, 74, 75; killed at the Gabbard, 77; 81, 82
Declaration of Indulgence, 171, 179
Denmark, 15, 48, 57, 58, 93, 97, 99, 129, 131; Norwegian harbours, 129, 131
Dieppe, 36, 156
discipline, 51, 58
'division of the fleet', 138–9
Dolman, Thomas, 157, 160
Dorislaus, Dr Isaac, 7–8
Douglas, Archibald, 163
Dover, action off, 4–6, 39; 25, 26, 61, 75, 80
Dover, secret treaty of, 169, 191
Dover Straits, 155, 160
Downing, Sir George, 101, 107, 108, 117, 124, 129, 171
Downs, the, 23, 25, 27–8, 31, 35, 37, 39, 41, 52–3, 70, 75, 138–9
Dryden, John, 121
Dungeness, 36; action off, 52–3, *54–5*, 74, 87
Dunkirk, 16, 32; siege of, 36; surrenders, 37, 70
Dutch Reformed Church, 8, 11

East India Company, Dutch, 12, 13, 23, 103
East India Company, English, 12, 93, 103
East Indiamen, Dutch, *32*, 116, 124, 129, 133–4, 179, 199
East Indies, 12, 71, 103
Edwin, John, 64
Elba, 49
Estrées, comte d', 172, 174, 181, 186, 188, 189
Evelyn, John, 135, 163, 169, 171, 172, 175
Evertsen, Cornelis, the elder, 52, 53, 56; at Portland, 61–8; 75, 86, 142, 144
Evertsen, Cornelis, the younger, 127, 155
Evertsen, Cornelis, the youngest, captures New York, 189–90
Evertsen, Jan, *112*, 117, 120; accused of cowardice and retires, 125, 127; reinstated, 150; 152, 155

Fairlight, the, 5, 62
Fighting Instructions, 73–4, 76, 85, 86, 113, 137, 149
Finisterre, 71
fireships, 18, 28, 30, 31, 33, 36, 73, 74, 75, 77, 81, 120, 124, 144–5, 153, 161, 163, 174, 176, 177, 188
Floriszoon, Pieter, 26, 52; at Portland, 61–8, 75, 86
Four-Day Fight, 139–47, *140–1*, *143*, 149, 177

France, 104, 127, 137, 169, 193–4; *see also* Louis XIV and Navy, French
Friesland, 101, 117, 133; Friesland admiralty, 18

Gabbard, battle off the, 75–81, *78–9*, 85, 97, 120, 128, 142
Galen, Commodore van, 49–50
Galloper sands, 145, 155
Genoa, 13, 14
Ghent, Willem van, 155, 160, 170, 172, 174, 175–6
Gillingham, 160
Goeree, 47
Grand Pensionary of Holland, office of, 10, 98, 116
Gravesend, 156, 160
Greenwich, 135
Gregory, Edward, 163
Gris Nez, cap, 69, 155
Guiche, comte de, 144, 147
Guinea, 104, 108, 115
Gunfleet channel, 75, 76, 115–16, 139, 150
guns, naval, 18, 20, 22, 29, 31, 34, 39, 41, 46, 47, 58, 64, 74, 76–7, 82, 116, 120, 138, 171, 199

Haddock, Sir Richard, 174, 176, 178
Haddock, William, 31, 33, 39
Hague, The, 101, 103, 117, 124, 129, 133, 148, 179
Harrison, Captain, 25, 26
Harrison, Major-General Thomas, Fifth Monarchist, 90
Harwich, 75, 127, 150
Helder channel, 82, 83
Helvoetsluys, 7, 50, 51, 133, 170
herring fishery, 11, 15, 23, 28, 93, 101
Holland, state of, 7, 8, 10, 12, 13, 17, 51, 91–2, 117, 178
Hollesley bay, 127
Holmes, Sir Robert, raid on Dutch forts in Africa, 104; *105*, 108; sent to the Tower, 110; resigns commission after Lowestoft, 127; 142, 149, 152; 'Holmes's Bonfire', 154–5, 167; attacks Smyrna convoy, 171, 172, 177; further appointment blocked by Rupert, 180, 202
House of Orange, 8, 10, 92, 99, 101, 171, 190; *see also* Statholderate
Howett, Samuel, 61
Hoxton, Walter, killed at Dungeness, 53
Huygens, Christian, 133

impact of first Dutch war on Dutch economy, 71, 81
Instructions, Fighting, for fleet, *see* Fighting Instructions
Isle de Rhé, 51, 56, 61
Isle of Wight, 31, 35, 62, 68, 73, 171, 172

James I, King of England, 12
James, duke of York (later James II, King of England), enthusiasm for war, 104; and Royal Africa Company, 104; 111; prefers gentlemen officers, 113; *114*, 115; and the battle of Lowestoft, 117–25, 127, 129, 134, 135, 144, 148, 149, 167, 169; and battle of Sole Bay, 172–4; *178*; suspected of Catholicism, 179; resigns as Lord High Admiral, 179; 180, 191, 192; his flight as James II, 192

Jordan, Sir Joseph, 121, 174, 177, 178
Joynball, Dirk, killed at Dungeness, 53

Kempthorne, Sir John, 149, 153, 174, 175
Kentish Knock, battle of the, 41–8, *44*, 51, 110
King of Denmark, *see* Denmark
Kirby, Robert, 125

Lane, Lionel, 61, 65
Laws of War 1653 (later Articles of War), 59
Lawson, Sir John, 22; and battle of Portland, 60–4; and battle off the Gabbard, 75–80; 89, 97, 108, 110, 113, 115, 117; wounded at Lowestoft, 121; 125, 201
Legge, George, 181, 184, 186
Leghorn, battle of, *49*, 50
Le Havre, 36
'line ahead' formation, *see* tactics: fighting in line
London, 106, 111, 121; plague devastates, 134–5, 200; 144; Fire of London, 156, 163, 179, 192
Longsands, the, 26, 53, 75
Louis XIV, King of France, 101, 104, 137, 157, 169, 171, 178, 191
Lowestoft, 117, 177
Lowestoft, battle of, 117–25, *121*, *122–3*, 127, 133, 134, 135, 137, 138, 155

Maas (Meuse) estuary, 35, 75, 116, 124, 180, 185
Margate Road, 53
Marlborough, earl of, 124
Marvell, Andrew, 135, 138
Mediterranean, 3, 12, 16, 36, 49–50, 56, 71
Medway, 139, 157, 160, 161, 163, 180; raid on, *158–9*, 160–5, *162*, 167, 171
Menillet, Commodore de, 36
mercantilism, 101, 103, 107
merchant captains accused of cowardice, 33, 34, 58, 127
merchant fleet, Dutch, 13, 16, 17
merchantmen, use of in battle, 116, 117, 125
merchants, Dutch, 11, 71, 81
merchants, English, 11, 14–15, 16, 90, 157
Mildmay, Captain John, 35; at Kentish Knock, 41, 45–6; 60; killed at Portland, 65
Minderhout, Hendrick van, 148
Monck, George, later Duke of Albemarle, 53, 59, 60; and the battle of Portland, 60–6; 71, 72, 73, 74; and the battle off the Gabbard, 75–81; and the battle of Scheveningen, 82–7, *84*, 89; role in Restoration of Charles II, 97, 98, 103, 111, 113, 129, 134, 135; and the Four-Day Fight, 139–47, 148, 149, 150, 154, 155; and the Fire of London, 156, 157; and the Medway, 160–3, 167; death, 172, 189, 193
Munnick, Captain de, 68
Myngs, Sir Christopher, 113, 134, 149

Narborough, Sir John, 172, 174, 175, 177, 180, 186, 187, 188
Navigation Act of 1651, 14, 15, 93
Navigation Act of 1660, 99, 101
Navy, Dutch, faction fighting within, 116–17, 125; 155; pressing of seamen, 55; ship numbers, 17–18, 20, 31–2, 39, 51, 74–5, 85, 98, 116, 138, 150, 171, 181, 186, 192
Navy, English, aristocratic volunteers, 113, 116, 125, 131; discipline, 58; faction fighting within, 111–12, 127–9, 135, 149, 155, 167, 172, 178, 180; finances, 48, 58, 108, 135, 157, 169, 179, 192, 199; gentlemen officers, 113, 178; manning, 111, 156; pressing of seamen, 58, 73, 111, 117; provisioning, 82, 111, 116, 129, 154, 156–7; sailors' pay, 58, 59, 135, 156, 163; ship numbers, 9, 16, 19–20, 31, 39, 58, 61, 85, 110, 149–50, 171, 181, 193; tarpaulins, 111, 113
Navy, French, 137, 139, 156; rebuilding under Colbert, 171; as allies of the Dutch, 137, 139; as allies of the English, 171–4, 180–1, 185–6, 188–9; criticised by the English, 178, 186, 188–9
Navy Board, 108
Navy Commissioners, *see* Admiralty Commissioners
Nes, Aert van, 142, 152, 156, 163, 177
Nes, Jan van, 144
neutral shipping issue, 16, 93, 99
Newcastle colliery fleet, 15, 71, 73
New Amsterdam, 104–6, *107*
New England, 58
New Model Army, 9, 66; *see also* soldiers aboard warships
New Netherland, 101, 104
New York, 104
Nicolls, Robert, 104, 106
Nieuport, 4, 39, 41
Northern Voyage, 23, 28–30
North Foreland, the, 26, 41, 139, 163
North Sands head, the, 27
Norway, 30, 58, 71; *see also* Bergen

Obdam, Jacob van Wassenaer, 98, 99; disliked by men, 116; and the battle of Lowestoft, 117–24, *119*; death of, 124; 125, 127, 137, 145
Orange party, 8, 17, 92, 99, 101, 108, 117, 155, 171, 178
Orangists, *see* Orange party
Orfordness, 75, 150
Ossory, earl of, 18

Packe, vice-admiral, fatally wounded at Casquets, 33
Parliament, 99, 103, 108, 137, 157, 166, 167, 169, 171, 179–80
Parliament, Cavalier, 103
Parliament, Purged, 72, 97; dismissed by Cromwell, 73
Parliament, Nominated, 73, 90
Pauw, Adriaen, Grand Pensionary of Holland, 7, 11, 17, 26, 98, 193
peace negotiations, First Dutch War, 90–3; Second Dutch War, 157, 160, 163, 166; Third Dutch War, 191
Peace of Munster, 13, 18, 98
Peacock, James, 61, 65
Penn, Sir William, 22, 28, 36, *38*, 113, 115, 120, 129, 133, 135, 142, 149, 163, 167; and Kentish Knock,

41–7; at battle of Portland, 60–6, 70, 73; and battle off the Gabbard, 75–6; after Scheveningen, 86; 113, 115, 120, 129, 133; and the 'prize goods', 135, 142, 149, 163, 167

Pepys, Samuel, 20, 108, *109*; visits the *Royal Sovereign*, 110; 125; visits the prize ships, 134; 139, 149, 156; reports distrust of the Court, 157, 160, 171, 178, 179

Pett, Peter, 160, 161, 201

Phillip II, King of Spain, 19

Pierce, James, 150

Plymouth, 3, 4, 31, 34, 35, 58

Poort, Captain, killed at Portland, 65

Portland, battle of ('three-day battle'), 61–70, 71, 74

Portsmouth, 53, 56, 62, 65, 66, 72–3

Portugal, 13

Presbyterians, 8, 11

privateers, 16, 17, 19, 57, 58, 157

'prize goods' affair, 134

prize money, 58, 86

Pulo Run, 93, 103

Reed, Nicholas, 39

Restoration of Charles II, 97, 99

right of search, *see* neutral shipping issue

Rip Rap shoals, 52

Rolling Ground, the, 127

Ross, Thomas, 116

Rotterdam admiralty ('of the Maas'), 18, 51

Rump Parliament, *see* Parliament, Purged

Rupert, Prince, Count Palatine of the Rhine, 16, 104, 111, 113, 120, 124, 125, 127, 128, 129, 135, *136*, 138, 139; and the Four-Day Fight, 144–7; 150, 154, 156, 167, 172, 178; and first battle of Schooneveld, 180–5; and second battle of Schooneveld, 185–6; and battle of the Texel, 186–8; denounces D'Estrées, 190; 195

Ruyter, Michiel Adrianszoon de, 31–4, 35, 37–9, *42*, 98; and Kentish Knock, 43, 46–7; and Dungeness, 52; and battle of Portland, 61–70; and battle off the Gabbard, 74, 77–80; and at Scheveningen, 86; African expedition, 108; 115, 116, 125, 127, 129, 133, 135, 138, 139; and Four-Day Fight, 142–7, 150; and St James's Day Fight, 152–4, 155, 156, 160, 161, 163, 167, 170, 171, 172; and battle of Sole Bay, 174–9; and first battle of Schooneveld, 180–5; and second battle of Schooneveld, 185–6; and battle of the Texel, 186–8, 189, 193

Sackville, Charles, earl of Dorset, 113

St Helens, 156, 172

St James's Day Fight, 150–4, 178

St John Oliver, Chief Justice, 8, 11, 16

'salute to the flag' issue, 3–4, 6, 15, 93, 163, 170–1

Sage, Jan le, 68

Salwey, Richard MP, 59

Sandwich, Edward Montagu, earl of, 99, 111; relations with Duke of York, 113, 127, 135; 115, 117, 120, 124, 125, 127, 128; Bergen raid, 129–33; *130*; condemned for taking prize goods, 134; side-lined to Spain, 135, 139, 142, 155, 167; reinstated as rear-admiral, 172; and battle of Sole Bay, 174–8, 193

Sansum, Robert, 113, 125, 127

Scarborough Castle batteries, 71

Scheldt estuary, 12, 80, 82, 83

Scheveningen, 97, 134, 142, 145

Scheveningen, battle of, 82–7

Schooneveld, 72; first battle of, 180–5, *182–3*; second battle of, 185–6

seamen (English), care of sick and wounded, 72–3, 82, 135; care of families, 72

sectaries, English, 8, 11

Sheerness, 150, 160, 166, 172

Sheffield, John, earl of Mulgrave, 113

Shetland Islands, 15, 23, 28, 71, 74

ship-money fleet, 19, 22

Ships: *Advice*, 65; *Amity*, 25; *Amsterdam*, 181; *Andrew*, 39, 43; *Anthony Bonaventure*, 52–3; *Antelope*, 19; wrecked, 48; *Assistance*, 61, 64; *Blaue Reiger*, 151; *Black Bull*, 146; *Bonaventure*, 33, 87; *Bourbon*, 185; *Brazil*, 25; *Brederode*, 4–6, 5, 20, 29, 30, 43, 51, 52, 62–8, 77–8, 81, 83; *Bristol*, 139; *Cambridge*, 149, 177, 181; *Charity*, 125; *Charles*, 19; *Charles V*, 163; *Conquerant*, 181; *Constant Warwick*, 19, *20*; *Convert*, 35; *Convertine*, 35; *Defiance*, 127, 142; *Delffland*, 133; *Delft*, 144; *Diamond*, 43; *Dolfijn*, 176; *Dragon*, 35; *Eendracht*, *118*, 124, 125 (new built in 1666), 142, 177, 181; *Essex*, 48, 124, 146; *Fairfax*, 19, 60; *Fan Fan*, 152; *Garland*, 52, 53, 87; *George*, 31, 32, 33, 75, 77, 121; *Glorieux*, 181; *Golden Dove*, 35; *Golden Leeuw*, 180, 181, 188; *Gouda*, 144, 145; *Greenwich*, 150; *Greyhound*, 43; *Groot Hollandia*, 175; *Guinea*, 43; *Hampshire*, 48, 80; *Happy Return*, 117, 150; *Hector*, 134; *Henry* (ex *Dunbar*), 110, 144, 152; *Henrietta Maria* (later *Paragon*), 19; *Hercules*, 53; *Holland*, 68; *Hollandia*, 124, 142; *Hunter* (fireship), 87; *Increase of London*, 25; *James*, 5–6, 19, 39, 41, 43–4, 75; *Jersey*, 104, 149, 150; *John and Elizabeth*, 25, 26; *Josua*, 177; *Jupiter*, 181; *Kentish*, 48; *Komeetster*, 188; *Laurel*, 61; *Liefde*, 120; *Lion*, 68; *London* (blown up 1665), 111; *London* (built 1670), 177; *Loyal George*, 143; *Loyal London*, 111, 150, 153, 161, 163; *Malaga Merchant*, 25; *Martin*, 65; *Mary*, 25; *Mary* (ex *Speaker*), 110, 124; *Matthias*, 163; *Merlin*, 170; *Monck*, 124, 134, 137, 150, *151*; *Monmouth*, 161; *Monnikendam*, 62, 68, 70; *Neptunus*, 33; *Nightingale*, 26; *Nonsuch*, 41, 45; *Oak*, 64–5, burned, 87; *Olifant*, 176, 186; *Oranje*, 124; *Paragon* (later *Henrietta Maria*), 19; *Pelican*, 43; *Plymouth*, 156, 201; *Portland*, 60; *President* (*Great President*), 3, 35, 20; *Prince*, 171–2, 174, 177, 186–8; *Prince Royal* (later *Resolution*), 19, 39, 110; *Prins te Petard*, 181; *Prins Willem*, 43, 46; *Prosperous*, 64, 65; *Rainbow*, 25, 61, 65, 150; *Recovery*, 3; *Resolution*, 28, 41, 56, 61, 70, 75–80, 83–6; *Resolution* (built 1664, burned 1666), 153; *Resolution* (built 1667), 177; *Revenge*, 110; *Royal Charles* (ex-*Naseby*), 110, 116, 124, 142–7, 150, 152–5, 161, 163, *164–5*, 170; *Royal Charles* (built 1673), 171, 181, 184; *Royal George*, 152;

Royal James, 117, 146–7, 150, 152, 154, 161, 163; *Royal James* (built 1671), 171, 174–8, *175*; *Royal Katherine*, 111, 124, 145, 152, 177, 181, 186; *Royal Oak*, 111, 121, 161, 163; *Royal Prince*, 120, 124, *145*, 146; *Rubis*, 156; *Rupert*, 152; *Ruth*, 25; *St Andrew*, 171, 174; *St George*, 187; *St Michael*, 171, *173*, 177, 186–8; *Sancta Maria*, 161, 163; *Sampson*, 35, scuttled, 65–6, 70; *Seven Oaks*, 143; *Snake*, 152; *Sovereign* (ex-*Sovereign of the Seas*, later *Royal Sovereign*), 19, 36, 39, 43–4, *45*, 47, 56, 61, 70, 110, 152, 185; *Speaker*, 19, *21*, 28, 39, 43, 60; *Stavoren*, 177; *Struisvogel*, 33, 66, 68; *Superbe*, *170*, 178; *Sussex*, 48; *Swiftsure*, 142–3, *147*, (captured and renamed *Oudshoorn*) 148; *Tholen*, 152; *Triumph*, 39, 52, 53, 60–6; *Tulip*, 85, 86; *Unicorn*, 19; *Unity*, 163; *Vanguard*, 25, 31, 33, 39, 53, 60–6, 86; *Victory*, 61, 65; *Vrede*, 161; *Walcheren*, 181; *Warspite*, 150; *West Friesland*, 156; *Worcester*, 19, 25, 85; *York*, 156; *Zeeland*, 120; *Zeven Provincien*, *138*, 142, 144, 152, 160, 177, 181; *see also* fireships, guns, merchantmen
signalling, 76, 82
Smith, Sir Jeremy, 127, 149, 150, 153, 155, 178
soldiers aboard warships, 22, 58, 61, 74
Sole Bay, 75, 82, 117, 129, 131, 155, 172
Sole bay, battle of, 172–8, *176*
South Foreland, 4, 25
Southwold, Suffolk, 31, 87, 89, *see also* Sole Bay
sovereignty of the seas *see* salute to the flag issue
Spaniard's Gate, 115, 133, 172
Spanish-Dutch relations, 12–13, 16
Spanish Netherlands, 169
Spragge, Sir Edward, 111, 139, 149, 167, 172, 177, 179; critical of Rupert's tactics, 180, 181, *184*; naval duel with Tromp, 185–6; killed at the battle of the Texel, 187
Start Point ('the Start'), clash off, 3–4, 37
States General, 7, 8, 10, 17, 18, 32, 50, 51, 81, 89, 92, 98, 127, 133, 178, 171, 179
Stop of the Exchequer, 171
Strickland, Walter, 7, 8, 11, 16
Stuyvesant, Peter, 106
Surinam, 163, 191
Svendsen, Hans, 143, 151
Sweden, 169
Sweers, Isaac, 176, 186
Swers, Captain, 65
Swin, the, 139

tactics: blockade, 81, 82, 87, 89, 128, 134, 157, 163; 'charging', 74, 85; deception, 82; development of, 113, 115–17, 120, 137, 146, 174, 178; failure to concentrate, 41–7; fighting in line, 73–4, 76–7, 85, 113, 115, 137, 146, 192–3; melée, 33, 77, 116, 120, 135, 137, 174, 177; 'smash and sink' versus 'disable and board', 65, 74, 76, 77, 116, 137; 'stand off and bombard', 74, 76–7; use of shoals by de Ruyter, 115, 125, 145, 152, 154, 172, 180–1, 185; *see also* guns, fireships
Talbot, Sir Charles, 155
Talbot, Sir Gilbert, 129, 131

Teddiman, Sir Thomas, 113; commands raid on Bergen, 131, *132*, 149, 156
Teil, Jean Baptiste du, 149
Temple, Sir William, 170, 171
Test Act, 179
Texel estuary, 71, 74, 75, 86, 89, 115, 116, 117, 124, 125, 129, 133, 137, 172, 179, 185; battle of Texel, 186–90, *187*, *188*
Thames estuary, 25, 53, 56, 57, 70, 73, 75, 117, 134, 139, 150, 156, 160, 163, 180
Thirty Years War, 13, 16
Thompson, George, MP, 59
Thurloe, John, 76, 77
Torbay, 37
Toulon, 137, 171
Treaty of Westminster, 98, 191
Triple Alliance (1668), 169, 171
Tromp, Cornelis, 116; uneasy relations with de Witt and de Ruyter, 117, 127, 133, 144, 152, 155, 120, 125, *126*; appointed commander-in-chief, 127; replaced by de Ruyter, 133, 138; and the Four-Day Fight, 139–46, 159, 152, 153, 154; banished for Orangist sympathies, 155; restored by William III, 180; and first battle of Schooneveld, 181–4; and second battle of Schooneveld, 185–6; and battle of the Texel, 186–8
Tromp, Maarten Harpertszoon, and action off Dover, 4–6, 18; moves against Ayscue, 26–7; and the Northern Voyage, 28–30; resigns, 31, 35, 39; resumes command, 50; and Dungeness, 51–3, *54–5*, 56, 57; and battle of Portland, 61–70, 71; and battle off the Gabbard, 74, 77–81; and battle of Scheveningen, 82–6; death and burial, 86, 87
'True Freedom', period of, 8
Turkey trade, 13
Tuscany, Grand Duke of, 50

union, proposal between England and United Provinces, 8, 11, 16
Upnor, 161, 163

Vane, Sir Henry, the Younger, 59
Varne *see* Rip Raps
Velde, William van de, the elder, 117, 138, 148, 177, 203
Velde, William van de, the younger, 176, 201
Vendôme, duc de, 36
Venetian embassy reports, 110, 116, 127, 155, 171
Vlie channel, 75
Vlie, raid on, 154, 157

Walcheren, 180, 185
Warwick, Robert Rich, second Earl of, 7, 19
West Indies, 12, 56, 71
Whistler, Dr Daniel, 72–3
Widt, Commodore de, 43; taken prisoner, 46, 68
William II of Orange, 7
William III of Orange, 8, 99, 125, 171, 180, 185, 191, 192, 201
Wilmot, John, earl of Rochester, 113, 131, 201–2
With, Witte Cornelis de, 26, 35, 36, 39, *40*, 99; at the

Kentish Knock, 41–7, 51, 52, 71–2; and battle off the Gabbard, 74, 77–81; and battle of Scheveningen, 82–6, 89–90
Witt, Cornelis de, 160–1, 163; at the Medway, 160–6, *166*, 167, 171, 178; accused of treason and murdered, 179–80
Witt, Jan de, Grand Pensionary of Holland, 10, 11, 97–9; and peace negotiations, 92–3; appointed Grand Pensionary, 98; negotiates peace with Cromwell, 98; centralizing policies of, 98, 101, 107–8, 117, 123; directs naval strategy, 98, 133, 137, 138, 155, 157, 160, 169, 171–2, 178–80; murdered, 179

Yarmouth, 43, 75
Young, Anthony, 3–4

Zaanen, Joris van der, 3, 4–5
Zeeland, 101, 116, 117, 156, 178; Zeeland admiralty, 18